WALL STREET JOURNEYMAN

SILVIO SANTINI

outskirtspress

DENVER, COLORADO

Outskirts Press, Inc.
http://www.outskirtspress.com

ISBN: 978-1-4787-1919-9

Outskirts Press and the "OP" logo are trademarks belonging to Outskirts Press, Inc.

PRINTED IN THE UNITED STATES OF AMERICA

Dedicated to my wife Luisa.
She has made me a better man and given me a better life.

Special thanks to my good friends Dave Noguerol,
Mark Orient and Erik Schmitz, as well as
my brother Mike and my sister Lisa.

Chapter 1

The phone began to ring incessantly. The harsh, shrill, loud noise brutally shattered the silence of the night. It rang four or five times. Then it stopped as the automatic messaging system kicked in. Then, as quickly as it had gone silent, it started ringing again. He grabbed the phone on the fourth ring of the second go-round. The lingering effects of the prior evening's excesses filled his mind with a fog that made it difficult for his brain to begin functioning. Six Budweiser's, a bottle of Shiraz and two joints of high test were a bit much to overcome with less than five hours of uneven sleep. He achieved a small measure of consciousness. He was not happy. Fucking yen he thought, it must be the fucking yen. Why did I listen to that stupid asshole Schlomo? I should fucking know better by now, he lamented to himself. What the fuck was I thinking?

He put the phone to his ear while still in bed with his eyes closed. His throat was so dry he could barely speak. "Yeah" he said in a low growl. "What the fuck is going on? Dollar/yen is tanking, isn't it?" It was Lorenzo on the other end of the phone calling from London. He was the chief dealer of the global Foreign Exchange (FX) options trading desk at a mid-sized U.S. based investment bank. Lorenzo ran the FX options desk for the bank in London and reported to him. The FX market was a largely unregulated OTC (Over the Counter) market where major financial institutions traded currency and currency products in a competitive, freewheeling environment. Trading in the FX

SILVIO SANTINI

market was not done on an actual organized exchange like the
New York Stock Exchange (NYSE), nor was it regulated by government agencies like the Securities and Exchange Commission
(SEC). Banks and major financial institutions traded with each
other through the telephone or more commonly using electronic communication systems that enabled transactions to be done
globally on an instantaneous basis. FX trading was done across
countries and time zones all over the world. Market participants
at banks were efficiently trading with people at other banks they
never saw, or may not even speak the same language with, in a
split second many times in a typical day. The market had taken
off in the early 1970s after President Nixon had abolished the
Gold standard for the U.S. dollar and allowed it to float freely
against the other major currencies. Large commercial and investment banks worldwide had jumped in and created a market
that quickly became one of their most lucrative trading platforms. The FX market had developed an amazing speed and ef-
ficiency long before the Internet revolution started. By now (the
year 2000) it had grown into a huge beast the Central Banks of
the world tried to influence but could not really control. The
daily dollar turnover in the FX market was now greater than the
dollar turnover on the NYSE for a whole trading year. The FX
market was open round the clock starting in New Zealand about
one PM Sunday afternoon NY time until trading finally wound
down around five PM Friday in New York. It was only closed on
weekends. The major trading centers were Tokyo, London, and
New York and the action passed from center to center each day
without pause. It was a big, tough market that was growing larger and becoming more unruly and difficult to trade every year.

He always had trading positions in most of the major currency pairs and had been getting phone calls in the middle of the night for years, so as to be informed of sharp market movements that affected his positions. When the phone rang at night, it was generally bad news. He had learned long ago that when things were going your way it was better to let your profits run while you were sleeping like a baby. But if things were going badly in a position, you had better find out about it immediately. He knew a lot of ex-traders that refused to take phone calls at night. You had to learn how to maximize your profits but control your losses if you wanted to stay in the game. The only problem with this system was the dread you had to live with most nights before going to sleep. If the phone rang in the middle of the night you were getting fucked and had to wake up and deal with it. Hoping the phone didn't ring was usually the last thought he went to sleep with. Lately, he had started requesting phone calls for extremely advantageous market moves as well. The possibility of good news helped him muster the will to grab the phone when it rang. He instinctively knew that this morning's phone call was bad news. There was no doubt about it.

Lorenzo was a young, Italian kid with brains, good looks, charm and an excellent ability to bullshit his way out of any problems he might run into. Lorenzo had not proven himself a particularly talented trader in his own right yet. But he was loyal. There was no question about it. Lorenzo would follow him into battle and die by his side. Lorenzo was loyal and this was more important to him than anything else. The rest was bullshit by comparison. "It's me, sorry to wake you." Lorenzo started as always in his thick, Italian accent. "The dollar/yen, it is collapsing. They break the stops at 108.20, the low was 106.63. The move, it was very fast. Now it is 107.20/23. What do you want to do?" I want to kill myself. That's what the fuck I want to do was the first thought that popped into his mind. He quickly dismissed this as a viable option. Too many sons of bitches out there that needed to go along for the ride if it ever came to that. "Sell twenty dollars and buy one hundred bucks of one month yen", he told Lorenzo. He was doing two trades simultaneously: a spot FX transaction and an FX options trade. The selling of twenty dollars was the spot FX transaction and meant he was selling twenty million U.S. dollars vs. buying the equivalent amount of Japanese Yen. Lorenzo would execute this trade immediately on an electronic dealing system. A record of the transaction would immediately go into the investment bank's trading system. To settle the trade, the investment bank's agents in New York would later deliver twenty million dollars to the counterparty of the trade bank's account in New York. Their bank agents in Tokyo would deliver the appropriate quantity of Japanese Yen to the investment bank's agent to confirm the dealing rate. Senior traders at banks would trade them up, sometimes doing hundreds of trades in a single dealing session, but the back office support staff would settle the trades with surprisingly few glitches.

This particular trading session had seen the dollar/yen exchange rate make a fairly sharp movement relative to the past several months and this kind of market action would have an immediate effect on prices in the OTC Japanese Yen options market. He knew that prices on implied volatility would be higher than they had been yesterday but that effective risk management required that he buy without hesitation. When he asked Lorenzo to buy one hundred bucks of one-month yen he was buying volatility for yen in the FX options market. Market participants could buy and sell their view of how much movement would occur for the underlying currency over any period of the time they chose, although most of the transactions globally involved tenors of one year or less. Lorenzo would execute the options trade either through a voice broker or by contacting other banks directly via an electronic but non-automated dealing system. He traded option portfolios for the different major currency pairs. These portfolios sometimes comprised hundreds or even thousands of different options of different amounts and various specifications. The aggregate risks of these options portfolios (commonly referred to as the Greeks in market parlance) were calculated by computer models. Then they could be quantified and traded as a single unit. In this instance, he had intuitively determined that the combined trades of selling the dollar/yen and buying the options were required to rebalance the risks in his Japanese Yen options portfolio. He rudely interrupted Lorenzo's queries concerning price levels and execution strategy for the proposed transactions. "Fuck it. I don't care what the fucking price is. Just sell the dollars and buy the options now. Don't play games. Let me wake up and then I will call you back and see what is going on."

He hung up the phone and began to grope around for his glasses on the nightstand. It was amazing how he could never find his fucking glasses after being woken up in the middle of the night to be informed of FX market movements. I mean, come on already. How hard was it to put your glasses somewhere that you could find them readily upon being awakened, especially when you consider how often he received phone calls in the middle of the night. Give me a break, he thought, as he continued to blindly grope around in the dark. I have got to be a fucking moron. Why am I so fucking stupid all the time, he silently cursed? He vaguely realized in the back of his mind that spending the prior evening getting slowly but surely wasted was a big part of the problem. By the time he had collapsed into bed around midnight he didn't even remember taking the goddamn glasses off. "Fuck!" he cursed out loud as he knocked over the half full glass of Coke that had been left on his nightstand for the past three days or so. It soaked his position sheets, making them a sticky mess before falling to the floor. His position sheets detailed all of the market risk for his various FX option portfolios. He dutifully brought them home every night and kept them by his bedside. Usually there were at least twenty pages crammed with numbers that he never looked at. He knew all the positions and the risks perfectly in his mind. Somehow, bringing them home each night made him feel more responsible and secure. But spilling something all over them was not actually that big of a tragedy, or that uncommon an occurrence. He finally found his glasses by rooting around on the floor underneath the bed. He grabbed them and put them on. He glanced at the clock. It was 4:30 AM. Might as well get up and catch the early train with this shit going on, he thought. He became aware that his bladder was about ready to explode and this provided the necessary motivation to get out of bed. On the second step he tripped over some junk his wife had left on the floor and he painfully banged his toes on the metal underside of the bed. "Son of a bitch" he mumbled to himself as he limped into the bathroom. His mouth was drier than hell and his head was starting to pound to supplement the intense pain in his toes. He was not well. He found his way into the bathroom and squinted as his eyes adjusted to the light. He quickly scanned all the current foreign exchange rates and the overnight price activity on his pocket sized pager while he relieved himself. He began to feel a bit better immediately. Scoring in the euro and dollar/canada. The aussie position was performing nicely as well. The sterling (British Pound) book was no worse than neutral, he was quite sure. No problems at all in any of the cross-currency books. All in all it could have been worse. Things could have been much worse indeed. This was nothing. Shit, he thought to himself. I am net positive P&L (Profit and Loss) for the day despite the debacle in the yen and that problem is now under control.

He jumped into the shower and let the steaming hot water cascade over his tightly shaved head. He rubbed his scalp and enjoyed the sensation of the water flowing warmly down into his eyes. The knots inside his brain began to loosen up and the thoughts began to flow. He was alone in time and space. He had returned to familiar territory and his thoughts were clear. He was back at the chess table again facing the grim, silent, opponent he knew so well. This opponent was larger than life and almost defied description. In fact she was much more than an opponent. She was a loving companion and an aggressive antagonist. She was beautiful and generous. She was ugly and greedy. She was a slut. She was a bitch. She was a whore. She had seduced him completely when she had come into his life fifteen years ago. Now she controlled his destiny. He slept with her. He woke up and spent the entire day with her. He dreamed about her. He could not stop thinking about her on weekends or during vacations, no matter how hard he tried. She built him up and stroked his ego. She made him feel strong and powerful. When things were at their best between them she made him feel like King Cock. But it was not always smooth sailing with her. Indeed things did not always go well with her. She had an evil side that could appear out of nowhere. She could become mean, vindictive, vicious and nasty in a flash. Things seemed calm and relaxed but she would suddenly turn on him without notice. He never knew when it was coming next. When things turned ugly with her for a protracted period of time she punished him mercilessly and drove him to the depths of depression. She taunted him, ridiculed him, and made him feel stupid and weak. She exposed all his insecurities and filled him with doubt and self-loathing. She crushed his pride and made him feel worthless. He had sworn to leave her behind countless times already but knew he was powerless to do so. He wasn't going anywhere. He knew it. She knew it. They both knew it. She was the beautiful whore he hated and loved with all his passion to the depths of his soul. The market.

Down through the years he had read articles and discussions about the FX market in various periodicals and business texts. Many well-respected university professors had written a plethora of academic articles on the FX market. He had read numerous dissertations that discussed the mechanics and machinations of the FX market written by the experts in the financial press. They would drone on endlessly about all the fundamental factors that determined currency values and drove exchange rate price changes. They would cite numerous macro-economic statistics to support their views. Much had been written about so called purchasing power parity. This was the theory that the same basket of goods and services in different countries should be priced the same on a relative basis adjusting for the FX exchange rate. In other words, a Big Mac should cost the same in Japan as it did in the United States adjusting for the rate of the Japanese Yen vs. the U.S. Dollar. He had spent three years living in Japan and knew firsthand how far off that theory was. Other theories focused on statistical analysis of the macro indicators used to quantify the economies of countries. Every major bank involved in the FX market had scores of economists that churned out research papers loaded with facts and figures and predictions about future currency movements based upon the analysis of Gross National Product (GNP), Consumer Price Index (CPI), interest rate term structure, you name it. The clients of the banks involved in the FX market clamored for this research but the traders who were risking the firms' capital in the market generally ignored it.

Before becoming an FX options trader, he had taken a class in International Economics at the prestigious graduate school of business he had attended. The professor for that class was renowned in the business press for his work on exchange rates and was a heavy duty consultant to Wall Street. When he first starting reading about the guy and his work on the FX market, he tried to remember the class lectures and what he had actually learned that had proven useful in trading currencies. The famed economics professor had spent much time in the classroom discussing the FX market and the fundamental economic factors that drove exchange rates. But he quickly came to the conclusion that he had not learned even one single thing of practical value in that class in terms of his professional career.

His whole career after receiving his MBA had been devoted solely to trading FX and FX options but the class with the so-called expert had not helped much. In fact, when he thought about it, all the theories and academic works he had read about the FX market were rubbish. They were completely devoid of any real meaning. What a fucking joke. The so-called expert economists had no clue about what was really going on in the market. They didn't know a thing that actually mattered on a practical level. They did not seem to comprehend that thousands of people worldwide of all different languages and nationalities were buying and selling these currencies on a daily basis in a frenzied chaotic fashion. The experts didn't have the slightest idea what was really driving the price changes in the FX market. They never seemed to consider the basic fear and greed that was influencing the decision making process of the market participants. The ecstatic joy of winning and the crushing pain of defeat felt by the thousands of traders in the market worldwide every day was the real driver of price changes. The experts could not begin to explain why the price of any currency was where it was and where it was going. The reality of the situation was that the research departments at the major banks were not much better than the academics. In fact, a good rule of thumb would be to always fade the predictions (go the opposite way) of the economics department of the firm you were working for. The good FX traders that he knew made their own decisions and used their own unique trading strategies. When he looked back upon it, most of what he really knew and used to succeed at this game had been self-taught. An education bought and paid for at the school of hard knocks was essential to the development of any trader. He had learned a trick or two from a couple of half-crazed Englishmen in the market that he had befriended. These were guys that had dropped out of school at the age of fifteen and had been trading FX for twenty years or more. They and others like them were switched on and had some understanding of what the hell was happening in the FX market and how to make some money trading on a consistent basis. The rest were simply talking out of their well-educated asses.

The shower continued its soothing cascade and he began to feel better. He felt alert and focused and ready for anything. He was back at the table playing the game he knew so well. It was his move and he suddenly knew exactly what to do. He instinctively anticipated what the term structure of the Japanese Yen volatility market would be now after the sharp overnight sell off in the dollar/yen spot market. He now understood the mistakes he had recklessly made in his Yen book with the prior day's trading. More importantly, he understood exactly what trades needed to be done to rebalance the exposures and strengthen the position. He intuitively knew that a particular strike roll in the Euro book would solidify that position and that there would probably be a good opportunity to get that done in London before the New York market opened. He knew what the levels in euro option volatilities would be without having to check. A strategy to improve his Canadian Dollar position was clear as day at the same time. There was not usually great liquidity (ability to buy and sell your amount easily without moving prices) in London for dollar/canada options, but it was worth a shot. Suddenly, he was quite sure the euro/sterling cross would pop and he had an idea how to jump in quickly now before the move started. He was back on the board, it was his move and he was back in control for the moment. He was excited to be in the game and was ready to take confident, aggressive action. He knew what the current move was and he had the next six or seven moves in a row clear in his mind now. In fact, there was no time to waste. He wanted to make his moves immediately. Push his pieces and see what came back at him.

He jumped out of the shower, grabbed his cell phone and called Lorenzo back in London. In rapid-fire staccato fashion, he barked out a series of complicated orders for Lorenzo, while standing in the bathroom naked and still soaking wet. He went through six different currency-pairs and at least two possible transactions for Lorenzo to execute in each pair depending on price, type of option, strike price of option (rate at which option can be exercised), maturity of option and principal amount of transaction. Some of the orders were to buy a certain type of option in a certain amount only if Lorenzo could sell a different option at the same time at another predetermined price. It was a lot of information communicated very quickly, but he knew Lorenzo could handle it all without anything needing to be repeated. Lorenzo listened attentively and only occasionally interjected something like "Yes, I understand, yes, yes, yes, you are a genius, yes, yes, yes, I love it, yes." He hung up the phone and began to dry himself off. He was starting to feel much better, indeed. His head had cleared and he felt invigorated and ready for action. His vicious attack dog had been set loose behind enemy lines. Lorenzo was a whirlwind of energy and there were few guys in the market better at getting trades done at excellent levels. In another hour, he would be at his office and back in the gunner's chair himself.

He would be swerving behind the turret and firing when clear shots presented themselves, while trying to avoid being strafed by the enemy's fire. The dealing room would be a chaotic symphony of ringing phones, shouting voices, and dealing machine alarms going off left and right. The sound and the fury of the battle would rage and consume his soul. He began to anticipate how great that first cup of coffee would taste on the train into the city. He would read the New York Post with the sounds of Miles Davis flowing through the headphones calming the choppy waters of his tortured mind-relaxing him and making him ready for another day in his life trading the Foreign Exchange market.

Chapter 2

He sat down on the train, took a swig of coffee and opened up the New York Post to the sports pages. The New York Yankees had won and were rolling along in fine form this season. Out of habit he checked on the Pittsburgh Pirates. As usual, they had taken it on the chin once again and were mired in last place. He had grown up in Pittsburgh and had been a lifelong Pirates fan, but his loyalty was waning of late. When he was a kid the Pirates were a great team, going back to the days before free agency when professional baseball teams stayed together for long stretches of time. Back in those days you got to know the team well and many of the good players stayed with the same team their entire career. Managers were not hired and fired at lightning speed, either. It created a feeling of bonding between the team and the fans of major league baseball teams that somehow seemed lost in the current days of multi-millionaire free agency. The Pirates had won the World Series in 1960, 1971, and again in 1979. His childhood hero had been the incomparable Roberto Clemente who had died at a tragically young age while still in his prime on a mission of mercy to help earthquake victims in Nicaragua. Clemente's plane crashed off the coast of Puerto Rico full of needed supplies that never made it. The Pirates had stayed strong in the 1980s but in the early 1990s they had lost all their top stars to free agency and had become perennial cellar dwellers. His allegiance had shifted to the New York Yankees. His interbank money market brokers got him box seats on demand and he probably took his sons to a dozen games every year. They all loved the Bronx Bombers. He had created a grandiose tradition for himself and his sons whereby they would start the evening at Sparks for the finest steak and lobster dinner in the city and then head up to Yankee Stadium for the game. In his mind, the Yankees shortstop Derek Jeter was developing into the closest modern day equivalent of Clemente. The guy did everything well; hit, run, field and Jeter played with the same grace and style as the great Roberto. More importantly, he was the clear leader of a championship team at a relatively young age. The Pittsburgh Steelers were a different animal than the Pirates, however. The NFL was a more competitive professional sports league relative to MLB due to team revenue sharing. The Steelers had a great championship record and were usually competitive year in and year out. They had a tremendously loyal fan base that traveled to away games week in and week out every season. He went to an away Steeler game with old high school friends every year. They had a blast getting away from their wives and kids for the weekend, getting pummeled, acting like teenagers and rooting for the Steelers. His sons had learned to love and support the Steelers as passionately as he did. It became a family tradition for most people he knew that had been born in Pittsburgh to become rabid Steeler fans.

His thoughts shifted to his father as they almost always did when he remembered his youth. His father had been a fucking maniac and was the kind of man that would have been put in jail these days, but in the 60s and 70s nobody did anything about domestic abuse. Women like his mother with five kids and no job and no money stayed in the marriage and did their best to hold the family together. The old man must have been bipolar or something of that nature. His father had been abused badly as a child and continued this terrible family legacy with much gusto. His old man had been a handsome; powerfully built man who could be extremely charming when outside of the house or around guests. The old man had been a fantastic cook and threw great parties several times a year. His father had been a traveling salesmen and a local politician and just about everybody the man knew outside of his wife and children loved the guy. From his father he had learned that community-zoning laws are an area of lucrative opportunity for local politicians. The new car wash would be built on land previously zoned residential and the old man would be off to the car dealership with a wad of cash to trade in his Buick 225 luxury sedan for a spanking new model. His wife and five kids knew all too well what a vicious bastard the old man was behind closed doors. When his father was in a good mood the man was generous and affectionate. But when the old man was in a bad mood, somebody was going to get a beating and that generally meant him, his little brother or less frequently, his mom. His younger brother was his little buddy and they shared a special bond. For some reason they were the targets for most of the violence dished out by the old man. He had terrible memories of all the yelling, screaming, insults, threats and occasional beatings the old man had dished out to his long suffering mother. But he also had horrible recollections over the thrashings that came out of nowhere that he and his little brother had taken. That was the most stressful aspect of his childhood. These vicious attacks from the old man came out of nowhere and were over in a flash. The old man had always stopped pretty quickly, otherwise one of them would have been killed. Some of the crap you could not forget. Like Christmas Day when he was seven years old and he was playing with his little brother, and the little guy fell and started crying with a bloody nose. The old man charged into the room punched him to the ground and beat him with his toy gun till it broke into a dozen pieces leaving him a crumpled, beaten, crying mess on the floor. You take a brutal beating out of nowhere on Christmas Day at the age of seven. How do you forget shit like that? He could vividly recall all the children watching Saturday night TV in the family room around seven PM when he was eight years old. The parents were due to leave soon for their Saturday night bowling league. His sisters had spent the afternoon making popcorn the old fashioned way and there was a huge pot of salted, buttered popcorn on the ironing board in the family room. The bar was going to be open on popcorn that evening. His favorite memories from his childhood were the times it was just the five kids hanging out. Things were calm and you could relax and let your guard down without fear. The parents were supposed to leave any minute but trouble erupted on their way out the door. His mother had washed his father's stinky bowling shimmy and in the old man's view this had ruined the shimmy. This discovery created an instant primal rage in the old man and his mother had been violently attacked. The old man started screaming vile profanities and they heard scuffling in the hallway. Then his mother was flung into the wall near the family room and the dry wall broke from the force of the blow. His father then grabbed his mother and flung her into the family room. She flew into the ironing board and landed in a heap on the floor. The big pot full of popcorn was knocked into the air and popcorn flew all over them as they all sat there cowering in shock and fear. He jumped up in a rage and flung himself at his father throwing little ineffective punches as he screamed, " I am sick of you Daddy, beating up on my Mommy!" Then his courage failed him and he quickly scurried into the bathroom next to the family room and locked the door. He remembered opening the window and planning to jump out the window and run away until the old man's rage had passed. But his actions had calmed his father down and now the old man was crying and asking him to open the door and come out. The old man made a big, weepy apology to all the kids and then they left for bowling. He still had painful remembrances of the beatings his little brother had taken for not eating peas or carrots. He had learned by the time he was five years old how to sneak disgusting things like peas into a napkin and into his pocket so that he could not be brutalized for not eating them. For years he wanted to teach his little brother the trick, but he suspected the little guy would probably get caught and that would end the game. So he never did. Eventually, he convinced his mother to stop cooking shit that his little brother could not eat so there would be one less reason for the little guy to take a brutal beating. He often wondered why he had to point this out to her and convince her. Mercifully, his old man had traveled a lot, so the man wasn't home during the weekdays all that much and they could have peace in the house. When the old man was out of town his mother always prepared cheap meals. This system made it possible for the meals to be extravagant when big daddy was home. The old man required fresh Italian bread and butter at every meal. God forbid if the bread was a day old or his mother made a mistake and put margarine on the table instead of butter. This would make his father get violent and go berserk. His father would sit down at the table and load his plate and start eating very fast so often the old man was sweating shortly into the meal. His father would usually demand salt and pepper in a loud grunting voice. He remembered quickly sprinkling some salt on his own food before passing it on to his father and for this he received a savage beating. The old man declared him ignorant and yanked him off the table by his hair, threw him to the ground and took off his belt and beat him quickly and thoroughly with sharp, snapping strokes of the thin, black, leather belt while screaming loudly about what a selfish, rude little motherfucker he was. His mother and brothers and sisters silently witnessed the all too frequent gruesome spectacle with a mixture of horror and fear. Shortly thereafter he thought about the experience. He had no idea what had set the crazy bastard off. But he suggested to his mother that she provide the old man with his own set of salt and pepper shakers. The rest of them could share another set. On the weekends with the old man the menu was usually steak with all the fixings on Saturday and home made Italian food on Sunday. His father had been a tremendous cook, there was no doubt about it. Most of what the old man cooked was delicious. But he fondly remembered eating hot dogs and baked beans or tuna noodle casserole peacefully with his mother and brothers and sisters during the weekdays. His father was a graduate of Pitt and would bet one of his friends a turkey on the outcome of the fierce local rivalry every year, the famed Pitt vs. Penn State football game. Penn State won a couple of years in a row and his father bought his friend a quality, fresh turkey from the local turkey farm. When he was nine years old and his little brother was six, Pitt beat Penn State handily. His father's friend decided to be a wise guy and left a huge live turkey on the porch tethered to the porch rail by a string. Around the poor bird's neck a tag was attached that read, "Here is your fresh turkey you Turkey!" It was Sunday morning and the old man immediately declared that they would butcher the turkey and roast it that very day. After they returned from Sunday Mass he and his little brother were drafted to assist in the process with very little discussion or explanation of the gruesome ordeal to follow. A huge pot of water was boiled to dip the bird's carcass in before plucking. Then the doomed turkey was led around to the back yard near the garbage cans. The old man had his huge axe with him and he and his little brother were becoming very nervous and apprehensive with the killing of the big bird imminent. The old man instructed his little brother to hold the legs of the turkey as he held the string that was around the doomed bird's neck and then they positioned the turkey over a garbage can. The old man's axe fell swiftly separating the head from the rest of the bird. The neck immediately began gushing blood like a geyser. The big bird bucked in its death throes and his little brother freaked out and let go of the dead turkey's legs. The writhing, headless turkey missed the garbage can and fell onto the ground and danced as it whipped around for a few seconds, while spraying an enormous quantity of blood all over the three of them. The old man immediately exploded into a rage and started screaming, "You stupid little bastards. Goddammit, you stupid little bastards!" Normally at this juncture, the old man would then administer a vicious beating to both of them. However, this time his father held a huge axe in his hands, so what came next could have been much more tragic than a beating. Like many neighborhoods in Pittsburgh, their street was on a hill and the backyard of their next-door neighbors was about six feet above the scene of this bloody debacle. At this exact moment in time, their neighbor, the elderly Mrs. Kowalski, had been right on top of them tending her flowers on the side of her house. She heard the shouts of rage and looked down to see the old man screaming in a violent frenzy at his two young sons while holding a huge axe, with all three of them covered in blood. Poor Mrs. Kowalski assumed the worst, and began hysterically screaming at the top of her lungs, and this caused his father to stop in his tracks and look up at her. The poor, frightened, elderly woman then fainted and almost rolled over the wall. Her husband came running out of the house to see what was going on. By this time, his father had put down the axe and walked up to Mr. Kowalski to explain away the situation. Fortunately, she was fine within a few minutes. When the old man came back down the dead bird was efficiently gutted and then dipped in the boiling water. His little brother and he had to pluck that bird clean before they were allowed to take off their blood stained clothes and go take a shower. He could never forget being in the basement as his father had savagely assaulted his mother when the old man discovered that she had not taken the expensive shooting gloves out of the pants before washing them. In the old man's mind, this ruined them and so his father screamed at her, hurling insults and profanity and beating her savagely. He had watched his father explode in rage and turn on his mother with hard punches knocking her down onto the disgusting part of the basement floor where the newspapers were. It was where their hunting dog that lived in the basement shit and pissed. He was ten years old when he saw his mother roll onto the shit and piss papers right in front of him after being beaten. She closed her eyes and grimaced in pain and humiliation. He noticed the crow bar leaning next to the wall near his father and considered whether he could grab it and attack the bastard and incapacitate him. But he instantly felt it was futile and froze in fear and loathing. The unpredictability of when the old man would explode into a violent rage created huge stress for everyone in the family. The old man would come home for afternoon naps when he was not on the road and this meant get the fuck out of the house and stay away til dinner. If you made noise that woke him up from a nap you were going to take a vicious pummeling. It was not a pleasant way to grow up, to say the least. Another unforgettable memory he had from his father was getting called into the bathroom to talk with daddy while the old man was smoking his non-filtered cigarettes and taking a shit. His father would ask him a few questions, profess his love for his son and demand a kiss on the lips. Frequently, this occurred when you could hear and smell the flatulence as the old man was explosively crapping.

As an adult, he was quite certain that the dysfunctional nature of the household had fucked up him and his siblings to varying degrees. Both of his sisters had spent years in therapy once they had become adults and moved away. His older sisters were both beautiful and brilliant and had shown him kindness and love his whole life. They had both moved away from Pittsburgh upon graduating from college and would never return. Both sisters went on to stellar professional careers. He and his two brothers had learned to self medicate (usually via pot and alcohol) at young ages. He distinctly remembered when he was twelve years old and an older friend of his turned him onto smoking pot for the first time. He loved it immediately and had never stopped smoking pot on a regular basis since. He had been shocked to learn that his friend had bought the pot from his own older brother who apparently supplied the whole neighborhood and school. When he confronted his big brother, his older sibling had said fine, he could buy at cost since he had already started smoking the shit on his own. His brother had not wanted to be the one who initiated him into getting high. Naturally, he quickly became a small-time pot dealer as well and remained one for many years. He could buy at wholesale and sell at retail and thereby fund his habit and keep money in his wallet. It was a no-brainer. Both his brothers were smart, good guys dealing with the same crazed upbringing. They both did fine later on in life and he always stayed close to both of them. He moved away from Pittsburgh after graduating from college and had never returned except to visit. His brothers were both typical Pittsburgh dudes who would never leave Pittsburgh. They would rather be unemployed in the "Burg" than move somewhere else to get a job.

There were some memories of his father that he looked back upon fondly and this had always complicated things in his mind. There were also numerous remembrances that did not involve violence, but were still a bit twisted. It was amazing how many things from your childhood stayed with you no matter how long ago they had occurred. It was not like you thought about them all that often but they were always there lurking, probably exerting some influence. The good memories of the crazy bastard generally involved food and/

or hunting and fishing which had seemed to be the great passions of the old man's existence, along with chasing pussy and terrorizing his family. They took a two-week summer vacation every year. The day before they left the old man would be in a foul mood as the car was meticulously packed full of every possible convenience considered necessary to cook extensively on the vacation. The old man usually lightened up once they got on the road, and the meals during family vacation were almost always outstanding. He distinctly remembered the vacation on the coast of Maine when he was ten years old. They were sharing a cottage near the beach with one of his old man's good buddies, Mr. Kellogg and his wife and three daughters. He learned later on in life that the illustrious Mr. Kellogg was the old man's running mate while they relentlessly chased pussy several nights a week. But when he was younger, it was Mr. Kellogg's family they vacationed with and they were fun to be around. It was always a bunch of kids in sleeping bags all over the main room and the parents in the two bedrooms. The meals were always the highlight. After several days in Maine, Mr. Kellogg and his father had taken them all fishing and they had all walked way out onto an ocean breakwater made up of huge boulders. He can still remember hearing the waves hit the boulders, smelling the fresh, clean ocean breeze, and looking down at the swirling tidal waters. He loved the ocean and later in life he bought a beach house as soon as he could afford it. No fish were being caught and several of the children had snagged their lines at the same time onto a buoy that was attached to a lobster pot that had been set relatively close to the breakwater. His old man had appraised the situation and suggested to Mr. Kellogg that they find out what the fuck was attached to that fucking buoy line. Mr. Kellogg readily agreed that this was a fine suggestion. Before his disbelieving eyes they pulled the buoy line in and hauled up this massive lobster pot that was teaming with large, wiggling, fresh Maine lobsters right out of the sea glistening in the sunlight. The old man declared to Mr. Kellogg that fishing was over and they better pack up their lobsters quickly and be on their way. Mr. Kellogg readily concurred that this was indeed a capital suggestion. Each of the eight kids was instructed to take off their jackets and a couple of lobsters were quickly stashed in each. Then they all held them over their backs in a makeshift sack like Santa Claus. The old man had tightly twisted each makeshift lobster sack so that the lobsters could not move much and they were all admonished to hold on firmly. His father and Mr. Kellogg packed up the rest quite abruptly, threw the lobster pot back in the sea and grabbed the fishing gear while efficiently hustling the kids back to the cars with the utmost haste. Only later in life did he understand the significance of this event. He later came to understand that they shoot first and ask questions later if you poach lobsters in Maine. These lobster pot rights are the lifeblood of families and are cherished and passed on to future generations. The old man and his pal Mr. Kellogg had poached lobsters in Maine with their combined eight kids who were all between the ages of eight and fifteen as their accomplices. That evening the old man's massive steamer pot was cooking hard all through the night or so it seemed. The mood at the cottage was festive and jovial. The old man and Mr. Kellogg were cutting up fresh steamed lobsters and putting out the meat in big chunks with butter and lemon as well as fresh cut French fries and home made cole slaw. He had never tasted anything

SILVIO SANTINI

so incredibly delicious as fresh Maine lobster. It was all you could eat and then some that night. They had lobster casserole, lobster rolls, lobster pasta, and lobster salad for days. He never got tired of it either.

The old man occasionally took him and his brothers on weekend trips either fishing or hunting. His father's good hunting buddy was Mr. Belano who had three sons roughly the same age as them. Mr. Belano had a hunting camp in the mountains several hours north of Pittsburgh. One early Friday afternoon in the fall when he was twelve they had left Pittsburgh for a weekend hunting trip with Mr. Belano and his boys. They all had arrived at the cabin around five PM and his father declared a headache and went upstairs to lie down. Mr. Belano quickly organized wrestling matches and moved the furniture and doubled up the carpet in the middle of the big room that made up most of the downstairs. Mr. Belano was acting as the referee as all three of the man's sons were grappling with his brothers and him. Suddenly he slammed Mr. Belano's son Danny down wildly and they crashed into a coffee table and knocked a big old ceramic lamp to the floor. It loudly crashed into many pieces. The old man came pounding down the stairs in a furious rage yelling and screaming appalling profanities. In his father's hand was a large wooden Polenta Paddle the old man had brought up to the cabin. When the old man noticed Mr. Belano's son Danny and him sprawled by the broken lamp his father charged over and started beating his son with the polenta paddle before it suddenly snapped in half. Mr. Belano and all the other boys looked on with shock and revulsion. The old man quickly threw his own sons back into the car, loaded up the still unpacked stuff and roared off at high speed in his big red Buick Electra 225. They had driven for about 20 minutes and were back on the expressway and were driving along in dark silence as usual. The old man did not care for the radio when he was driving so you drove in silence and you had better not talk too loud and annoy the man. He was in the front seat and got up the nerve to speak. He said, "You know the whole wrestling tournament was Mr. Belano's Idea. It was Mr. Belano who moved the furniture and the rugs and organized us to start wrestling. You told us to listen to Mr. Belano before you went to take a nap. We were following your instructions when you broke the polenta paddle and made us leave." He had diplomatically not mentioned that the old man had broken the fucking Polenta paddle on him. The old man didn't look at him but responded in a rational voice "So it was Mr. Belano's idea for you boys to wrestle? Mr. Belano organized the whole thing?" At this juncture the old man's calm tone gave his two brothers the balls to speak up and they immediately began to reiterate the same message. The whole sordid wrestling travesty had been Mr. Belano's baby the whole way. They had just been playing ball. Suddenly, the old man slowed down and made a high speed u-turn on one of those highway turn-arounds reserved for cops and emergency vehicles. After they got off the expressway they stopped at the rural store where his father knew the butcher. They all went into the store together and watched the butcher custom cut 1 ½ inch thick Porterhouse steaks to the old man's specifications. His father bought all manner of food to go with the steaks to make an amazing meal. They showed up back at the cabin and his old man informed Mr. Belano they would be staying after all and dinner would be ready in about an hour. His father suggested that Mr. Belano go ahead and re-start the wrestling matches, but they had all lost the passion for that. The fucking dinner was extremely delicious as usual.

They always went deer hunting with Mr. Belano and his boys on the weekend after the hyped up opening day Monday of deer season in Pennsylvania. The season was for bucks only and usually on that Saturday, the only one who would shoot a buck deer legally would be the old man. But one deer would never satisfy his father and Mr. Belano's desire for a large stock of venison. The old man did not believe that game laws or bag limits had any relevance. That Saturday night they would take off into a nearby farmer's field in Mr. Belano's four-wheel drive pickup truck. Mr. Belano would drive and his old man would be up front with his loaded rifle. All six boys would be bundled up and riding in the back of the pick up truck, bumping along off-road. His older brother would be holding a large spotlight wired directly into the truck's battery. They would drive deep into the huge field and then the truck would stop and they would sit silently in the dark and cold under the bright stars burning through the clear winter's night sky. After some time the old man would whisper to his brother to get ready the light was going to be put on. The spot light would shine brightly, revealing many deer grazing in the meadow with their eyes frozen and locked staring into the sharp spotlight. The cartridge in the old man's rifle held six bullets and six shots would crack out sharply into the night. There would then be six dead deer in the field every time. The old man was an excellent marksman and never missed. His brother would hold the light, illuminating the field and the old man and the rest of the boys would run out and grab the still, warm, dead deer and haul them into the back of the pickup truck. The old man knew if he field gutted the poached deer it was possible game wardens might stumble onto their game. When they got back to the cabin, the deer were efficiently gutted, skinned and butchered and packed into big ice chests that were waiting. The old man and Mr. Belano would set up an assembly line with all the boys helping to cut up the meat and pack it in plastic wrap and then freezer paper. This process would usually last until two or three AM that Saturday night. The next morning Mr. Belano would launch into an improvisational mocking version of the Latin Catholic Mass with his old man playing along bellowing Amen at the correct times. It would usually end with some kind of plea for the Pittsburgh Steelers "to kicka da shit outta da Cincinnati Bengals" and they would all shout out the final big Amen. He loved Mr. Belano and thought the man was hilarious. Then his father would prepare a massive Sunday brunch of pancakes with real maple syrup, eggs, fried potatoes, fresh deer liver fried with onions and fresh deer tenderloin sautéed with mushrooms in red wine reduction sauce and large hunks of fresh Italian bread. They all ate massive quantities with extreme gusto. The old man and his friend Mr. Belano efficiently jack lighted deer each year using their sons as their willing assistants. He had to admit he found it exciting, and enjoyed the experience immensely. They all did.

One summer the old man decided they would all try flyfishing. His father bought them all cheap fly rods and some fly gear and they woke up early on Saturday and drove to a campsite and set up camp near the famed Yellow Breeches. This was a so-called "fish for fun" stream where you could only fly fish and had to release all fish except for one trophy trout over twenty inches per day. This beautiful, scenic stream was teeming with good-sized trout. They spent the whole day thrashing around the stream but did not catch a single fish between them. Fly-fishing successfully required expensive equipment and great skill and experience, none of which any of them had. That night around the campfire the old man explained that the game plan for to-morrow's fishing was being revised. They would sneak in worms inside their waders and they would split up and fish with worms once they were alone on the stream. All trout caught would be kept and put into plastic bags and then hidden inside the waders as well. If a trout was flipping about too much inside your wad-ers as to possibly call attention to yourself the old man advised biting the trout on the head to kill it instantly. He was very good at fishing for trout in a stream with worms - better than the rest of them put together and that included the old man. Moving quietly by himself on the stream and finding nice little holes to fish he caught large numbers of nice pan-sized trout and his wad-ers were stuffed with fish. It was like taking candy from a baby for him in those waters that theoretically were never invaded by bait fisherman. That day he crammed his waders with about two dozen trout between ten and fifteen inches or so. When the old man got a look at his booty back at the campsite he was praised profusely indeed. Those trout and the many that followed in the ensuing years found their way to the old man's smoker. Smoked trout is very delicious he had to admit. They went on poach-ing expeditions several times a summer to all of the finest trout streams in Pennsylvania and always returned home with an ice chest full of trout ready for the smoker. Once on the famed Letort, not long before dusk he hooked into a huge, power-ful fish. He knew he was fighting a trout of enormous size. He raced downstream after that fish in similar fashion to Brad Pitt landing a giant trout after an epic battle in Robert Redford's brilliant movie "A River Runs Through It." More than once he thought he would slip and fall into the water or spear his head on an outcropping tree branch but somehow he finally subdued the magnificent fish and had it hovering calmly in the shallows right next to him. His heart was pounding and he had never felt so exhilarated. The colors and deep red spots on that fish were beautiful. He did not know the true size of that monster Brown Trout but he looked back on it and figured it was over thirty inches and probably twelve pounds at least. It was definitely a once in a lifetime fish to catch in a stream like that on a fly rod. He wondered if it had been landed fair and square by a legitimate fly-fisherman could it perhaps be a state record or something of that nature? The old man would go crazy over that fish. Then he thought about it. It was the last day of the trip. The ice chest was already full of poached trout. He probably had a dozen more beauties in his waders. They would not run out of smoked trout for months. He wasn't even sure he could get that huge trout back to the car with out attracting attention. It certainly would not fit in his waders. More importantly, he began to think that maybe that fish deserved more. It took many years and a lot of good fortune for a Brown Trout to reach that kind of size living in a stream. Then he thought maybe he deserved more too. He reached down and took out the hook and gently released that huge Brown Trout. He would never forget watching it swim slowly away. He never told his father or his brothers about catching that fish. It was just between him and the big trout. He continued fishing as an adult and eventually became a big proponent of catch and release.

He had a natural ability as a kid to get the edge in competitive situations. He almost always won the games of Risk or Monopoly when they were kids. His strategy was sound, but he also was not averse to slipping extra money from the bank or pieces back onto the board if that's what it took to win. He was much better than all the other kids in the neighborhood at ping-pong. For years he organized elaborate tournaments for money. He would set up a point spread structure whereby he was spotting all the other players points to some degree. He knew enough to make sure his matches were always close and he would be sure to lose a tournament once in awhile. He never let any of them know just how much better he was than them. He instinctively understood what most big time Wall Street operators knew; if you gave a patsy a little something now and again you could keep him around for a long time to be consistently fucked. He had a childhood friend whose father was some kind of low-level mobster. One of the nicest men he ever met in his life. His friend's grandfather lived with them and had also been a mobster in his younger days. The man would captivate them with tales of the good old days when the tiny old geezer had been a hard-nosed enforcer for the top hood in the city. The old guy's favorite mantra was "You want to make money in gambling, then take bets don't make bets!" Later in life on Wall Street, he found how right the old mobster had been. A vast majority of the so called great trades on Wall Street were all about getting someone to sell you something for less than it was worth or getting a sucker to pay you more for something than it was worth. Most of the money made on Wall Street was as simple as that.

When he was fourteen, he had gone to the movies with some friends. One of the kid's mothers had dropped them off at the theatre. His mom had agreed to pick them up after the show. They were outside the theatre waiting for her. Suddenly, he saw his old man's unmistakable red Buick Electra 225 pulling up to the traffic light. He naturally assumed his father was picking them up instead and ran ahead of his friends to the car. He got up to the car and looked in the driver's side window and locked eyes with his old man. Some floozy in a low-cut dress was draped next to the old man on the front seat and was in the process of putting her cigarette into his father's mouth so the old man could take a drag. The light turned green and the old man turned his head and drove away quickly without opening the window or saying a word. When his friends asked if that been his father, he replied no. A couple of minutes later his mom picked them up and the incident was not mentioned. A few days later he entered the basement and his father was there reloading rifle bullets as was his custom in spare moments. The crazy bastard was always smoking even when he was making bullets and had open canisters of gunpowder nearby. It was a miracle the old man had never blown the house up. His father called him over and stubbed out the cigarette. After a little small talk the old man asked him directly "You saw me with the woman in the car by the theatre the other night, didn't you?" He looked his old man in the eyes and simply said, "Yes." His father than replied, "Well, Mrs. Clemming was stranded at Agnello's gas station and needed a ride home so I was just trying to help out." He did not respond. His father pressed him a bit, "You don't believe me do you?" He calmly replied, "No." The old man asked, "Did you tell your mother about this?" He once again gave a single word response, "No." The old man reached for his wallet and pulled out a twenty and handed it to him. "Thanks" was his one word reply. He did not feel bad about keeping the money. His wallet was a better home for that twenty instead of the old man's as far as he was concerned. Also, he had already come to the conclusion that the old man was out running around. This little episode verified the situation.

By the time he was twelve years old or so the domestic abuse had slowed down considerably. Not coincidentally his older brother had matured quickly and Fausto was probably able to give the old man a good fight by this time. The violence finally ended for good when he was fifteen. He had come home from wrestling practice and had something in his eye and needed to take his contact lens out. The old man started yelling at him about some chore he had not done in a timely fashion. He had sprinted past his father and gone into the bathroom because when the old style hard contact lens got something stuck it felt like someone was sticking a knife in your eye and you needed to get it out immediately. The next thing he knew, his father had charged into the bathroom after him and grabbed him by the hair and smashed his face into the sink. Instinctively he threw out a hard elbow and caught the old man right under the chin slamming his head into the wall. The old man must have bit his tongue, as blood started coming out of his father's mouth. He ran out of the bathroom and into the den with the old man in hot pursuit. Then he did something that caught the old man by surprise. He turned and squared up with both fists clenched. "Come on mother fucker let's go", he screamed in anger. "I'm going to kick your ass, you miserable, vicious bastard, let's go", he shouted. His father still considerably outweighed him so this was an altercation he would most likely lose but he was a tough kid, ready to fight back and excited about at least getting in some good shots. Then the old man did something that shocked him even more. Instead of advancing to start the fight, his father reached back and grabbed a fire poker off the hearth and started swinging it slowly but menacingly. This fire poker was basically the same size and heft as a crowbar. He could not believe it. He lost his mind. He started screaming at the top of his lungs "You crazy fucker, you want to kill your son over nothing, go ahead kill me, kill me you fucker!" He ripped off his shirt and screamed "Go ahead stab me in the heart, cut your fucking son's heart out, go ahead I don't fucking care anymore you bastard!" Then he looked his father in the eye and noticed something interesting. In years past when his father was yelling screaming and administering a beating the old man's eyes always seemed to take on this clouded distant look. But suddenly his father's eyes looked clear and the old man had stopped swinging the fire poker. His father did not say a word. The old man put the fire poker back in its place and walked out the door and got in the car and drove away. They never discussed the incident but as near as he could tell the old man had never gotten violent again before dying a rough death from lung cancer seventeen years later. In reality, his father had been a pretty decent guy after that blow out altercation with the fire poker. His high school friends had all loved the old man. His father's parties were legendary. The diagnosis of cancer had come suddenly and it did not take long. His mother had nursed his father at home during the final, torturous months. Chain-smoking non-filtered cigarettes his entire adult life had caught up with the old man in the end.

Chapter 3

In the summer of 1977 before his senior year in High School he began to consider where he should attend college. Despite his frequent drinking and pot smoking, he had an impressive academic record, as school had always been easy for him. He had a GPA of 3.93 and had scored 1470 on his SATs. He was a varsity athlete and an accomplished musician. He figured he probably had the credentials to get into an Ivy League school or some top-flight university on that kind of level. He had not investigated the process very thoroughly however. His father had paid for both of his sisters to go to college. The old man had also paid for his older brother's first year in college but his sibling had gone off the deep end into heavy drug usage and had flunked out. One evening he decided to test the waters with his father. He started the conversation, "So you know I am going into my senior year. I have a very strong academic record and so I am considering trying to get into a premium university." The old man's reply was a bit of a shocker, "Well that sounds like a good plan and I wish you all the best in your pursuit of college at the highest levels. There is really no need to waste time discussing any of it with me. I don't know much about it and since I am not going to pay one penny towards your education I can't see that it is any of my business." His relationship with the old man had been frosty but polite since the fire poker altercation of a couple of years ago but this was shocking news nonetheless. He pressed the issue a bit, "What do you mean you are not going to pay for my education; that does not seem fair. You paid for the girls, you paid for Fausto?" The old man replied tersely, "That's right, I stupidly paid for your fucking dope head brother and he fucking flunked out, wasting my fucking money didn't he? You think I don't know you smoke that shit just like him? That means you will become a fucking loser just like him and flunk out, so I am not going to waste anymore fucking money on any of you smart ass dope heads." He made one last feeble argument, "It is not a fair comparison. Fausto's record in high school was heading south by his junior year. I have made straight As including the highest-level courses. It is not fair to judge me by that standard." The old man smiled and softened his tone, "Listen, do us both a favor and save your breath. I'm done. I am almost broke now anyways, and I don't have any more money to waste. You are all on your lonesome. If you are half as good as you say you are, you will figure out a way to pay for it on your own. It will make a man out of you. I am sure you will do just fine. Remember, reach for the stars and you just might grab a little piece of the moon." With that the old man got up and walked away and they did not have any further discussions about his pursuit of higher education.

Realizing he had to pay for his own college education was a shock that required a couple of months to fully sink in. Eventually, he decided to just enroll in the local state university since it was far and away the cheapest alternative. He never even put in an application anywhere else. His friends told him that with his record he should at least apply to some top schools and see if he could get a scholarship. For some reason, he did not even try. He learned later this had been a mistake on his part. You should strive to get into the best possible college and then figure out how to pay for it. Fair or not, the perceived quality of the university you attend has a direct influence on employment opportunities after graduating. His father did use connections to get him a summer job working as casual labor in a steel mill located on Neville Island on the Ohio River outside of Pittsburgh. He made enough money there between the union wages and large amounts of overtime, that he was able support himself and pay for his college education, supplemented by part time jobs during school and small-time pot dealing. The standard job for summer casual labor was working as a Lid Man on top of the coke battery. A coke battery is basically a big oven where coal is baked at high temperatures for twenty-four hours to turn it into coke, an essential product in manufacturing steel. Coal is loaded off of barges onto huge conveyor belts that take the coal into a large vehicle on rails, which transports the coal into the coke ovens. The job of Lid Man is to open and close the big lids on top of the coke battery. The work environment is so hot and full of noxious gases, that the standard practice is to work one half hour on/ one half hour off throughout the working day. On his first day working as a Lid Man, he was sitting in the filthy steel mill locker room on his half hour break drinking water and wondering how he was going to make it through the fucking summer. He needed the money and was grateful for the job but this had taken the concept of work to a whole new level. Suddenly, he was surrounded by four hulking, filthy steel workers. The biggest one poked him in the chest and asked him a question in a loud voice, "Hey college boy, we have one important question to ask you. Do you jerk off?" He was totally taken aback and wondered what the hell was going to happen next and so he feebly replied, "Sorry, I am not quite sure what you mean." The big guy got in his face, "I think my meaning is pretty fucking clear, do you jerk off? Do you choke the chicken? Do you beat your meat? I am only going to ask you one more time. Do you fucking jerk off?" The verbal assault was so unexpected and forceful he blurted out, "Yes, of course I jerk off. I do it all the fucking time as a matter of fact." This brought on great guffaws of laughter from the grizzled steel workers. The big dude slapped him on the back and said, "Good man. We don't like fucking liars around here." They then walked away happily and he breathed a sigh of relief. He never did quite figure out what that little incident was about, but he never had any issues with any of the union mill workers during his three summers at that plant. He learned great respect for the effort and hardships endured by industrial labor. But the experience also convinced him that he would make his living in some kind of white-collar fashion. The working conditions in a major steel mill had to take years off your life if you spent too much time there.

He had several humbling experiences right around the time he started attending college. A few weeks before school started he drove into the city of Pittsburgh with his friend Steve to buy tickets for an upcoming concert at the Stanley Theatre, a legendary music venue. He would later attend the last concert ever performed by Bob Marley there on September 23, 1980. Marley, the Reggae legend would die an early death from cancer in 1981. It was a memory he would never forget. On this particular day, he drove up to the Theater box office and illegally parked as he usually did to buy tickets at the box office. In these pre-internet days you could not buy concert tickets conveniently online. When he walked back to his car a few minutes later there was a police car parked in front of him and there was a ticket under his windshield wiper. When he got to the car he picked up the ticket and turned his head towards the cop car and said, "Thank you." A few seconds later as he was starting the car and not paying attention, the big policeman had bolted out of the car and ran up and grabbed him by the hair. He would later assume that the cop had thought he had said, "Fuck you", instead of, "Thank you." In any event he was in a state of shock and heard Big Cop bark, "Fucking smart ass are you?" Then Big Cop spied their open cans of beer in the car and began chortling happily while still pulling him by the hair, "Oh my, we got some underage drinkers here don't we?" The drinking age in Pennsylvania was twenty-one and they were both seventeen so the cop had them there. Then Big Cop ordered him and Steve out of the car and had them put their hands on the car roof and spread their legs. A few seconds later, Big Cop pulled a half a doobie out of the ashtray and the man became ecstatic as his own heart sank. Big Cop bellowed loudly, "We got some smart ass, pot smoking, beer drinking tough guys here don't we?" Big Cop ordered them both not to move and then brought the open cans of beer and the half a doobie back to his cop car to confer with the big bastard's fellow police officer. Big Cop walked back towards them a few minutes later just as a police paddy wagon pulled up. Big Cop ordered them both in, without handcuffing them. Big Cop jumped into the back of the paddy wagon with them and the van began moving. They were both shitting themselves thinking about what was to come next. Big Cop got in his face and began taunting and insulting him in every way possible. The verbal onslaught went on for a few minutes, but both he and Steve looked down and did not reply. Finally, Big Cop poked him in the chest and declared in exasperation, "Where is that tough guy I saw out there a few minutes ago? Aren't I the biggest asshole you ever met in your life? Don't you want to bust me one, tough guy?" He replied very politely, "No sir. Absolutely not." Big Cop seemed to get angrier, "Come on tough guy, you know you have had enough. Let's have a fair fight. I will give you the first punch. Go ahead and hit me anywhere you like." He kept looking down and humbly replied, "No sir. It is a criminal offense to strike a police officer. No sir, I will not fight you in any way." At this juncture, Big Cop turned to his friend Steve and started taunting him for about thirty seconds before Steve started crying and blurted out, "My father is going to kill me. I won't be able to go to college now. My life is ruined!" Steve then started blubbering uncontrollably. He found it a bit embarrassing even considering their dire circumstances. In reality, it probably saved their asses. Steve had made them too pathetic to abuse any further. Big Cop turned around and pounded on the front of the paddy wagon and did not say another word to them. The paddy wagon stopped soon and the doors opened and they were right in front of their car. Big Cop handed him his car keys and advised him to stay out of the city of Pittsburgh for a while. He readily agreed this was indeed a fine suggestion. They drove away with Steve still blubbering like a little baby. Several weeks after school started he had an even lower experience. One of his good buddies from high school had gone to West Virginian University (WVU). The drinking age was eighteen in that state and Morgantown was a true college, party town. A number of his good friends came into town for a weekend of serious revelry. Late that Saturday night they were roaming the streets of Morgantown after the bars had closed, when they came upon several hookers who were ready to call it a night. After some friendly banter, the girls invited them back to their apartment to party. The ladies had a serious stash of high quality marijuana. One of his friends convinced him to steal this huge potent bud and eat it. He just swallowed it right down with a swig of beer. In a little while things began to get quite hazy and then he had no further memory of what transpired next. Apparently, they took off to a late nightclub and he got separated from the group. He remembers starting to slowly achieve consciousness the next morning, feeling terrible. He heard a loud buzzing noise and something was pinching his leg. He was also being beaten in the midsection in a slow rhythmic fashion. Someone was speaking but he struggled to decipher what was being said. He opened his eyes and began to apprise the situation. He was lying on his back on the front porch of some old row house in Morgantown. A small dog was furiously growling as it chewed on his lower leg like a large bone. A very fat, ugly old woman in her nightgown was standing over him, beating him with a broom. He began to understand what she was saying. She was repeating herself, "I have called the police. They are on the way you drunken bum. They will be here any minute." He began to grasp the situation. He stood up abruptly and she screamed. He ignored her and took off in a sprint down the road. He cut back and forth between the row houses to get as far away as possible before the cops arrived. After about ten minutes of running he puked his guts out. He then managed to find his way to the bus station and bought a ticket for Pittsburgh. He went home with his tail between his legs and didn't even consider trying to get back to his friend's apartment for his stuff. He had had enough fun for one weekend.

He majored in Mechanical Engineering because he was sure he could get a job with that degree upon graduating. The first two years of the curriculum were loaded with more general scientific and academic courses like high level mathematics, physics, chemistry, probability and statistics and even English and writing. He excelled in that kind of course work and did very well. In his junior year the curriculum shifted heavily into real engineering course work. He did not have much natural aptitude with machinery and struggled in the basic engineering courses. He was terrible at drafting as well. He really began to hate Mechanical Engineering and began to wonder if he had made a big mistake with his major. During that year he had a group of friends that he had occasionally done blotter acid with. Blotter acid was LSD on a small paper square that you let dissolve on your tongue. He and his friends loved tripping and going to parties where they would sit by themselves and engage in heavy duty discussions he could never remember much about the next day. He liked the way lights and colors looked so magical when you were on acid and the "trails" that would follow people as they moved. One Saturday night when he was working, one of his friends died from an overdose. The autopsy revealed that she had taken a blotter that had roughly five times the normal dosage. The experience was shocking, sad and chilling. He thought it over and realized that there could not be much quality control in illegally manufactured recreational drugs. He swore off hard drugs forever and he never wavered. It was a decision that served him well when he

SILVIO SANTINI

started working on Wall Street and so many of his colleagues seemed to be cokeheads. He even gave up pot and alcohol for a few weeks but it didn't take long before he slithered back to his old standbys. He also came to the conclusion that he needed to make changes in his life, so he impulsively applied to transfer out of the School of Engineering and into the College of Arts and Sciences. His advisor signed off on his transfer request without comment but to his surprise he was summoned to meet with the Dean of the School of Engineering. The Dean sat him down and pointed to a huge stack of papers on his desk, "Do you see that stack of applications on my desk? Those are all applications from students trying to transfer from the College of Arts and Sciences into the School of Engineering. I would guess that less than 10 percent of them will eventually get in." The Dean then held up his transfer application and said, "This represents all of the applications I currently have for students trying to go from the School of Engineering into the College of Arts and Sciences. More importantly, I notice that you are currently 16th out of 128 in your class, so you are obviously capable of doing the work to finish your degree. I would like to know why you want to do this." It struck him that he probably had not thought this decision through very well and so he kind of stammered with his response, "Well I have been having some personal issues. A good friend of mine died recently and it was very destabilizing to me. It has struck me that I just do not like Mechanical Engineering so I thought I would get a degree in Business instead." The Dean paused for a moment and then spoke, "I am sorry to hear about your friend. But I would like to ask you a question. Why do you suppose all these students are trying to transfer into the School of

Engineering?" He responded, "Because employment opportunities upon graduating are much better for engineers than for most other majors." The Dean smiled, "Exactly. Now let me ask you another question. What interests you? What kind of work do you want to do when you graduate?" Once again he realized he did not have a very good answer for an important question, "I guess I am not really sure. I have been supporting myself since I was seventeen and I am paying for my own education so mostly I have thought about making more money, first and foremost. I suppose I lean towards the business side of things. The hard core engineering stuff really doesn't interest me so much." The Dean leaned towards him, "Listen to me carefully. I want you to reconsider this transfer. I think you are making a big mistake. Tough it out and finish your degree in Mechanical Engineering. Get a decent job and in a few years you will figure out how to move towards the business side of things. Maybe you will consider getting an MBA. I would advise you to take the GMATs while you are still in school and your test taking skills are still sharp. How about we put this transfer on hold and you think it over for a week and come back and tell me your decision then?" He knew when he was getting good advice so he did not hesitate, "There is no need for that sir. You have already changed my mind. Please rip that transfer application up. Thank you very much for taking the time to help me realize I had made a foolish, impulsive decision." In his final semester at school he took the GMATs and scored 730, a very good performance. Several years later when he applied to graduate business schools, the same Dean wrote his academic letters of recommendation.

At the end of his junior year he drove to Ocean City, MD with some friends for one week's vacation before starting work for the summer. They drove at night and since he was behind the wheel he was drinking coffee all night as his friends were pounding beers and smoking pot. Their plan was to crash in the car for the balance of the night when they got there and then sort out a cheap place to stay for the balance of the week in the next morning. Early May was the off season and from last year's experience they knew they could find a cheap place to stay near the beach and the boardwalk, near plenty of bars. They got to the parking lot at the beach around 2 AM and all of his friends fell soundly asleep immediately. He was all hopped up from the coffee and so decided to go for a walk on the beach. After walking on the beach for five minutes he came upon a bonfire where a group of biker dudes and their chicks were sitting around a nice fire. It was back in the day when the local police were more lenient toward nighttime bonfires and bikers in the off-season. As he got closer to the group he could see one biker guy sitting on a piece of driftwood playing guitar and singing. The man was performing an acoustic version of The Rolling Stones' Wild Horses and doing a bang-up job. He became overcome by the sound of the sweet music on top of the clean ocean breeze and the rhythmic beat of the pounding waves. He blatantly walked right into the middle of the group and walked straight up to the guitar player and stood less than five feet away from the player and swayed while the classic song ambled to its slow finish. He remembered looking around at the harsh, arrogant looking bikers and the dirty chicks that seemed stunningly beautiful despite their obvious lack of normal hygiene or grooming. He thought to himself that surely he would be a great success in life because he could easily mix in with any-one, anywhere at anytime. He certainly never considered how irritating it must have been for these bikers to have a preppy little fuck like him in his little Izod shirt with the neat collar and little alligator insignia crash their overnight beach party out of nowhere. The song ended and suddenly there were ten seconds of complete silence except for the sound of the waves. The guitar player turned to him and quietly said, "Dude, if I was you, I would get the fuck out of here now." Suddenly, he could feel the group focused on him with hostile, angry energy. He thought to himself that surely they were going to kill him and bury him in the sand. He briskly walked away from the group with his head down. Somebody smacked him in the head and knocked his Pirates baseball cap off, but he just kept moving. When got about 50 yards away from the bikers he broke into a hard sprint back to the car. When he got there he immediately started it up and began to drive away. When one of his friends woke up and started to grumble he told him there was too much light and they needed a better place to sleep. He had noticed a bunch of motorcycles on the end of the parking lot and had decided the best decision was to get the fuck out of there. He drove 3 or 4 miles uptown and they fin-ished the night on a quiet side street. A few days later, he went into MacDonald's with his friends and saw the biker group there eating at a number of tables. The guitar player biker dude had his Pirate cap on and he thought about asking for it back before deciding that was probably a really bad idea.

One month before he graduated from college, his girl-friend informed him she was pregnant. They got married and had two sons one right after the other. His wife had also come from a violent, dysfunctional family. She became more erratic and difficult as the years went by, even after he achieved financial success. In all honesty, he could not say he had always behaved like husband of the year. It was a lonely marriage. Eventually they got divorced. In any event, he left college with big responsibility on his shoulders. He took a job as a field engineer with a major service company in the gas and oil drilling industry. The Arab Oil Embargo shock had hit in the early 70s and this, combined with rampant inflation, had caused a big surge in oil prices over the past decade. This had triggered a huge boom in the domestic drilling industry. He was sure this would be a great growth industry to get involved with. The job entailed a hands-on six month training program before you became a field representative with your own territory and a company car. He was certain he was on his way to prosperity and would be able to take care of his new family in style before too long. Shockingly, the price of oil collapsed that summer. This created carnage in the domestic oil patch and many over-leveraged drilling and production companies went bust. His company's business suffered and he had been on the job less than three months when he received a huge shock. The company had decided to suspend the field-engineering program indefinitely. New hires like him could stay on with the company as equipment operators at a reduced salary and if conditions improved they might restart the program at a later date. With a pregnant wife he did not have much choice except to stay on in this new role while he started mailing out resumes trying to find a new position somewhere. They had him driving the acid truck to well sites where they performed hydraulic fracturing operations. Hydraulic fracturing is essentially the high pressure pumping of gas or liquids mixed with sand down into freshly drilled wells to create splits in the rock strata which theoretically increases production yield. The real money for his company was in selling chemicals to throw into the mix during the process. The true job of a successful field engineer was chemical sales to the production companies that owned the wells. The acid truck had two 1000-gallon liquid containers on it, which usually were filled with 750 gallons each of a liquid mix used in the hydraulic fracturing process. This meant that the truck shook and the steering wheel vibrated greatly as you drove this truck, due to the liquid sloshing around in both tanks. You would usually get a wake-up call at 3 AM or so for the jobs and you went to two well sites a day. On his first day driving the truck, he ran through a red light in a small town because no one had explained to him how you had to gear down to stop a big truck. You could not just hit the brakes like you would in a car. They had just assumed he could drive a stick shift. It was insanity having him drive and operate any of these equipment trucks. This was certainly not an area where he had any natural aptitude. By the third day of these new responsibilities he was exhausted. Driving home from the second job he fell asleep at the wheel. Suddenly, he woke up with the truck bouncing madly as he went smashing through a cornfield at high speed. Somehow, he maintained control of the truck and got back on the road without wrecking. When he got back to headquarters, he was sitting in the workers lounge having a cup of coffee when he was called down to speak with the head mechanic. The burly mechanic eyed him from top to bottom, scratched his beard and asked him a question, "Hey bud. Let me ask you something. Did you by any chance drive through a cornfield today?" He paused before responding, and then answered with a question, "Why would you ask me something like that?" The mechanic hardened his tone, "How about you get down on the ground and take a little peek under the truck?" He dutifully did as he was told and was not surprised to see the whole undercarriage of the truck stuffed with cornstalks. The mechanic then said, "I have no idea why these stupid pricks running this company have you college whiz kids running trucks all of a sudden. But if this shit keeps up I'm getting out of the fucking profit-sharing program." It was hard to argue with that logic. The next week he went on a job where the well site was on top of a mountain in a remote area in the Allegheny National Forest. It was pouring rain and the road up to the well site was a muddy, rough dirt road hacked out of the mountainside. It had just started to get light outside when he hit a rough spot and the truck lurched violently to the right, almost sending him cascading down hundreds of feet to certain death. Naturally, this scared the shit out of him. He then started hugging the inside of the road. A little while further, he hit another bump and this time he had the impression that he had run over the water pipe that ran along the inside track of the dirt road up to the well site. He quickly forgot about this as he concentrated on driving that truck up that dirt road without killing himself. Generally, it took several hours for the set up before a hydraulic fracturing operation. Naturally, he slipped away and burned a fattie to try and take the edge off and calm his fucking nerves. When they started the operation on this day they had to immediately stop because the water supply was not working. He watched the commotion and then remembered the debacle earlier when he ran over the pipe. He thought about it for a moment and then approached the job foreman who was known as a pretty outspoken tough character. He went up to the foreman and explained the situation. To his surprise the foreman did not explode in anger at him. The man just told him to get in the pickup truck and direct them to where this may have occurred. Sure enough a section of pipe had been flattened and needed to be replaced. He had never spoken to this particular job foreman before and was surprised at what a decent, thoughtful man the guy actually was. On the ride back up to the well site the foreman said to him. "Kid, it is not right that they got you driving a fucking acid truck out here. It is a waste of your education and it is not a good business decision on their part. Frankly, it is not safe either, no offense intended. Now the job will be delayed an hour or two and then it always takes me 3 hours at least to do these damn calculations and fill out the job report when I get back to the shop. It is my son's birthday and I won't get home till nine now." The foremen on the jobs had to make a number of calculations and fill out detailed reports. He had ingratiated himself to some other foremen when he was still in training by doing the reports for them. He could crank that stuff out with his eyes closed. He told the foreman, "Let me crunch the numbers and do this paperwork for you. It will be done before we leave the job site and you can still make your son's birthday dinner." For the rest of his time with the company that foreman arranged for him to ride with him so he could do all his paperwork for him. They became good friends riding together. The foreman was known as a badass because he aggressively dressed down slackers on the job site. But he was an intelligent man and they had many long, interesting discussions on a wide variety of topics while they were riding together. The foreman was a good family man and played drums on the weekends in a country band. He sat in on several of the band's gigs playing piano and had a ball. One thing the foreman could not make sense of was why the price of oil could swing up and down so rapidly. In fact he found it fascinating that all these guys making a living in the oil patch had no idea why the price of oil fluctuated so dramatically even though their livelihood depended on it. This was when he first became interested in financial markets. He wondered how the fucking price of oil could go up for ten straight years and then as soon as he was getting into the game it violently collapses and messes up his life. He pondered that one for some time.

After several months he found an engineering job with a consulting firm that had a huge mandate at a major, inland logistics base for the Department of the Navy. The base had many warehouses full of equipment and rows of office buildings where thousands of civil servants and consultants worked. Most of the work entailed writing reports and sending detailed letters back and forth. Within a short period of time, he realized that his mind would turn to mush if he did this kind of work for too long. It did not take him too long to figure the scam out, either. The Naval Officers that ran the base were a year or two away from retirement and this kind of outpost was where they finished out their careers without too much stress or pressure before retiring. All of the senior managers with his consulting firm were retired Naval Officers. It was pretty obvious that the game was to keep the consulting gravy train running full throttle so that all the retiring Naval Officers had lucrative slots waiting for them with the consulting firm.

The consulting firm had a number of employees known as triple dippers. They had retired from the military after twenty years of service and so they had a full pension from that. Then they had worked for the civil service for another five years or more and thereby qualified for a civil service pension, as there was a loophole whereby they could double count their active military service along with their civil service to qualify for another full pension. Then they were getting paid by the consulting group to complete the triple dip. The triple dippers were doing quite well for themselves courtesy of Uncle Sam. He befriended one triple dipper at his firm who was a huge ex marine they all referred to as Jarhead. The man had an enormous head with a crew cut and was literally the size of Hulk Hogan; Jarhead must have been six foot eight and weighed 350 pounds or more. It was the dawn of the computer age and all of the Navy's logistical information was getting loaded into databases. Jarhead would sit there all day slowly entering data into the system with one finger while constantly asking for help. He was glad to help the man, as the big fellow seemed quite pleasant for such a massive dude. One day after work he went to a bar to have a few drinks with three of his colleagues, including Jarhead. The big man sat down at the bar and quickly polished off two double boilermakers, and then slowed down to nurse a third. A group of tough looking biker type dudes were standing at the bar next to them. One of his friends was talking and waving his arms around, and accidently knocked over one of the biker's drinks spilling some on his pants. The biker dude grabbed his friend by the shirt and started making threats. Quick as a cat, Jarhead bolted out of the bar stool and grabbed the biker roughly. One massive hand, which was probably the size of a grizzly bear's paw, went around the biker's neck and the other one grabbed Biker Boy by the balls. Jarhead then picked Biker Boy up and slammed the suddenly helpless dude against the wall while holding the man three or four feet above the ground. Biker Boy's face was turning red and the man's eyes seemed to be ready to explode. The dude's legs were spread apart and feebly wiggling as Jarhead ruthlessly crushed Biker Boy's testicles. The biker's friends looked on in frozen horror. Jarhead leaned his face in close to the poor bastard and belched and then asked Biker Boy a question in a loud voice. "Do you want me to fucking kill you?" Biker Boy shook his head no and they could hear him pathetically whimpering from the pain. Jarhead pulled Biker Boy away from the wall and gave the man a little love tap of a head butt. The guy's legs must have felt like jelly and Biker Boy collapsed to the floor of the bar as Jarhead sat back down in the bar stool and quietly ordered another boilermaker. Biker Boy's friends helped the man up and they all hustled right out of the bar. They were not so stupid. They had ascertained the grim reality that Jarhead could go through all of them at the same time like a hot knife through butter. It constantly amazed him throughout his life how some people would aggressively initiate conflict for very little reason with adversaries whose capabilities they did not understand.

His younger son had been born with significant medical issues and they were extremely strapped for money. He determined that he needed to work on weekends to try and keep them afloat. He took his responsibilities as a father seriously. His first part-time job was as a picture salesman. The guy who owned the business had developed a nice little racket.

The man would ingratiate himself to hospital administrators and would convince them to present a certificate for a free 8" by 10" baby picture to all couples that had babies delivered. This would enable Picture Man to get their names and phone numbers. Picture Man's staff would contact them when the babies were around nine months or so and get appointments for a photographer to stop by and take the little one's picture. The Picture Man's army of salesmen would then get the packages with the babies' proofs and go back to see the couples so they could select their free 8" by 10". Obviously, the point was to get them to buy some fucking pictures, not to select their free 8" by 10" and send you on your way. The sales people had to pay 10 dollars for each packet and then were paid 40% commission on the balance of the sale. He took a weekend gig working for Picture Man and very quickly was making three to four hundred dollars every weekend. But it was tough money to make. It was in the pre-cell phone era, which made the extensive phone calls and driving very inconvenient. He also began to see how wrong pre-conceived notions could be in business. When he started selling the baby pictures he assumed that you would make more money selling to affluent couples as opposed to working class people. But quite the opposite was true. The women in the big five bedroom houses in affluent neighborhoods tended to be cheap bitches and you had to work hard and squeeze to close a shitty thirty dollar order and break-even. On the other hand, most of the time the working class women in lousy neighborhoods went crazy over the pictures and would reach for bigger packages. They also usually paid cash, which was fantastic. For cash orders he would write them up for ten or twenty dollars less than he had actually charged whenever he felt he could get away with it. In this way he made 100% commission on that small part of the order. One Saturday he was having a bad day with just one appointment left. It was a cold and blustery day and he was in a funk because it was homecoming weekend for his Alma Mater. While his old college buddies were partying down and attending a big football game at a reunion weekend he was driving around the countryside selling baby pictures and had only made about fifty bucks for the whole damn day. His last client lived in a rural trailer park and it had been hard to find. The baby was a doll and the pictures were adorable but the woman would not buy anything. She told him they could not afford any baby pictures and would not budge. He launched into his last resort, which was to get them to pay ten bucks for all the proofs so at least he could get his money back for the packet. Even this effort failed. He got angry and frustrated and crossed the line with a snippy comment, "Well these are such beautiful pictures it really is a shame because we destroy all non-purchased proofs to recycle the chemicals. How would you feel about that if God forbid something should happen to the little fellow?" Suddenly the poor woman burst into tears and blurted out, "Oh my God! How did you know my baby was so sick?" Before he could try to apologize and make amends the whole fucking trailer shook and the curtain behind the kitchen table swung open. Her husband had been in there the whole time and burst out after him. This was a big, fat man with long hair and a beard in his boxer shorts with his big hairy belly hanging out. The man screamed, "You son of a bitch!" and grabbed him by the shirt. He had on his big steel toed work boots and instinctively nailed the guy with a vicious kick to the shins. It caught the crazed husband by surprise and the man let go of his shirt and fell down, causing the trailer to shake even more. The woman started screaming and the baby started crying. It had turned into a horrible debacle. He always thinks of the old Lynyrd Skynyrd song "Gimmee Three Steps" when he recalls this incident because that was the break he was looking for. He quickly bolted for the door and got in his car, started it up and began backing out of there as quickly as possible. While he was pulling out, Big Boy ran out of the house and punched a dent in his car as he was fleeing the scene of the crime. He didn't care too much about that, as the car was a piece of shit anyhow. So in the end the woman got the proofs as well as his case full of sample plaques and his winter coat. At least he consoled himself that the coat was too small for Big Boy. Needless to say, this signaled the end of his fledgling part-time career as a baby picture salesman.

His next part-time job was loading freight Friday and Saturday evening from midnight to nine AM. They lived near a large freight hub. It was boring work and a depressing way to spend your weekend but it was fifteen bucks an hour he desperately needed. There was a stack of Playboy magazines in the lunchroom and one Sunday morning at four AM on lunch break he read an article in Playboy about average salaries in different fields. He was surprised to learn that investment bankers were number one. They made more money on average than even doctors. He did not know what investment bankers did but he was very interested to find out. Several weeks later his sister got married and his wife was paired in the wedding party with the groom's cousin. The cousin was a good-looking, polished man and he also heard that the dude was an investment banker with Morgan Stanley in NYC and made a shit load of money. His wife and the investment banker seemed to be having a fine time at the main table chatting and even dancing. He was stuck at a table with his mother helping her care for his infant sons, feeding them and changing diapers. Mercifully, his mother elected to leave the wedding somewhat early and take the boys home for bed. He then smoked a couple of joints with his brothers outside and then started to hit the whiskey pretty hard to make up for lost time. When he was half kicked in the ass he walked up to the main table and sat down next to the investment banker. He started a conversation, "I hear you are an investment banker with Morgan Stanley and do quite well. Can you explain to me exactly what a fucking investment banker is and how do I become one?" The investment banker replied, "I need some information and there is no sense in bullshitting me. Where did you go to college, what did you major in and what was your GPA? Have you taken the GMATs and what was your score? Also, briefly describe your work experience since graduating." He spoke for a few minutes and the investment banker seemed dutifully impressed with his background. The investment banker then said, "Listen, you can make this happen. You have the necessary credentials and abilities to make the move, I am sure of it. All you need to do is quit your job and go back to school full time for an MBA. It is a two-year program. You have to go to one of the top schools. There you will learn all about investment banking, and with drive and determination you will get a job on Wall Street when you graduate. But the school you go to is important." The investment banker then wrote the name of eight top graduate business schools on a napkin and handed it to him. "Get accepted to one of these schools and make the move. Do not let anyone discourage you. Make the move and never look back. You will not regret it." Once again, he knew when he was getting good advice. He applied to four of the schools and got accepted to all of them. He decided to attend the graduate business school with the most quantitative program. Most of the family on both sides tried to discourage him. It seemed crazy to all of them that he would dare quit his full time job and go back to school with a wife and two kids. His mother especially nagged him about what a foolish move he was making. He never wavered in his decision. His younger son's health had stabilized, which removed his only real concern. Other than that, he was working his ass off seven days a week and didn't have a pot to piss in so what the fuck did he really have to lose? Interestingly enough, only his father was genuinely supportive. The old man said, "It takes a lot of balls to make a move like this. In fact, it takes a man. It tells me you will be a big success in life because you have balls and are not afraid to take a chance. I wish I had taken more chances in my own career." His quest to work on Wall Street began as they packed up and moved to the Windy City.

Chapter 4

The investment banker he had met at his sister's wedding was absolutely correct that he would figure out what investment banking was all about at graduate business school. From day one at that school there was a big focus on recruiting. The first year students needed to find summer internships and the second year students were looking for full time jobs right out of the block. The school provided many resources to help the students research companies and industries and look for jobs. The school also held a number of conferences and cocktail hours focused on recruiting. Most importantly, many top companies actively interviewed students directly at the school. He had to give the administration a lot of credit. They put significant effort into helping students find quality employment. When it came to post MBA careers there was investment banking, consulting and then everything else. Students were spending a lot of money to be there, especially when you considered lost wages for two years and so there was a big focus on high paying job opportunities above all else. He loved the curriculum at that school and made straight As. In reality, undergraduate engineering was more difficult but finance was much more interesting to him. Unlike most students, he did not have the luxury of not working while attending graduate school. He had loans to cover tuition and housing but still needed to come up with money to support his family. He lined up a couple of part-time consulting gigs for the first semester. He had become an expert in U.S. Naval procurement procedures and was surprised at how valuable a skill this was. He helped several local manufacturers close out a number of big deals with the Navy that fall. The procurement procedures were very convoluted and difficult to implement without an insider's knowledge. This was not the business he had gone back to school for however. He was determined to work on Wall Street. He also took a weekend job as a night-time desk clerk at one of the school's undergraduate dorms. The area around the school was a small, moderately upscale neighborhood surrounded by miles of pretty rough inner city. After he had been there a couple of weeks he left the dorm at six AM on a Sunday morning as usual. He opened his window and fired up a joint to burn on the short drive back home to their student-housing apartment. When he was making a right hand turn onto the main drag a big black Cadillac roared past him and just barely missed hitting him. "Mother fucking ass-hole, mother fucking asshole!" he shouted to himself in the car. He drove up to a red light and pulled up on the right side of the black Cadillac that had almost hit him. The window on the Cadillac opened and the driver was a menacing looking black dude who was wearing dark glasses and pointing a pistol at his head. In a loud voice Bad Dude asked a question, "What did you say Motherfucker?" His heart sank. He figured the hood was going to shoot him in the head and that would be the end. Instinctively he lowered his gaze away from Bad Dude and found a voice to reply, "Nothing Sir. I said absolutely nothing." Bad Dude waved the gun and laughed. He interpreted this as a good sign that the man was just fucking with him. Sweet relief flooded through him. He reasoned that if this fucker was just going to randomly shoot him it would have happened already. Then Bad Dude spoke, "Sir, my name is now Sir? A second ago it was mother fucking asshole. So what is it, Sir or mother fucking asshole?" Without looking up he replied, "Sir. Without a doubt it is Sir." He then heard the engine of the Cadillac roar and looked up to watch the car moving quickly away through the still red light. He read the license plate but quickly decided there was no point in reporting this shit. He had always hated cops anyhow.

Not too long after that startling incident he noticed an interesting posting on the bulletin board in the campus recruiting office. A major brokerage firm was looking for a first year MBA student to work full-time at night servicing clients and executing financial futures transactions on overnight exchanges. This was exactly the kind of opportunity he was looking for. He had already begun stressing out about having to get some kind of summer internship in finance. He was at a disadvantage to many of his fellow students due to his engineering background. But you needed some kind of job in the industry to get the Wall Street firms to notice you for full-time recruiting. He sent in a resume and also made several phone calls but got nowhere on this job opportunity for two weeks or so. He got the idea to call after midnight in hopes of talking to existing staff of the night desk and at least get some information. He got through to the current manager of the desk and struck up a conversation. The guy had graduated from business school at the end of the summer and had worked the job for almost two years. The firm had promised to move the man to a sales job on the exchange floor as soon as they found a replacement. The current desk manager was of the opinion that they were being extremely picky about hiring a replacement because they were not in a hurry to let the man move on. He knew he had found a good opening with this guy and suggested he stop down to the office with a pizza. The guy accepted his offer and they spent a couple of hours shooting the breeze that night and really hit it off. Within a couple of days he had an interview with the head of floor trading at the firm who was known by all as Mr. Coffee. As soon as he met the man he understood why the staff at the brokerage firm all called the dude Mr. Coffee behind his back. The man was very tall, wiry and athletic looking. Mr. Coffee raced stock cars on the weekend and had the look of a man not to be fucked with. The serious dude spoke a mile a minute and none of it was bullshit. To start the interview, Mr. Coffee relayed a lot of information about the position very quickly. He in turn responded with multiple reasons why he was a great choice for the job. He made sure to speak briskly and in staccato fashion similar to what he had heard from Mr. Coffee. The interview was over in twenty minutes and so he was sure he had blown it. But when he called the desk manager that night he was told to relax, Mr. Coffee had loved him. He got called back to interview with the top guy at the office. The Boss was the head of the institutional futures business for the entire firm. He later learned that The Boss was the only official A.E. (Account Executive) at the office and all commissions flowed through the man's fingers. The Boss would take his cut first and pay all the salesmen and balance of staff as he saw fit. The man was apparently making thirty to forty million dollars a year. His friend the desk manager had told him that The Boss was also an amateur painter and the paintings on the wall in the man's office were all personal work. He would always say afterwards that The Boss was the most impressive man he ever interviewed with. The top guy looked sharp, exuded confidence and talked like Marlon Brando's character, the Godfather, in the movie based on the classic Mafia novel. Early in the interview, he had made it a point to comment positively on the amazing paintings pretending that he did not know The Boss was the artist. This got things going in the right direction. At one stage he remembers The Boss leaning close and saying, "The people that have worked hard and been loyal to me are all millionaires. But the people that do not work hard or are disloyal end up with nothing." He responded with a heartfelt soliloquy about his work ethic and loyalty and somehow mixed in his responsibilities to his two young sons as well. He had also noticed pictures of The Boss's six kids all over the office. He got the job.

He worked Sunday through Thursday night six PM to five AM. It was a pretty tough gig to go along with full time enrollment at school but he was used to working like an animal and surviving on minimal amounts of sleep. The desk would normally be staffed with three other daytime floor clerks who wanted the overtime. They were supposed to be there from seven PM to eleven PM but most nights he would cut them all loose by nine PM and sign off that they had stayed until eleven PM so this helped him make friends quickly. It was thrilling to be working in the financial markets, discussing economic news and price movements with clients and executing futures trades. His learning curve concerning practical market knowledge quickly accelerated past most of his classmates at graduate business school. The clients for his desk were a combination of the institutional clients of the firm and scores of local futures traders from the Chicago futures exchanges who could trade on a "give-up" basis. This meant they would call to execute trades and then the trades would be given up directly to their brokerage firms to be cleared. They just paid a trade execution fee but did not clear their trades through his firm. Keeping the institutional clients of the firm happy was the most important aspect of his job and for many of these clients his desk provided more of an information service than an active trade execution capability. In those pre-Internet days, these kinds of night desks represented the most efficient method for traders to monitor the overnight market risks on their positions. A big part of his job was a nightly sheet with call levels in different markets for institutional clients of the firm. It was critical that you never miss a call level. The local traders were much more active in actual trading at night and he learned a lot talking with those guys and executing trades for them. He met an interesting cast of characters at the firm. One of the daytime floor managers he got to know well was a very charismatic character who could pontificate elegantly about the bond and currency markets. The man later went on to become a lead market analyst on a major business television network. He befriended a middle-aged guy named Arnold who was there practically every night because the man needed the overtime. Arnold had experienced a fairly incredible rags to riches to rags life. Arnold was married with five kids and living in a 2-bedroom apartment in a low income section of town, barely making ends meet. Arnold had grown up in a rough section of the city. The man had started working on the floor of the CBOT (Chicago Board of Trade) at a young age. In the 70s, Arnold had become an executing floor broker, which meant the man did the actual trading in the futures pits on behalf of futures brokerage firms and was paid a commission per trade. In the hyperinflation environment of the late 70s the soybeans futures market exploded and Arnold made a killing. For a few wonderful years the man was making five hundred thousand dollars a year and started living like a king. Arnold had apparently bought a huge house in the exclusive North Shore area of Chicago, acquired multiple sports cars, enrolled his children in expensive private schools and began taking extremely lavish vacations with his family. It is a sad fact that most people can learn how to spend money very quickly once they have it, but the reverse process is usually much more difficult and extremely painful. After the decisive actions of then FED chairman Paul Volcker began to tame inflation in the early 80s, the commodity markets quieted down and the trading in these futures markets slowed considerably. It had not taken poor Arnold very long to run out of money because the guy had overextended himself to such a large extent. At this stage, Arnold had decided to become a local trader in the pits since there was very little opportunity to make money executing trades on behalf of brokerage firms. This meant the man was buying and selling futures for his own account on a speculative basis as opposed to being paid a fee to execute trades for others. Arnold wasn't very good at speculating and in no time at all the man lost everything, including several hundred thousand dollars of his father's retirement savings. Now in late 1985, Arnold found himself broke, racked with guilt over the hardships his family was now enduring, estranged from his father and working sixteen hour days to barely make ends meet. Despite all the personal hardships, Arnold was a nice guy to work with who patiently taught him a lot of practical market knowledge. He felt great empathy for the man. Arnold used to constantly tell him that they were ships heading in different directions. Arnold told him his time would come to make a lot of money but you could not count on it lasting for too long. Arnold implored him to save his money when that happened so he didn't end up destitute like poor old Arnold who considered himself a disgrace and often spoke of suicide. He never did forget about Arnold and heeded that advice when he began to achieve significant financial success in the industry.

Some of the clients of the firm that he spoke to frequently were quite memorable. He could not forget a man named Pete who was considered a premier client. Mr. Coffee had succinctly instructed him that he had better keep Pete happy. Pete was easy to keep happy. The guy was a very active trader at night and always was extremely pleasant despite the fact that it seemed that the man's positions were constantly losing money. He had started working on the desk shortly after the historic Plaza Accord the G-5 (United States, Germany, France, Japan and United Kingdom) had signed in late 1985. The U.S. dollar had been on a massive bull run since Reagan had taken office and this had created huge trade imbalances and significant stress in global financial markets. For the first time in history, the Central Banks had publicly declared their commitment to substantially devalue the dollar and had made clear their intentions to actively intervene in currency markets to achieve this end. On his desk they were trading currency futures, which were denominated in Dollars per currency. So this meant the futures went up when the Dollar was going lower. It seemed to him that currency trading was the easiest game he had ever seen. Just stay long currencies (short Dollars). The Central Banks had made clear the direction they wanted to move the market. Most nights, the currency futures he was monitoring and executing trades in would all go higher. Every once in a while the currencies would fall back in a small retracement due to significant profit taking action in the market or some kind of headline designed to slow the move down and keep it manageable. Two years after the Plaza Accord the Dollar had in fact devalued by roughly 50% across the board vs. these other major currencies. Indeed, staying long currencies during this period was as close to a lay up trade as you will ever see in financial markets. But for some perverse reason, Pete had a hard-on to be short currency futures. The man was always short currency futures in Japanese Yen, Swiss Francs, or Deutsche Marks and would have take-profit orders (orders to buy back his futures contracts lower if the Dollar appreciated and book his profit on that trade) as well as stop-loss orders (orders to buy back his futures contracts higher if the dollar went lower to take his loss on that trade). He could not understand Pete's motivation, but would dutifully call Pete on a regular basis to inform the man of market movements and news releases, as well as to notify him of the latest stop-loss trade execution. Many clients were quite terse and rude when you called to inform them of stop-loss trade executions, and frankly this was understandable. In later years he would learn how unpleasant it was to be woken up in the middle of the night to be informed you were losing money. But Pete never seemed to get angry when informed of more losses on the never-ending long Dollar bets and they started to make frequent small talk concerning sports and other current event topics. Finally one night there was an extremely large retracement in the Dollar and for the first time Pete bought back currency futures lower and booked a profit. When he called Pete to give him the good news the man was very excited. Pete insisted on ordering him a steak dinner to be delivered to the office. He just could not understand what was motivating Pete to trade this way. When he asked Pete why the man was playing the currency futures from the short side despite the Central Bankers clear intentions to devalue the Dollar, Pete launched into a big patriotic speech about how the Dollar was stronger than all these other currencies put together no matter what the Central Bankers said or did. It made no sense. He got up the nerve to ask Pete if trading currency futures was his only livelihood. The answer was astonishing. Pete had owned a construction company the man had built from scratch and sold for over twenty million dollars three years earlier. Pete had then decided to trade futures full time and freely admitted that losses totaled around ten million during that period. When he asked Pete why the man didn't just stop (Mr. Coffee might have fired him for asking a question like this), Pete informed him that it was impossible to stop now because there were significant tax-loss carry forwards to apply to future trading profits. Pete could not seem to grasp the concept that you actually had to make a profit for the year to apply the tax-loss carry forwards. He often wondered how much longer it took for Pete to go bust because that result seemed inevitable. Pete epitomized the trader with pre-conceived notions who ignored what the market was communicating. "Don't fade the tape" is one of the oldest market sayings around, but traders do it constantly and probably always will.

He contrasted Pete with another client known as Top Dog. This guy would call out of the blue a couple of times a week and ask questions and sometimes leave large orders always speaking in a low confident voice. The man was a senior trader at a major commercial bank. Top Dog would call every time the Eurodollar Futures (short term interest rate futures) made a move based on central bank interventions or news releases about the Dollar even though there was technically no correlation between these markets. Typically the Eurodollar Futures might have moved quickly from 8135 to 8145 and Top Dog would suddenly call and leave an order to sell five thousand contracts down to 8140. These meant start selling at 8145 and keep selling until you either sold five thousand or the price was back below 8140. Usually he might sell several thousand and drive the market back down below Top Dog's lower level. It was very infrequent that he was able sell or buy the full amount requested by Top Dog. Once in a while when he called Top Dog back to report his trade fills the man would request a lot of information that he would quickly retrieve from the Telerate system. Sometimes Top Dog would explain the relevance of the data requested. The man never made any idle chit chat about sports or any other current event; the only topic of discussion was financial markets. Speaking to Top Dog on a regular basis was an incredible educational opportunity that helped him move up the learning curve quickly. The man was a real pro and it was an amazing opportunity to learn how a true professional analyzed financial markets and made intelligent trading decisions.

For the first few months he was absolutely thrilled just to be there doing the job for his relatively low wages. The firm knew there were a lot of MBAs who would love to have that job for the experience, opportunity and resume building power so there was no need to pay much. The financial futures market back then was a much more freewheeling, less closely regulated environment than now exists. The commissions were significantly higher making financial futures a very lucrative business. There were big waves of money washing back and forth across his trading desk and he was itching to find some way to get in on the action and make some extra cash for himself and his family. He started to figure out all the little games that were going on under the radar. All of the senior sales people and floor managers at that firm had personal trading accounts. Being alone in that office in the middle of the night, he had access to the entire daily trading ledgers and floor reports and started to figure some stuff out. Winning trade errors always found their way into somebody at the firm's personal account whereas losing errors went into the error account. The cagy desk managers on the exchange floors all had locals (independent floor brokers) that were their buddies. When they had big orders to execute that were going to move the market their buddies would get tipped off in a slick fashion so they could jump ahead of the order and make some quick money. The locals would then kick back some of their winning trades into the floor managers' accounts so they could get a taste of the honey. Also, many of the professional traders who had large institutional trading accounts with the firm also had separate personal trading accounts. Mr. Coffee was an animal. The man called at least four or five times to check on currency markets every night. He learned to keep a running update of the market information the man wanted and any news item of interest every hour on the hour so he could succinctly deliver the right stuff on every call. This habit stayed with him throughout his later career as a trader. Mr. Coffee had a very slick little nighttime trading program. Every night the man left four orders that had a code name as opposed to an actual trading account number assigned as all trades were legally supposed to have before being executed. They were smart orders. The orders were always to buy Swiss Franc futures lower so that if by some chance the dollar had a temporary bounce overnight they were buying the Swiss Franc futures lower. It was essentially the opposite of the strategy being employed by clueless Pete. Whenever these orders were filled he called Mr. Coffee to inform him and then put the tickets on the man's desk. Mr. Coffee had three big clients who had large institutional accounts and personal accounts. Whenever the trades were winners the original trades and the subsequent take profit trades went into Mr. Coffee and the three amigos personal trading accounts. If the trades became losers all of the opening trades and the subsequent loss taking closeout trades went into one of the three amigos institutional accounts on a rotating basis. In this fashion winning trades were converted into personal cash and losing trades were harmlessly absorbed into the institutional ledger. It was a nice little money machine for the four good buddies.

He befriended a few of the local traders that left orders and executed trades with him. Most of these guys were market makers (traders who make prices) in the currency futures options pit at the CME (Chicago Mercantile Exchange). Their overnight currency futures orders enabled them to rebalance and optimize their currency futures options portfolios at night since the actual FX market never closed. He began to learn some practical options trading skills from his conversations with these dudes. One night one of these locals called right after the Swiss Futures had made a quick move lower based on some bogus news story and he confidently told the local it was a false break and would soon sharply rebound. The local told him to go ahead and buy some Swiss Futures with a tight stop-loss but then the phone got cut off. He should never have actually executed a trade on such an imprecise order. Trade orders needed to be specific and all conversations were being recorded. He was so excited the local supported his view that he very cavalierly bought Swiss Futures and the market almost immediately exploded higher so he made the man a quick five grand. If the trade had been a loser he could have been stuffed, to use market parlance. This means the local would not have been obligated to accept the trades because he had not really given a specific order that had been repeated back to him for verification. This could have created big trouble for him with Mr. Coffee. But the trade was a winner and that made all the difference in this situation. Apparently the guy had been high on something because the man called back several hours later to verify nothing had actually been done. When he informed the local he had made him a quick five grand the guy became ecstatic. About an hour later the man showed up at the office and visited with him on the trading desk around two AM. He had to take the elevator down to the security desk and sign the local in. The guy had a bag of cocaine and wanted to turn him onto some lines. He had sworn off the hard stuff and so he politely declined. Then he suggested a better way for the local trader to pay him back. How about the local let him use the man's account to trade and then they square up in cash on a regular basis in some discreet fashion. The local agreed to this under pretty tough terms. If he lost money in the account he had to pay the guy back all of it. If he made money he would get 1/3 of the profits in cash on a monthly basis. The local would keep 1/3 for the man's share and 1/3 to cover taxes. He took the deal since it was the only way he could get in the game. After the guy left he realized this might not represent such a great opportunity. It represented an enormous bogey to cover and left very little margin for error and he did not have any money to lose. He pondered for a few weeks and then the answer came to him. He could trade a sure thing if he waited until Top Dog made a move. Then he could cover the range in some unobtrusive quantity every time. The Eurodollar futures were worth 25 dollars a tick, so if Top Dog came in to sell at 8215 down to 8212 it meant you were assured to make 3 tics. In this example, if he was able to sell more than five hundred contracts for Top Dog at 8215, he might allocate 40 of these to the local's account and he would simultaneously put in a bid for the local to buy back the 40 at 8212. It was guaranteed that Top Dog's order would drive the market down to 8212. It never failed. In this example the trade would be worth 40 x 3 x 25 = $3,000, which would make his cut $1,000. Obviously, this was totally illegal and he would have been instantly fired had this activity been discovered but he didn't think that was likely to occur. He was very careful to keep his mouth shut and with all the shenanigans going on in that office, he didn't think anyone was looking at stuff too closely. This was before the days of diligent compliance departments at major broker-age firms. In retrospect, it was reckless and foolish to take this kind of career risk just to make some extra money. Moreover, it was extremely unethical towards Top Dog to allocate even one of his contracts to another account. But he was hungry and was determined to get his snout into the money trough and damn the consequences. He made between two and four thousand dollars cash steadily per month with this methodology for the rest of his time at that firm and his family's lifestyle improved quite nicely as a result. This technique is known as front-running customer orders.

Landing this job saved him from even having to interview for a summer internship during his first year at graduate school, but he determined to actively seek a fulltime job on Wall Street when he graduated. He had made up his mind he wanted to be a trader and not a salesman so he did not really have interest to remain with his firm after graduation. His firm was purely brokers and did not offer any principal trading positions, only sales opportunities. The full time recruiting for Wall Street jobs was broken down into two broad categories; either Investment Banking or Sales and Trading. Investment Banking referred to positions in Corporate Finance, M&A (Mergers and Acquisitions), or any of the other advisory, fee based businesses Wall Street firms were involved in. These were the graduates who had to work extremely long hours doing face time in the first few years of their careers. When big deals were imminent, they often had to work several days in a row, never even going home to bathe. Basically, these jobs involved doing all of the grunt work for the Wall Street firms' deal making machines and were essentially very arduous screening programs with fantastic long-term opportunity if you paid your dues and made the grade. All of the major Wall

Street firms had Sales and Trading training programs whereby you spent your first four months at the firm being trained, and rotating around all of the major trading desks at the firm. At the end of the training program you would be placed on a trading desk in either a sales or a trading role, depending on your interests, the needs of the firm and how well you had sold yourself during your rotations on the various desks. His experience put him in a strong position to land one of these coveted Sales and Trading slots. He went through the process and got offers from two of the major investment banks that were recruiting in this area. He accepted one of these offers and was sure that this ended his interviewing experiences at the school. However, he received an invitation to interview with Grossman Zachs near the end of the recruiting season. Even though he had already accepted a position and reneging on a job offer was severely frowned upon by the campus recruiting office, he determined to take the interview simply because the mighty Grossman Zachs was considered the premier Wall Street firm. It was a bizarre interview. For some reason the interviewer seemed to have a real chip on his shoulder. The interviewer from Grossman Zachs made some disparaging remarks about how it must have been impossible to attend school properly while working at night despite the fact that his GPA was 4.0. Every other firm had been impressed with his work ethic. His normal interview sales pitch did not seem to impress the man from Grossman Zachs in the slightest. Halfway through the interview, the guy asked a very complex question concerning bond duration, which he had no idea how to answer. After he stumbled through this one, the guy followed it up with another tough, technical question concerning convexity analysis that only a cash bond trader with some legitimate experience could have handled. These were extremely unfair questions. No other firm had asked questions that only a seasoned market participant could have handled. His experience was in financial futures and FX, not cash bond dealing. It was a set up. This type of trading analytics was not covered in the curriculum. At this point the Grossman Zachs interviewer actually made a phone call using the phone in the room right in the middle of the interview, ignoring him for a few minutes. The interviewer then hung up the phone and pushed his resume back at him saying something to the effect that Grossman Zachs needed individuals with strong quantitative skills and he seemed to be lacking there. He got angry and grabbed his resume and glared at the interviewer, "Fuck you and fuck Grossman Zachs you fucking asshole. I have a suggestion, how about you and me continue our little chat out in the parking lot when you've finished your schedule?" He stood up and got in the interviewer's face. Mr. Tough Guy interviewer from the powerful Grossman Zachs looked a little startled but stayed very calm and asked, "Are you threatening me?" He replied, "Never in a million years would I work for Grossman Zachs." He then stormed out of that interview without another word. He never understood why Grossman Zachs had invited him to an interview to subsequently treat him so rudely. From what he could later ascertain, Grossman Zachs was not actually looking for the individuals with the strongest quantitative skills, best academic record, or the most applicable work experience. All of the students who he knew that landed jobs at Grossman were preppy little fucks that had gone to graduate school directly out of undergraduate school. They were all little rich dudes that had grown up leaning on Big Daddy's money. What they all had in common was that they had fathers who were some kind of honchos on Wall Street or in corporate America so that hiring them might lead to some kind of business opportunity for Grossman Zachs. In retrospect, he realized it was possible that the mighty Grossman got the best bang for their buck from recruiting MBA graduates using this hiring criteria. From this day forward, he completely despised Grossman Zachs. In this regard, he was ahead of his time. Twenty-five years later, 99% of the people in America felt the same way as Grossman Zachs become the symbol of Wall Street greed and corruption in the post-crash of 2008 world.

Chapter 5

He kept working on the overnight futures desk until after he graduated from business school. He had expected Mr. Coffee to break his balls over quitting but the man had surprised him. Mr. Coffee had acted like a complete gentleman when he resigned, and wished him all the best. Afterwards, he realized that Mr. Coffee was too smart to get shitty with him. There was always the possibility he could become a client down the road. He had arranged to work for his new firm during the summer before the MBA program started in the fall. They had an opening on their overnight FX trading desk and he had the experience to jump right in. With a wife and two kids and plenty of debt from graduate school he didn't feel he was in a position to take the summer off. Working on the FX overnight desk was a whole new ball game compared to running the overnight futures desk at his prior firm. Although the trading activity at his new firm was completely client driven, it was principal trading in the interbank FX market as opposed to executing futures trades on listed exchanges for commissions. Basically, they were quoting prices to clients and then covering the transactions with another bank, hopefully at a better rate than the price given to the customer. The clients had money on account with his firm and so they took the other side of the client FX trading activity as opposed to executing the trades on an exchange. This is the key difference between principal trading and executing trades on behalf of clients on an exchange and charging commissions. It was a very exciting transition to make and he did so seamlessly. Clients called in for information and prices via the telephone and then they all used the electronic dealing network provided by Reuters to trade with banks worldwide. They worked together as a team to get the best prices and extract maximum profit on each transaction and there was a good spirit on the desk. He worked the 4 PM to midnight shift, which meant they were initially dealing with banks in New Zealand and Australia. Then Tokyo and the rest of Asia would come on line halfway through the session. His salary was now considerably higher and they had also been provided a rental apartment at a subsidized rate through the firm. He later learned that the firm was "parking" apartments for a real estate client. This meant they were given a below market rate on their apartment but they signed an agreement to not renew the lease after it expired. The real estate company was trying to turn the building into a condominium and did not want to grant new leases that could not be broken because of the stringent NYC rental laws. He had a fine time with his family getting used to living in New York City.

Near the end of that summer he was involved in one of the most bizarre trades of his career. He answered the phone in the late afternoon on a Sunday and the caller identified himself as the CEO of the firm and requested to speak to the desk manager. After the desk manager hung up on the call he explained in a very excited voice that the C.E.O. needed them to sell over 500 million DEM (Deutsche Marks) vs. the Dollar. This was an enormous transaction during that period and was an especially large trade for the early Monday morning Asian time zone trading session. The DEM traded in the FX market under European terms, which meant it was denominated in Deutsche Marks per U.S. Dollar. Typically, market participants would talk about buying or selling dollar/mark, which meant buying or selling U.S. Dollars vs. the Deutsche Mark. In this case the C.E.O. had requested to sell Deutsche Marks, which meant he was buying U.S. Dollars. The dollar had remained in a long-term downtrend since the Plaza Accord in late 1985. For the month or so prior to this call the dollar had been getting pounded lower across the board on a fairly consistent basis and by most technical market standards was probably quite oversold and vulnerable to a retracement rally at some stage. There were dozens of banks that would quote them in this time zone but most of these calls were limited to a twenty million dollar maximum principal amount per trade. They had to carefully coordinate all the banks they were going to call and then attempt to sell the Deutsche Marks as efficiently as possible, spreading the trade over many counterparts. The team executed the trade swiftly and brilliantly. Clearly, they had caught the market short dollars because after they completed the trade the dollar experienced an explosive rally. It drove the exchange rate up by two percent or so, which represented a very big move for the DEM. There was a lot of discussion about how much profit to book for the department on the deal since it was an internal transaction for the firm. In general, it was always easier to take a bigger mark-up on a trade if the client was quickly in the money on the deal. But it was a bit trickier to decide how much pinch to take from a trade executed on behalf of the C.E.O. Before this decision could be made, he answered the phone and the caller identified himself as the C.F.O. of the firm who also requested to speak to the desk manager. It seemed that the C.E.O. had gotten confused and dealt on the wrong side of the market,. The trade they had actually needed to do was to sell dollar/mark, which meant buying DEM vs. the Dollar. He later ascertained that the firm was acquiring a German brokerage firm and the negotiations had been concluded that weekend. Therefore, the DEM needed to be secured to establish the exchange rate and pay for the acquisition. The C.E.O. had gotten excited and decided to execute the FX trade himself without making sure he was dealing correctly. Because of the sharp reaction that the trade had created in the marketplace, the incorrect deal had generated a profit of approximately six million dollars. The overnight desk manager knew that this issue had gone beyond his decision-making level and so he contacted his boss, the Chief FX Dealer of the firm. The Chief FX Dealer ordered the overnight desk manager to sit tight. Within an hour, the Chief FX Dealer and several of the most senior spot FX dealers had arrived. They were cagey enough to know that they needed to wait for the London trading session to open. This would give them greater access to liquidity and they would be able to reverse the trade, while dealing with banks that may not have been aware of the earlier transaction. The Chief FX Dealer also knew this was a big profit windfall for his department, so everyone on that desk was sworn to secrecy about this deal. At this time, the C.E.O. was considered one of the most dynamic young leaders on Wall Street. Several years later, the Board of Directors of the investment bank ousted him in disgrace after a series of well-publicized mistakes. It certainly did not surprise him when that C.E.O. got bounced. What he remembered most was reading that the C.E.O.'s exit package for screwing up and getting fired was in excess of thirty million dollars. He often fantasized about how great it would be to get fired and receive over thirty big balloons on the way out the door. In reality, the C.E.O. probably convinced himself at the time that he was getting fucked. Wall Street was full of dudes making more money than they had ever dreamed of, but instead of feeling grateful, they were bitter and angry and felt they were getting screwed. He fell into that way of thinking himself for a time. In any event, he recalled being simply astounded that the C.E.O. would jump into a trade and fuck it up only to make a lot of money for the firm by accident. When he asked the overnight desk manager his impression about this deal, the man smiled and said, "In this business it is always better to be lucky than good." That quote stayed with him throughout his career.

At the end of the summer, he had a private conversation with the Chief FX Dealer. The man assured him that he had done a great job that summer and had thoroughly impressed everyone in the department. He was offered the opportunity to work Sunday evenings for extra money. Sunday evening was Monday morning in Asia and it was generally the busiest day for the overnight FX desk, so they could use an extra hand. He lived close to the office and he was always looking to make more money so he was happy to accept the extra work. The Chief FX dealer also told him to keep an open mind while going through the MBA program, and then come back to the FX department where he surely had a bright future. He had a great time that fall in the MBA program. It was a truly unique opportunity to learn about all the different business lines the firm was running in Capital Markets. There was also a lot of pressure on the MBAs because they needed to make a positive impression somewhere to get placed. He really didn't feel any pressure since the open invitation to stay with the FX department was in his hip pocket. Most of the MBA graduates would eventually be placed in either Fixed Income or Institutional Equities, but they got a chance to rotate through many other trading desks as well. He found several of the trading desks that did not usually hire any MBAs to be the most interesting. The Stock Loan department was a revelation to him. Most of the graduates took the day off when they were scheduled to be in Stock Loan since it was common knowledge that they would not hire any MBAs and preferred you not even show up. This intrigued him, so he made a point to get there early and spend the whole day. The firm had a huge number of brokerage clients that held their stocks in "Street" name, which meant in the name of the brokerage firm. They had developed a big business charging interest to lend these stocks to other brokerage firms. In order to sell stocks short you needed to be able to deliver borrowed shares of the stock. Selling a stock short meant you were betting on a price decline in the stock. It is a pretty simple concept that most people find somewhat confusing because the idea of selling something you do not actually own sounds strange to people outside of Wall Street. Stock loan sounded simple but in practice it was a very lively and complicated business. The stock loan department was full of Italian dudes from Brooklyn who spoke with heavy accents and wore a lot of gold chains, bracelets and rings. These guys were on the phone all day cutting deals, chasing down stock, and pushing people at other firms to accept their terms. They were probably the most lively and colorful group of people he ever met in the industry. He fell in love with that business but was politely told at the end of the day that he had zero chance to get hired there. They were not going to let any MBA punks break into their racket. The other department, which did not usually hire MBAs, but intrigued him, was the NASDAQ trading desk. The NASDAQ at that time was essentially a computer bulletin board system to show stock prices but it did not actually connect buyers and sellers. The actual trading at that time was done in the OTC market, which for the most part, meant dealing over the phone. It was a business where Wall Street firms openly colluded. The different brokerage firms had tacit agreements to make prices in certain groups of stocks and maintain a standard bid/ask spread when dealing with each other. But actual clients had to pay a much wider spread. For example, the market maker in a particular stock might make a price of 6 ½ at 6 ¾ to fellow NASDAQ firms, which meant he would buy stock at 6 ½ or sell stock at 6 ¾. But the price to a retail client would be 6 ¼ at 7. It was a great system for the brokerage firms, since you would only have to take risk in a certain number of stocks, while being able to make principal trading profits on many other stocks. In addition, they charged commissions on the trades as well. The OTC stock traders impressed the hell out of him. They were engaged in true "seat of the pants trading" which almost reminded him of a big poker game, with the same kind of bluffing and gamesmanship they needed to employ to succeed. Black Monday (the stock market crash of October 1987) occurred while he was going through the MBA program. For a while, they were all concerned that the firm might cancel the program and sack them all. Fortunately, this did not occur. He was offered a position in NASDAQ stock trading, but made the conservative decision to stay with the FX department because he had significant experience in that area and had already established credibility there. He remembered the final dinner he had with his fellow MBA graduates before they went off to start their careers in the various departments. They were all seated around a big table in the executive dining room of the firm, having dinner with the Senior Executive Vice President who ran the MBA program. The man was a very polished, impressive individual. Near the end of the meal, the guy sitting directly across from the Senior Executive Vice President picked up the remnants of his veal chop and began to masticate loudly as he attempted to chew every last bit of meat off of the bone. His name was Andy and he was definitely the most rough and tumble member of the MBA class. The rest of them watched him in silent amusement until another dude, who was the most arrogant member of the group, offered Andy his bone to chew next. This offer made the rest of them laugh and should have humiliated Andy, but he seemed quite unaffected. About ten years later, the same Mr. Wise Guy was indicted on some sort of money laundering charges. Meanwhile, Andy started his own hedge fund in the 90s and by now is probably worth in excess of a billion dollars personally.

He joined the FX Department to start the New Year. The head of the division that contained the FX department was a trip. The man was universally known as the White Rabbit. This guy was very dapper and was always impeccably dressed. The White Rabbit had small round glasses and very large front teeth. It was considered common knowledge that the man had a strong proclivity to indulge in the white powder; hence the name. The White Rabbit liked to stand at attention in the middle of the Dealing Room when it was busy and bark out orders like the captain of a ship - never mind that he wasn't actually trading anything. On Friday afternoons, the White Rabbit often would show up in the Dealing Room with sexily clad young women who most people assumed were hired help. The White Rabbit's favorite saying, which the man repeated often in a deep baritone was, "Our long term strategy is to make money today!" On his first day with the FX Department, the White Rabbit had personally welcomed him into the Division with a magnificent breakfast in the Executive Dining Room. The man spoke in an impressive, grandiose fashion and after that experience he was sure he had made a good decision. He had pushed the Chief FX Dealer to place him on the Options Desk. The Options Desk consisted of a three-man team the firm had hired from another bank in late 1986. They had kicked ass in 1987 and were considered stars in the Dealing Room. They apparently had a reputation for being a bit lax and sloppy on the operational side of the business, and this had helped him get placed on the desk. The Chief FX Dealer had given him a choice; he could fill an opening and start trading his own book immediately as a Swiss Franc Arbitrage trader, or he could join the Options Desk. The FX Department had traders in all of the major currencies that quoted clients and traded FX with other banks. They also had arbitrage traders in every major currency pair that arbitraged the spot FX market vs. the currency futures on the CME. Arbitrage generally refers to buying and selling essentially the same thing simultaneously on different markets to lock in profits. The FX arbitrage traders wore headsets to trade directly with the CME futures pit and also had a series of voice boxes where they traded with interbank money market FX brokers. The futures and spot FX markets were basically interchangeable, adjusting for interest rate differentials. By diligently doing offsetting transactions in both markets each day, a good FX arbitrage trader could build up a very strong P&L over the course of a year with almost no risk. The Chief FX Dealer advised him to take the Swiss Franc arbitrage trading slot since he would immediately have his own P&L ledger. This would put him in a position to earn a good bonus his first year on the desk if he was profitable. If he joined the Options Desk he would report directly to the Head Options Trader and he would be responsible for all the desk grunt work; preparing the daily trading blotters, entering all trades into the risk management system, checking out trades with brokers and salesmen, making daily P&L estimates and coordinating all aspects of business processing with the Back Office. It would be up to the Head Options Trader to decide when he could actually begin trading his own book. Despite his personal ambition and usual impatience he chose to join the Options Desk. He was burning to get into that game and was willing to pay his dues.

The FX Options Market had started in the early 80s and was growing rapidly. Options for any financial asset provide leverage and very precise hedging and risk management capabilities in regards to market direction. The new market that options created was trading the volatility of the underlying currency pair. This meant trading based on how actively or inactively the spot market might behave, instead of just being focused on the direction of the market's movement. At this time, options were still a new product and not well understood by senior FX managers. Spot FX positions were very simple to monitor and account for. Many of the successful spot FX traders in the room made their money during the day and went home flat (without a position). On the other hand, the Options desk traded many different options and maintained large portfolios of options in various currency pairs. The analysis of risk and the revaluation of options required computer systems to crunch through a number of easily attainable variables like spot value, interest rates, strike (price at which option can be exercised), time, as well as the implied volatility, which was not so readily available. There were no market pages available with this information on any of the market information providers. The Options Desk had built up big inventories of options in all of the major currency pairs and they provided their own marks for the implied volatilities to revalue their portfolio each day. It is never a good idea to let a trading desk control the revaluation of its portfolio. The Options Desk basic strategy was to always stay net long options and build up extremely large long volatility positions in Japanese Yen options prior to the monthly release of the U.S. Trade Balance. This meant they were anticipating that the currencies would have greater movement than the options market had estimated. This had been a very effective strategy in 1987. One of the driving factors of the Plaza Accord had been the big global trade imbalances and this had become the most highly anticipated monthly economic data release during this time period. The exploding volume of Japanese imports of automobiles and electronics was a highly controversial issue, and thus the Japanese Yen consistently had the strongest reaction to the release of U.S. Trade numbers each month. He worked hard and did his best to ingratiate himself to his new boss on the Options Desk. He came in early and loaded the man's options pricing system with fresh data. He cheerfully fetched coffee, newspapers or food from the deli whenever he was asked. He reorganized all their trade processing procedures and the desk interactions with the back office worked flawlessly under his control. The Options Desk traded with customers through sales people, exchange floors, over the Reuters dealing system and with interbank money market voice brokers. The interbank money market voice brokers had built a tremendous business in spot FX and FX options by this time. Their business consisted of facilitating trading between banks using brokers who had voice boxes or direct phone lines onto the trading desks at the various firms. It was a very lucrative business in those days and active traders could expect lavish entertainment and/or freebies like tickets to professional sporting events or Broadway shows. Technically, all the banks had internal rules that limited gifts that traders could accept from vendors but this did not seem to be enforced in any way, shape or form. Very early in the New Year there was an explosive market move after the release of U.S. Trade numbers and the Options Desk made a killing. They had further cemented their status as the kings in the room. After several weeks on the desk he was invited to join the rest of team and have dinner with one of their money market options brokers. They went to a restaurant called the Quilted Giraffe that was a hot spot in Manhattan at that time. The dinner was quite notable because Woody Allen and Diane Keaton were having dinner at the table next to theirs. Woody Allen had the same whiny little voice in person as in the movies. It was a very expensive dinner and the Head Options Trader ordered many bottles of very pricey wine. He had never sampled such amazing wine before, but he realized he could make the adjustment quite easily. Afterwards he remarked to the Head Options Trader that he had not known the man was such a wine expert. His boss laughed and replied, "I don't even care for wine all that much, I just wanted to get them to spend as much money as possible." He figured out pretty quickly that the Head Options Trader was taking cash kickbacks from a CME broker. They traded a ton of options with that guy. One day the broker came into town and took the Head Options Trader to lunch. Late that afternoon, his boss was sitting at the desk, brazenly counting one hundred dollar bills. The Head Options Trader was wondering out loud whether to get a car service home because of the ten thousand dollars in cash. He told the man that if the decision was to walk home, he would personally follow him and mug him. The Head Options Trader ordered car service and took it home. The man was not very generous, to say the least. The Head Options Trader would snag free Knicks tickets from his money market brokers and then sell them at face value to basketball fans in the room. The Options Desk needed to do many rebalancing spot and forward FX trades per day to hedge their FX option portfolios. They also needed to maintain a number of hedging forward FX positions as a part of their portfolios. He determined that the FX Forwards Desk (the trading desk focused on trading the short term interest rate markets in the various currencies) was taking excessive pinch on their dealings with the Options Desk. He prepared a detailed report documenting the gouging going back three months and presented it to the Head Options Trader. The sneaky little bastards on the Forwards Desk had been stealing thousands of dollars a day from the Options Desk on all the daily interest rate adjustment trades that were required to run spot and forward FX positions! His boss was delighted with the report and rushed off to an angry confrontation with the Chief FX dealer. The Forwards desk was forced to trim the spreads in all future dealings with the Options Desk. The Head Options Trader rewarded him by giving him the book in British Pound options to trade. He was still the bitch of the desk doing all the grunt work but he had his own book to trade and generate P&L - he was in the game for real.

It did not take the mighty too long to fall. When you are long volatility with FX options it means that you profit from large movements in the currency. This was the opportunity but there was also risk associated with this position. You also had something called time decay which means the position loses money every day you fail to properly capture enough movement in the currency through a series of spot trades to rebalance the options positional risk. The value of the position also varies directly with the value of the implied volatility used to revalue the options. When you are net long options you make money if volatility goes higher and lose if it drops. The Head Options Trader had held maximum long volatility positions from the summer before Black Monday and had maintained this positioning well into the New Year. After a couple of months this strategy stopped working so well. After a long stretch of highly turbulent market movements, the environment in global financial markets was beginning to calm down. The Dollar had bounced significantly from the post Plaza Accord lows early in the year and was now range-bound and stable. The stock market had rebounded nicely from the lows in the fall and now seemed to be back in a stable bull market. There started to be less and less opportunities to trade spot profitably in order to capture market movements vs. the option portfolios. The Head Options Trader told him to stop updating all the different tenors of implied volatilities for the various currency pairs as he had been dutifully doing several times a day. His boss indicated that from now on, it would no longer be his responsibility to change the volatility marks for their option books and he should not worry about it. The Head Options Trader explained that moving the volatility marks so rapidly as he was now doing was over-complicating their hedging strategies and costing them money. He knew that was a line of bullshit and thought to himself that what was losing them money was all the fucking time decay and lack of spot trading opportunities, but he kept his mouth shut. The previous monthly release of the U.S. Trade Balance had not triggered a very big move in the currencies, and things had slowed substantially in the month since then. The Head Options Trader was clearly betting the ranch on this month's release of the U.S. Trade Balance, with the biggest overall long option position they had ever carried. He personally thought it would be a non-event and they were at significant risk unless there was somehow a big surprise in the numbers. In general, the game of trading on U.S. economic data releases involves positioning that either pre-release market estimates for the statistics will be proven correct or widely out of line. He positioned his book modestly short volatility in GBP options and felt his maximum risk if he was incorrect was one week's worth of customer driven revenue. The Head Options Trader told him that he was making a big mistake and he should realize that he was not going to get a bonus if the desk made a lot of money but his book lost money for the year. The man also said that it was his right to position his book as he saw fit. Several days before the release of the monthly Trade Balance figures, he did a revaluation behind the Head Option Traders back and determined that they were falsely revaluing their option portfolios by hundreds of thousands of dollars. When the number was released it was so quiet in the Dealing Room you could have heard a pin drop. The number was right in line with market expectations. It seemed the trade situation had stabilized for the moment and nobody gave a shit about the current rate in U.S. Dollar / Japanese Yen. Suddenly, the room was blasted by the noise erupting from the voice boxes for all of their interbank option voice brokers. Implied Volatility had been way overvalued and now it was getting destroyed. He had never heard and felt such a furious force emanating from those boxes. He was scoring in his little GBP options position but that was like a fly on the back of an elephant compared to the rest of their long option positions. Going into the number they were officially back to flat P&L for the year, although he knew that in reality they were actually in the hole. However, it was being hidden by the incorrect volatility revaluation marks being controlled by the Head Options Trader. Relations between the Chief FX Dealer and the Head Options Trader had gotten quite testy. He had recently overheard the Chief FX Dealer admonishing his boss; "You guys made a ton of money in the first few weeks of the year. How the hell could you piss it all away so fast? You are not acting like a professional trader. You are behaving like a compulsive gambler. I want this risk taken way down and the focus shifted to customer business for awhile to rebuild some

P&L nice and steady." The Head Options Trader and his equally cocky number two man looked like deer caught in a headlight as volatility collapsed violently that morning in the FX Options Market. As the day progressed, the Chief FX Dealer smelled a rat and came over to the desk. The Head Options Trader had conveniently run out to lunch and so the Chief FX Dealer challenged the number two guy on the desk, "I need to know what is going on right now. How much money have you guys lost? Have you cut any of your positions? How much risk do you have left? I want some answers now!" Number Two was already massively stressed out and so the man loudly blurted out, "Get the fuck out of my face!" The Chief FX Dealer was a tough, hardened veteran of the business. The man had worked his way up at the firm the old fashioned way and was a no-nonsense manager. At this point, the Chief FX Dealer quietly told Number Two that they needed to go have a private conversation in the office. He watched in fascination through the glass wall of the office as they angrily got in each other's face. Suddenly, Number Two charged out of the office, grabbed his suit jacket and abruptly left without a word. It was obvious the guy had just been fired. He thought to himself that Number Two had at least gone down swinging and therefore had salvaged some dignity. After the Head Options Trader returned from lunch, the man spent the rest of the afternoon sequestered with the Chief FX Dealer behind closed doors. The White Rabbit stopped by the desk to chat with him and the other junior option trader as they sat there stunned in the aftermath of the firing. The Rabbit went on a long rambling speech about how the Options Desk had gotten carried away after their triumphs last year and they needed to get back to the basics of making money off customer flow, with much less reliance on taking proprietary risk. The Rabbit then grabbed the erstwhile number two's HP 12C calculator on the desk and asked them if it belonged to the firm. He realized that the Rabbit wanted to take the calculator. So he said it had been Number Two's and that he would take care of it now. He then took it out of the Rabbit's hand. He still has it to this day and the initials of Number Two stayed forever etched on the back of the calculator.

That evening he stayed late at the office and pondered the situation. The Head Options Trader had not remarked the volatilities in their system. They had officially lost one million dollars or so on time decay but he had calculated that with correct volatility marks they would be down another three million dollars. The Chief FX Dealer spied him alone on the desk and summoned him into the office. The Chief FX Dealer began to speak with him quite calmly, "What you observed today is not typical of the professional manner in which I manage this department. But I had warned your boss that he was no longer hot and he had recklessly lost his P&L for this year. I told him to cut the risk and focus on customer business but he did not seem to want to listen. I want you to explain to me what I should know about the positions on the Options Desk." The moment of truth had arrived and he understood clearly where his loyalties belonged. He began, "Most of the books are positioned well long of volatility. This means they pay time decay, profit if spot moves a lot, or lose if it doesn't. The revaluation of the portfolio is driven by the marks for implied volatility for the different option tenors and currency pairs. I had been remarking the volatilities to market in the system several times a day including the close, but several weeks ago the Head Options Trader instructed me to stop. I would like to mention that my book, the British Pound portfolio was positioned short volatility and made good money today." The Chief FX Dealer responded, "I see. So I would assume from what you are telling me that the current volatility marks are too high, especially after a day like today, and if we were to mark the books to market properly we would lose additional money. How much do you roughly estimate that we are out of line?" He answered, "Approximately three million dollars." The Chief Dealer showed no reaction and spoke calmly, "Do you understand that the number of the loss is not so important as the fact the loss is being willfully concealed by a senior manager?" In reality, the Options Desk had made over twenty-five million the year before so it really wasn't that big a loss when put in that context, but it was certainly unethical professional behavior, almost bordering on fraud. He again answered. "Yes. I understand completely." He figured he had already said what he needed to say and the less he said now, the better. The Chief FX Dealer smiled warmly and shook his hand, 'You did the right thing coming forward like this. You have completely justified my faith in your abilities and professional standards. I want to commend you for your honesty and concise analysis. But I do have another question. How can I ensure that the back office gets access to the correct volatility marks each day so that they can remark the books independently?" He responded without hesitation, "We do a lot of business with a number of money market voice brokers. We pay them significant commissions on a monthly basis. They know where the volatilities are better than anyone else. I get my marks from them. I would make it clear to them that a requirement for continued business is to fax an updated sheet of closing volatilities in all major currency pairs to the back office on a nightly basis." The Chief FX Dealer patted him on the shoulder as he walked him out of the office, "Yes, that is an excellent suggestion. Please keep our conversation to yourself. Nothing will happen for at least several weeks and it is very important that you simply continue to work as normal." That is exactly how he played it. Around this time, large money market brokers had just started to realize the data they created through their broking activities was extremely valuable and could be stored, processed and sold to the Street.

Several weeks later, early on a Monday morning he was called into the Chief FX Dealer's office. He was introduced to a serious looking guy about his own age. He was informed that the previous Head Options Trader had resigned from the firm and this was the new Head Options Trader. He realized that he was too unseasoned to get the gig but deep down he had held a small modicum of hope that he might get the nod. He was sure he was ready. His new boss had run the desk at another bank for the past three years and he quickly found out that the man knew his stuff. During the next six months, the Options Desk began to crank out consistent profits under the steady hand of the new Head Options Trader. He realized he still had a lot to learn and his knowledge of the business accelerated rapidly working with his new boss. They hired a guy out of the back office to do all the grunt work and he became the senior trader on the desk as the new Head Options Trader effectively took on more of a strategic management role. He began to actively go out for expensive dinners with the FX

Options brokers. Every morning, shortly after six AM, he used to get a call from a young female broker from the Forwards desk at one of the interbank money market brokerage shops. She would give him a concise run down of the forward levels that morning so that their options system could be updated to price and value options correctly. She was very pleasant and they developed a friendly relationship. He found something amusing to say about the markets or current events and got her to laugh on a daily basis. He didn't think too much about this until one day one of the forward dealers asked him a question out of the blue, "I heard you are friendly with Jessica over at Marlow's. Do you realize she looks like a fucking supermodel?" He replied they were just phone friends and had never met. Several weeks later, Jessica excitedly informed him that she had been promoted and could now take clients out on expense account. She asked him when would he like to get out for dinner and drinks. He readily accepted the invitation trying to think of it as just another broker dinner, despite the fact that he didn't even actually do business with Jessica. Her firm was providing his desk with this information on a daily basis as a courtesy. When he met her at the 50s-themed bar and grill she introduced him to one of her colleagues, a guy his own age that had played major college football. She had a Latin look and was tall and lean and very pretty and sexy, with an infectious smile. They sat down at the bar and wolfed down big cheeseburgers and fries and began getting pounded. Around ten o'clock, after they had been having a million laughs and were well sauced up, Jessica excused herself to go to the ladies room. At this point her colleague shocked him, "Dude, you are the luckiest bastard in the world as far as I am concerned. She broke up with her boyfriend last year before Christmas and has not gone out on a date since. Now you are all she talks about. She told me to leave at some stage this evening so you guys could spend some time alone. When she gets back I am going to bid you both Sayonara. Nice to be you." After she got back and the dude excused himself, she ordered another round of tequila shots and the rest of the evening became a blur. The bar and grill had a back room where a big screen was playing old 50s black and white movies and there were a number of replicas of old cars. It was set up to simulate the drive-in movie experience from a bygone era. Around one AM he found himself making out with her in the front seat of one of those old car replicas and she suggested that he go home with her. He dug down deep into his addled, twisted, lusting mind and realized he was acting like a complete heel. He could not let this situation go any further. He had not actually lied to the girl, but had certainly misrepresented himself in their friendly banter over the past several months. He had not mentioned that he was married with two young children and had instead tacitly presented himself as a young, single professional guy new to the New York scene. He told her that there was a big number out the next day and surely he had to go home now or his head would explode and he would not be able to trade effectively tomorrow. She readily agreed with this logic and so they said goodnight and parted company with a passionate kiss. He had not resolved the problem but had at least called a temporary timeout. The next morning she called right on time with the forward rates and started raving about how great it was to finally meet him. She asked what would he like to do this weekend. His little brother was coming into town for a visit that night so he latched onto this excuse to punt the football until Monday. She seemed a bit hurt and asked why they both couldn't get out with his little brother. She promised she would introduce his little brother to one of her hot friends and if the guy was anything like him she was sure they would hit it off. He came up with some further crap about elaborate plans that could not be changed and then excused himself due to some breaking market news. He tried his best not to think about the unresolved Jessica situation for the rest of the day. That Saturday night he was having dinner at a top-flight New York City steakhouse with his wife and his little brother. For no particular reason his little brother and his wife were seated on one side of the table and he was alone on the other side. Not five minutes after they had sat down, to his horror he saw Jessica breeze into the bar with three similarly hot friends, all of them dressed to kill. He could not believe it. What kind of miserable, unbelievable coincidence that they could decide to have drinks at the same fucking steakhouse where he was having dinner with his wife and little brother? It could not be possible. Before he could even begin to work out some kind of plan, he looked up and she caught his eye, gave him a big smile, and sexily sauntered right over to their table. It was all happening faster than his shocked brain could deal with and it struck him that by all appearances, his little brother and his wife were the couple and he was flying solo. Jessica came right up, planted a kiss on his lips, put a hand on his shoulder, and then turned around and said. "This must be your little brother. Welcome to New York City, I'm Jessica." Then she held out her hand to his little brother. It was suddenly crunch time and he had to make an immediate decision. He stood up and coldly said, "Hey there, Jessica. This is my little brother and this is my wife." Jessica stared at him for a second in obvious shock and then she tried to recover. " I'm his broker" she stammered, "We do business together." His wife replied dryly, "I'll bet you do indeed." He spoke again, "So Jessica, what do you say you buy us a bottle of wine or something?" She readily agreed that this was a good idea and then beat a hasty retreat back to her friends. Within a few minutes, he saw Jessica and her friends leave the bar. The waitress came over with a nice bottle of red wine and told them the woman who just left had bought it for them. His wife excused herself to the ladies room and his little brother leaned over and excitedly spoke, "Jesus fucking Christ she is amazing. You're fucking her aren't you, you lucky bastard?" He replied, "No way. The girl was a bit tipsy so she got a little carried away, that's all." Later in the evening when his brother went to the can his wife asked him the same basic question. "So are you fucking that whore?" she flatly asked. He forcefully denied that anything was going on once again. That Monday morning a new young dude from that money market broker shop called with the forward rates and he never spoke to Jessica again. That was one way to solve the problem, he wryly thought to himself afterwards.

He enjoyed watching the senior dollar/mark trader in action when the market was busy. The man was a heavy set Italian who had a bad perm and wore scads of gold necklaces, bracelets and rings. He had nicknamed the guy Picasso because when the man traded a large amount you could hear him loudly scream, "Prices dollar/mark, now!" Then Picasso would wildly wave his arms and contort his face in anguish while yelling and screaming. He felt the man was truly some kind of avant-garde visual artist. When the bank traded large amounts with clients in spot FX (generally, greater than one hundred million dollars) the dealers would often have the other traders and even some of the sales people in the room make calls to other banks. This was done to quickly cover most of the risk and hopefully lock in some profit if the trade was well priced and executed. Picasso's shirt was always rumpled and the man's shirttail was always out. He could sometimes see Picasso's big belly heaving in the Dealing Room frenzy. The man seemed to know what he was doing because the dollar/mark P&L was consistently number one in the room. One morning in the early fall of that year, a very slow, boring dealing day was suddenly shattered by unexpected, shocking geo-political news out of Germany. The DEM began to collapse violently and the room exploded into chaos. Phones were ringing of the hook and sales people in every direction were screaming for prices in dollar/mark. He watched Picasso stand up to face the furious onslaught. The man's face turned beet red and Picasso stumbled backwards and collapsed in a crumpled heap on the Dealing Room floor. He was sure the man was dead. Shock rippled through the Dealing Room. Within minutes a nurse was attending to Picasso and shortly thereafter paramedics came into the room and took the man out on a stretcher. Meanwhile, the Chief FX Dealer had jumped into the role of senior dollar/mark dealer and was banging out trades a mile a minute with confident precision like a champion. He heard later that the Chief FX Dealer made a million bucks or so after Picasso collapsed that day. The next day they heard that Picasso was going to be okay. It was not even a heart attack; it had probably just been a severe panic attack. Several weeks later, Picasso was welcomed back to the Dealing Room with much fanfare. It was announced that Picasso would now be handling the dollar/canada spot trading in the room. Dollar/Canada tended to be a sleepy backwater in the FX markets back then and was a gravy slot to quietly make money off customer activity without taking much risk or having too much excitement. Several days later explosive geo-political news out of Canada hit the market and the dollar/canada spot market erupted into a frenzied, explosive move higher. In the words of the great Yogi Berra, it was déjà-vu all over again. Sales people surrounded Picasso in a violent frenzy, demanding prices in various amounts for various clients. Picasso stood up and his face turned deeply red once again and before all their eyes the man seemed to melt like the Wicked Witch of the West in The Wizard of Oz. The Chief FX Dealer rushed out and quickly ushered Picasso into the sanctity of the office. Then the Chief FX Dealer jumped into the dollar/canada chair and began efficiently banging out prices and printing money for the room. The next day they were all advised that Picasso had retired from the business.

Near the end of that year he was called into a conference with his boss and the Chief FX Dealer. They told him that the future of the FX Options Business was global books with trading in all the major FX centers. They all knew they were missing out on profitable business with their London FX desk because they did not have an options desk there. The London FX desk was covering their customer business directly with other banks in the interbank market and they were missing out on all the gravy. They wanted to know how he would feel about going to London to start their FX Options Desk in that major center. He immediately told them he was very excited about the opportunity. At that time it was well known that ex-patriot positions in foreign cities were well compensated and it helped improve your profile in the industry. London was an even bigger FX market than NY and most market profession-als considered it the most important of the three major trad-ing centers. He was very pumped up about going to London. They told him to give them a few weeks to explore the pos-sibilities and then they would get back to him. Several weeks later they had another conference. They told him they had ac-tually gotten approval to open FX Options Desks in all three major centers, meaning Tokyo, London, and New York. They had decided to send him to Tokyo instead and hire someone else to run their London desk. They indicated that since the desk in Tokyo was being launched from scratch, they needed someone they could trust who they knew could handle the responsibilities and make money. A week later they hired a young dude from another major investment bank to run their London desk. About two weeks later, it was a Friday morning and his last day at the New York office. He and his family had airplane tickets to Tokyo the next morning. He was called into the office of the White Rabbit. He sat down across a beautiful, large mahogany table and looked the White Rabbit in the eye. The man began a long-winded discussion about what a fine job he had done for the division in such a short period of time. The White Rabbit then launched into congratulations for the opportunity he was being given to move to London and start their FX Options trading activity there. The Rabbit then began a rambling spiel about how lovely cab rides along the Thames River at dawn were with the new day's sun burning brightly on the water. He was thinking to himself that the White Rabbit had probably had many such cab rides on business trips to London after long nights of debauchery with drugs and hookers. Then it struck him that he had a real predicament here. The White Rabbit was continuing to blather about London and had moved onto extolling the virtues of the senior FX professionals in the London Office of the firm. He wondered exactly what the fuck he should say when his time to speak finally arrived. Clearly, the Rabbit was about a month behind the thinking of the FX Department and was not aware that they had already hired an options trader in London and that he had tickets to relocate with his family to Tokyo tomorrow. It seemed impossible that the head of the whole division could be so out of touch. How could he extricate himself from this mess, he asked himself? He had heard that the White Rabbit had a fleet of vintage automobiles. On the mahogany table there were a number of exquisite replicas of old cars and the White Rabbit was rolling an orange Bentley back and forth as the man continued to pontificate about the wonders of London. Then God showed mercy and the White Rabbit's secretary interrupted them to inform the man that there was a very important phone call that required immediate attention. The White Rabbit shook his hand warmly and offered some final words of encouragement and then ushered him out of the magnificent office. The next morning he flew to Tokyo with his family and his next grand adventure started in the Far East.

Chapter 6

His first impression of Tokyo really surprised him. Clearly, Tokyo was cleaner, more modern and more civilized than New York City (NYC). Indeed, the whole country of Japan appeared to be more technologically advanced than the Unites States. This came as a real shock to a guy who had always considered the United States the center of the world. The subways in Tokyo were immaculate, quiet, and significantly better organized and more efficient than the subways in NYC. Most of the many small shops that abounded in Tokyo had sharp, clean glass doors that opened and closed silently on an automatic basis. Shop owners and workers were neatly dressed and professional and courteous at all times and the stores were clean and well organized. The elevators were swifter, quieter and operated more crisply than any he had ever seen in the U.S. The Shinkansen (Bullet Train) traversed the entire country of Japan providing efficient train service, traveling at over 200 miles per hour with a smooth, quiet ride. In comparison to the Shinkansen, Amtrak was a bad joke. The buildings in Tokyo seemed much newer with more interesting designs than most of the buildings in NYC. The lights and sounds in the busy sections of Tokyo were exciting and seemed futuristic. There were appliance and electronics stores all over the city in big tents. At the end of the day, the shop owners would close and latch the rope barrier on the stanchions and go home and nothing would ever get stolen. In NYC, dudes in trucks would have cleared these shops out on the first night. Tokyo was an extremely crowded city but the people were infinitely more patient and courteous than the denizens of NYC. Uniformed officials with clean white gloves literally pushed people into crowded subways and nobody seemed to get angry despite being packed in like sardines. There seemed to be cops on every corner in Tokyo, standing immobile on platforms, looking stern and baking in the hot sun wearing their gray uniforms. Rarely did you ever see the police in Tokyo actually do anything because the crime rate was so low. When he first arrived in Japan in late 1988, it was the height of the great asset bubble. Japan had become the monster exporter of automobiles and electronics to the rest of the world. In the early 1960s, Japanese cars and electronics had been considered low quality and unreliable in America. But twenty-five years later they were dominating global commerce and putting their U.S. rivals to shame. Japanese products were cheaper, more reliable and technologically more advanced. The major U.S. exporters were whining and crying about unfair competition and putting significant pressure on the U.S. government to take action to curtail Japanese inroads into U.S. markets. Certainly, pressure from major corporations within the U.S. had been a major factor leading to the Plaza Accord in 1985, which subsequently doubled the value of the Japanese Yen by the late 1980s. This currency rate adjustment essentially doubled the cost of Japanese cars in American but they still sold the hell out of them because their cars were better and much more reliable than U.S. automobiles at that time. If the Japanese Yen rate had never doubled in value from 240 Japanese Yen/U.S. Dollar to 120 Japanese Yen/U.S. Dollar the Japanese would have never stopped kicking our asses in automobiles and electronics. Instead, by the early 1990s the higher exchange rate had led Japan down the path of social unrest, political upheaval and putrid deflation. The FX market can exert significant influence on a nations economy in the global market place. In the late 1980s, the U.S. automobile companies could not sell any cars in Japan because the Japanese thought U.S. cars at this time sucked and they were right. The Japanese loved German cars and imported significant amounts. Driving a German car was a status symbol in Japan and all the car service limousines seemed to use luxury German sedans. The Japanese did love American cars from the 50s and 60s and you saw many of these restored perfectly roaring down the streets of Tokyo. This era of Americana was very popular in Japan. The Japanese seemed to instinctively always know what the good shit was whether it was cars, electronics, music, booze or whatever. The Japanese stock market was bubblelicious in those days with outrageous valuations. Equity analysts were justifying Price/Earnings Ratios (P/Es) of 500 or more for established industrial Japanese corporations, which represented roughly twenty times the PEs of competitive U.S. corporations. At its peak valuation on December 29, 1989, the Nikkei -225 Index stood at a lofty 38,957.44. On this date in history, the Dow Jones Industrial Average closed at 2,753.20 a level that essentially equaled its peak level from August 1987, before the crash on Black Monday in October of that year. At this point in time the ratio of Dow Jones to Nikkei was approximately 7.1%. Twenty-two years later on December 29, 2011 the Nikkei -225 index closed at 8,398.89 vs. 12,287.04 for the Dow Jones Industrial Average. The ratio of Dow Jones to Nikkei was now 146.3%.

The stock market indices had corrected by twenty fold and Japanese P/Es were back in line with U.S. P/Es due to the effects of globalization. Several decades later, Japan had not become the dominant economic power of the world after all. Japanese real estate valuations were even more stretched back in the late 1980s. At its peak, the city of Tokyo was worth more than the United States of America, at least on paper. He met the long time branch manager of a major U.S. bank in Tokyo by chance at lunch on his first day of work in Japan. The man had been there fifteen years and had been shrewd enough to buy a modest house in the Hiroo area of Tokyo back in 1975 for around 200 thousand dollars. The man told him what a lovely neighborhood Hiroo was. They moved into a fully furnished four-bedroom apartment in Hiroo within a few days of his arrival. He even got a magnificent white Yamaha piano delivered and got his chops back big time while living in Tokyo. Their apartment building had its own park as well as a very nice pool. Hiroo was a gorgeous little neighborhood with the best shopping center in Tokyo, with all the American brands. There was also a beautiful park with a lake full of huge carp. The Japanese would crowd that lake fishing in the summer but the point was just to fish not to catch anything. He eventually figured out that all the fishing rods were fancy and brightly colored but they did not even have hooks on the end. You were probably not supposed to catch any fish but he didn't care. He went with his kids and took a fishing rod and reel and fished with canned corn and caught a lot of massive Carp on the weekends. These fish were mostly five pounds or more and would put up a tremendous fight with the light tackle he was using. He had a ball with his kids catching and releasing those fish. Hundreds of Japanese that were fishing with their beautiful fake fishing rods and lines, would silently watch him and his kids fight and land those fish without saying a word ever. Not one fucking peep out of any of them. They released every fish they caught. He bought a used scooter and rode it without a license to work and out at night for the next three years. Hiroo was a premium neighborhood where so many ex-patriots rented pricy apartments courtesy of their banks that it had become facetiously known as the Geijan Ghetto. Geijan was the derogatory term that Japanese used to refer to foreigners. Another basic fact he discovered about Japanese people was they were convinced they were better than anybody else in the world by a wide margin. They seemed to have forgotten that we had brutally kicked their asses back in WW2 and forced them into submission despite all their pride. Or maybe they remembered that all too well but were too polite to let on? He was not sure. The bank manager sold his house in Hiroo in 1989 for approximately ten million dollars and retired from banking and bought a big spread on the Malibu coast in California. Tokyo was still an expensive city these days, but prices had come way back and were more in line with other major cities in the world.

When he arrived in Tokyo, Japanese banks were flush with cash due to the booming economy and high savings rate prevalent in that country. The Japanese banks were rushing into the global capital markets looking to compete aggressively with western banks. FX options were a hot area where easy money was being made by the western banks. He quickly figured out his firm had made a good decision getting him out there to trade that market. It was a good situation. Most of the Japanese banks did not know what the fuck they were doing. They had guys that had been assistant branch managers in Osaka, sitting on their asses for the past five years engaged in conventional banking and suddenly they were trading FX options and had no clue. They did not understand how to quantify all the Greeks (the risk characteristics of the options) so that they could understand their market exposures, systematically control their strategy and properly account for their cash flows and profitability. In his opinion, the Japanese people he met that worked for the foreign banks seemed a lot sharper than the staff at the Japanese banks. The people working at the Japanese banks all attended the University of Tokyo or some other prestigious university in Japan, whereas the workers at the foreign banks were mostly educated at universities in the United States. The Japanese kids that could not get into the premium universities in Japan all went to college in the U.S. as their back up plan. Therefore, they spoke better English and could think original thoughts. The U.S. banks all marked their options positions to market. For example, if you sold a particular option and received one million dollars in premium and at the end of any given business day it was valued at nine hundred thousand dollars, you would have a million dollars of positive cash flow, but your unrealized profit would be one hundred thousand dollars, and there would not be any realized profit. Under Japanese tax code, if you sold an option for one million dollars, you showed one million dollars of realized profit immediately. Only when the option was closed out or assigned into a spot FX position would there be another P&L event. Therefore, every fucking company in Japan was selling the shit out of FX options. The FX market was deep, liquid and non-regulated. The Japanese firms could sell options to foreign banks and get a lot of cash up front and deal with the back end later. It seemed too good to be true to them. They were selling options and booking the profits immediately and then had no clue how to measure the risk, value the options correctly or properly hedge the exposures. Every day the Japanese banks would come into the interbank FX option voice broker market and sell options either for themselves or for their many exporting clients or insurance companies. The interbank voice brokers had a great racket in Tokyo. They were mostly British firms that had been in the money markets broking business for many years. In Japan they had joint alliances with all the major Japanese brokers. So the traders at Japanese banks talked to Japanese brokers and traders at foreign banks spoke to English brokers and the brokers facilitated the trades for pricey commissions. His firm was always making an effort to get Japanese firms to trade directly with them to avoid paying all these high commissions but it was not easy to accomplish. During the first couple of years he was in Tokyo, the action was fast and furious, but there were constant stories about big blow-ups at Japanese banks, major corporations and insurance companies. They would sell a bunch of options and show big profits up front. For awhile it might work, but eventually they would have to honor option contracts that had gone way against them, and they would be forced to take big losses that often came as a huge negative surprise to shareholders and the financial media. These big option losses certainly played a role in the long bear market decline in the Japanese stock market since those lofty days. After announcing a big loss, the Japanese bank or corporation would pull away from the market for a while and try to learn how to manage the business properly. By his third and last year in Japan, the edge relative to New York and London had tightened up and the easy money was mostly gone. The easy money never lasts too long in financial markets, but its sweet while its there. During his time in Tokyo, he was paying his voice brokers around one hundred thousand dollars a month in commissions, but he was making his bank in excess of one million dollars a month on a consistent basis, so it was worth it. These high commissions had the added benefit of enabling traders to demand lavish entertainment from these brokers. It only took him a few weeks to identify a broker that had a regular line on some sweet blonde Lebanese hash so this dude moved to the top of his list by keeping him well stocked. He took several trips to Australia for vacation with his family and his brokers would pay for a charter sport fishing boat to take him and his sons out fishing for blue marlin. That is pretty nice entertainment payback for commissions. There were a lot of great, pricy restaurants in Tokyo so it was nice to have brokers pick up all the tabs.

His desk consisted of a computer, a phone, six voice boxes to speak with brokers using a microphone, a Reuters dealing system and information service. He had a Japanese assistant. She would enter trades into the system and keep his trade blotters and fax them to his firm's New York back office. He was there only a few days when his chair started rolling back and forth in the middle of the afternoon. He chillingly realized that it was some kind of tremor he was feeling, sitting in the 35th floor office. In disbelief he observed that business was going on as usual in the office and nobody seemed in the least bit concerned. He was in a state of panic. He asked his assistant,

"Haruka, is that not an earthquake? Shouldn't we be evacuating the building immediately?" Haruka smiled sweetly and replied, "When your chair is gently sliding back and forth you never need to feel afraid. But if your chair ever moves up and down violently, then be very afraid!" The firm would actually process all of his business out of NYC so it was a pretty simple operational set up. He was in a big room with equity and fixed income traders and sales people but he pretty much did his own thing. It was simple stuff. Each day he would make a plan of what options to buy that day and what options they would sell against them in the London and New York time zones to lock in profits and hedge the positions. The prices for options in volatility terms were always lower than what fair value had been perceived to be when the New York market had closed since all the option traders at foreign banks knew the Japanese only had interest to sell options. When he first started trading in the Japanese market he would aggressively over bid the competition for the type of options he wanted to buy in the first several hours of the day since the prices represented a great bargain relative to what they would have had to pay in the New York market for the equivalent. One day he received a phone call from the head trader at the prestigious French bank that was one of the early leaders in the FX Options market globally. The man invited him to dinner at Pachon, one of the finest French restaurants in Tokyo. After he had accepted the invitation he became very puzzled about the purpose of this invitation. In New York, he had rarely socialized with any of the competing traders in the market at other banks. He had dinner with the head trader and two of the man's colleagues and the food and wine was fantastic. Near the end of dinner the head trader got serious and spoke business for a few minutes. The man emphasized what a lucrative market it was for FX options in Tokyo and if they all worked together on prices, they could make more money. He figured out that it had been a very elegant market maker's collusion dinner. The head trader from the French bank was suggesting he be less aggressive and he could buy the options he wanted but get them at more attractive pricing. More importantly, he would not be narrowing the acceptable spreads in the market, which would cost all the foreign banks some money. He knew when he was getting good advice and he backed off and started to trade less aggressively. His number of daily transactions declined on balance and he started making more money. He went to a series of sales meetings with institutional salesmen from his firm to a number of Japanese corporations and Insurance companies to solicit direct business in FX options. It was always a long shot that they could make any traction into the local corporate market and after a number of fruitless meetings he phased this practice out. What he most remembered from these meetings was standing with his sales colleague in some fancy conference room at the potential client's office, surrounded by six or more junior staffers and their manager. They would go through this convoluted process of formal greetings, bowing and exchanging business cards and taking time to look at each one as if it was something special to behold. The manager usually spoke decent English but the staffers never said a word. He would try to tell a joke and if the manager ignored it so did the staffers. If the manager laughed then all of the staffers would laugh immediately rite on cue. It would have been considered non-prestigious for the Japanese firms to deal directly with a foreign investment firm instead of with a Japanese entity so he figured out these meetings were a waste of time. Not long after he had gotten started in Tokyo another French bank launched an FX Options desk there. The dealers contacted him via the Reuters dealing machine and encouraged him to ask them directly for FX options prices. He called them several times for standard stuff of either one-month or two-month duration and their prices were wide and useless. Then one day when a surprise news release had rocked the market and spot prices were moving rapidly, he called them for an option of only three days duration. These options were called short dates and back then were not usually available via the voice brokers. The voice brokers only covered the gravy Japanese flow and the standard dates like one month, two month, three month, six month, or one year. In those days the short dates were a trader's best guess and pricing should reflect your existing book and its risk management requirements, as well as your market view. To his amazement they made a wide price but the bid was way too high. It was worth a clean thirty grand to sell the three-day option to them and so he happily did so. In normal market parlance, this was known as a pick-off. They had fucked up and made the wrong price but rather than suggest that perhaps they needed to rethink their price, he just traded immediately without comment. He never understood why he would ever do anything different in this situation, but some dudes in the market believed this was bad etiquette. He figured that all was fair in love and war. A trade executed with a voice broker was a done deal and could not be broken. For a direct trade, the general rule of thumb was that if the counterparty started bitching and moaning within a minute or two before pricing and confirming details you had to be willing to break the trade. But once you confirmed the deal and ended the Reuters dealing session the trade stood. The traders at the new French bank in the market closed out the deal and were extremely friendly in the process and never called back to whine later. He started to call them for a price on a short date every time the markets made an unexpected move and two times out of three he could stuff them on an overpriced bid and make some quick cash. They never seemed in the least bit upset with any of the deals. After four or five profitable trades for him they invited him out to dinner and he got a chance to meet them. They were young, well-educated French men, only a few years out of university. At this time, France still had a military draft, but by working overseas for a few years they fulfilled their military obligation. They were essentially legal, upper-class French draft dodgers. They didn't know what the fuck they were doing when it came to trading FX options. Over the course of a nice meal and fine wine they let on that their mandate was to have a respectable presence in the market and not lose more than ten million dollars in their first year. He could not believe his ears. He made up his mind that if they were budgeting ten million to donate to the market he should work diligently to at least get ten percent of the booty and this he accomplished until they unceremoniously closed their desk down eighteen months later.

He learned some of the nuances of the life of the Japanese Salaryman as well as the differences between American and Japanese culture. The Japanese salesmen at his firm seemed to go out for dinner almost every night. They were big drinkers. He would often see them in the men's room early in the morning at the office, splashing cold water on their red faces trying to wake up and start a new workday. Apparently, the wives controlled the money in most Japanese households. But the men all had liberal expense accounts so they had their fun going out for nice dinners and drinking on the company dole most work nights. The Japanese also had a much more casual attitude towards sex and prostitution than most Americans. The more natural and relaxed attitudes about sex were probably prevalent in most of Asia. The business districts in Tokyo were full of these so-called Hostess Clubs. Japanese men liked to frequent these establishments after business dinners. You paid a fee to enter the Hostess Club and then pretty young girls would sit with you while you were drinking. They would say very little but smile prettily and hand feed you little snacks. He later ascertained that for extra fees you could go into the back room and fuck them or indulge in whatever fantasy you were willing to pay for. One of the Japanese sales guys he had befriended tried to explain the local attitudes to him. Prostitution was considered a normal part of business entertainment and therefore his wife did not give two shits what might occur with whores during any of his business night outs. But if the man were ever caught having an affair with a secretary or something of that nature there would be hell to pay. He went on a business trip to Singapore. One of his voice brokers had arranged for him to meet a broker there for a drink. When he showed up at the bar, he could not help but notice three very sexy Singaporean ladies sitting at the bar. He had been secretly lusting Asian women since coming to Japan and these three were some of the most beautiful he had seen yet. They were all three dressed to kill with slinky tops, mini skirts and spiked high heels. Their black hair shown and they were all heavily made up in a very alluring fashion. He thought to him-self that he might sell his soul to the Devil to have his way with one of those hot little Asian vixens. The broker showed up with a squat little man named Mr. Kono from some Japanese bank. They all had a glass of some top-notch whiskey and then the broker grunted and waved his hand at the three little vixens that were still sitting at the bar. The girls immediately walked over and stood obediently next to the broker. The man reached into his jacket pocket and pulled out three hotel room keys. The broker handed a key to each of them and indicated that they had two hours in the room and then they would meet back at the bar for a nightcap. He was given the honor of pick-ing which girl he wanted first. He could not believe it. You talk about something falling into your lap. Later that night when he was laying in bed thinking about the incredible sex he had ex-perienced with the professional Asian escort a disturbing thought popped into his head. He remembered his thoughts when he first sidled up to the bar and started ogling the sexy ladies. Could something so profound have happened in such an insidious, careless fashion? Had he in fact just sold his soul to the Devil for the princely sum of exactly two hours of sex with a prostitute in Singapore? In market parlance, if this was true then he had just hit a low-ball bid. He had given away the ranch for next to nothing. He quickly laughed to himself and dis-missed this as a viable possibility. After all, he had not pricked his finger and signed in blood or done anything else to verify a deal had been made. In reality, he was not a very religious per-son. It always seemed to him that religion was the biggest source of conflict and violence in the world. This attitude started to become more prevalent with the rise of militant

Islam in the post-911 period. He had identified the main tenant of most religions as the suspension of reason, meaning that blind adherence to the religious creed was called faith and considered the highest possible virtue. The second major tenant of most religions was the requirement to proselytize and bring in new members. The major point of organized religion seemed to be how to make money and increase power and influence here on Earth. Several weeks after he returned to Tokyo he arranged dinner with a Japanese woman that ran options trading at the branch of a U.S. bank in Tokyo. It was not a big FX trading institution. He had done several trades with the woman through the voice brokers market and had arranged an introduction so he could take her out to dinner and try to solicit direct trading with her. Her name was Misaki. They had a nice dinner and he found her very pleasant to talk with. Her English was pretty good and he felt she was bright. She was probably a few years older than him and was very petite and pretty. She was probably five Feet tall and ninety-five pounds or so. One thing that stood out was the poor condition of her teeth. This seemed quite prevalent in Japan among both men and women. He surmised that dentistry must be one area where American technology still remained superior. Over dinner she told him that she had to cover all business directly with a counterpart. She did not like to pay the high commissions in the interbank voice brokers market. Grossman Zachs had solicited her and for a short time period she had given them all her business. But after a few months of fair pricing, they had begun to gouge her ruthlessly and she had discontinued the dealing relationship. Boy, that was big surprise. Grossman Zachs had got their claws into her and then started to rip her off after a few months. She told him that she was not so stupid as Grossman Zachs thought she was. She was very capable of determining what the correct price was. He assured her that he would like to deal with her on a fair and equitable basis. He would show her the fair price every time. He could price any combination of options she wanted. If she felt the price was not fair he would discuss it with her and try to adjust pricing to reach compromise and deal. If this did not work, she could then execute the trade in the voice brokers market with no offense taken. He stressed to her that he was sure they could work together for mutual benefit. He could tell she was intellectually curious and offered to teach her professional options analysis and risk management technology. She would be welcome to come to his office for lessons on his firm's risk management system. She seemed very happy and told him she would like to do business with him very much. After dinner she wanted to drink whiskey. Damn, could she drink a lot of fucking whiskey for a tiny wisp of a girl. They got pretty drunk and he was telling jokes and she couldn't stop giggling and laughing. She turned serious and started telling him a little tale that took him quite aback. She said she had come home early from a business trip several years earlier and found her husband in bed with another man. She was quite sure her husband was gay but they had a good marriage that worked for them. They did not want children and were very compatible outside of sex. In fact her husband had not fucked her in more than two years and she was very anxious to get fucked. She thought he was a very nice, handsome man and would he please consider fucking her? He considered for a minute and realized that infidelity was something that came a lot easier once you had broken the ice. Much later in life he came to understand that fidelity in a committed relationship was based on the corner-stones of mutual love, respect, honesty and trust. His first marriage did not have a sound foundation. He readily agreed that he would indeed be very happy to fuck her. He paid the check and they went to a nearby Love Motel. Tokyo was full of these so-called Love Motels that rented rooms by the hour so couples could check in and have sex. The interesting part of this business was that in reality most of their clients were mar-ried couples. Tokyo real estate was so expensive, and the city was so crowded, that many Japanese lived in small houses or apartments with multiple families together. For many Japanese couples the Love Hotels were the best way to have sex with some privacy. In typical Japanese style, the Love Hotels be-came quite gaudy with all manner of colors, motifs and special amenities available. He pounded her with everything he had and still she could not get enough. She seemed quite insatiable. After an hour and a half he was exhausted and still she would not settle down and stop moaning and begging for more. He asked her for a back rub. She climbed up and down his back giving him a very nice massage scampering across him naked. He saw her on an occasional basis for the rest of his time in Tokyo for the normal program. They would enjoy a nice steak dinner while getting drunk on whiskey and then check into a Love Motel to fuck for two hours. He got a kick out of picking a Love Motel with a different motif each time. He turned her onto smoking hash and she loved the stuff so much he had to bring her a little extra as a present to take home each time he saw her. When his stocks were low this part of the program became slightly annoying. He never felt guilty about his affair with Misaki. He figured it was business not personal.

The White Rabbit unexpectedly showed up at the Tokyo office for a business visit one Monday morning. He attended a fantastic lunch with the White Rabbit, the Managing Director (MD) of the Tokyo office and several other senior traders. The White Rabbit magnificently pontificated in a deep baritone about all the outstanding opportunities in Asia and what a great job he and the other senior traders at the firm were doing. It was obvious that the MD and the White Rabbit were good friends and had known each other a long time. The formal head of the firm in Tokyo was some Japanese dude he was never officially introduced to his whole time in Japan. But the real head of the firm in Tokyo was the MD. The man was definitely extremely savvy concerning financial markets. The MD was also known as quite the partier and womanizer. The man was married to a much younger woman and had three small children, but was carrying on simultaneous affairs with two American sales women at the firm. The only people in the whole office who seemed unaware that the MD was doing them both at the same time were the two women themselves. The next morning the White Rabbit was gone as was the MD. He had befriended the MD's assistant and this was his source for all the inside information at the firm. He asked the MD's assistant where the White Rabbit and the MD had gone. There was an issue he had hoped to discuss with the White Rabbit while the great man was in Tokyo. The assistant informed him that he was out of luck as they were both gone for the balance of the week. The guy asked him if wanted to know the official version or the real version of where they had gone.

Naturally, he wanted to hear both. The official version was that the White Rabbit and the MD were traveling throughout the Asian region visiting important clients of the firm. The real version was they were off to Thailand that morning. The program for the two good buddies was to spend the first night in Bangkok where they would each hire two sweet, young, lovely professionals for the balance of the week. Then it was off to the scenic resort city of Phuket where they would stay in magnificent beachfront suites at a luxury hotel with their new young friends. Halfway through the week they would switch girls to keep it fun and interesting for everyone involved. He had to give the White Rabbit credit. The man had fun and enjoyed the pleasures of life with reckless abandon.

The cash market long bond trader for the firm in Tokyo was a cocky asshole. The guy loved to brag about trading profits, large bonuses, fucking Japanese girls, exploits in squash and golf, and just anything else a man could brag about. He had learned that you never talk about your trading P&L or your bonus at a Wall Street firm. Neither one was anyone's business except your superiors at the firm. The arrogant bond trader could be pretty funny at times. He had to give the man credit for that. The Japanese Head of Fixed Income sales at the firm was a fat, middle-aged, mean spirited, obnoxious man. The Little Troll delighted in publicly dressing down his subordinates, especially some of the pretty young girls in the office. He had often seen Japanese girls out in the hallway crying after receiving particularly harsh tongue-lashings in public. The grumpy sales manager had a habit of falling asleep on the desk in the afternoon with a newspaper on his lap and then loudly snoring. One afternoon, he heard through the grapevine that

the bond trader was going to set the Little Troll's newspaper
on fire. Sure enough, in the middle of the afternoon he smelled
smoke and turned around in time to see the sales manager leap
up in terror and scream loudly with puffs of burning newspaper flying in the air. The fire alarms went off and it took some
time to calm things down in the office. They were all doing
their best not to laugh out loud. Nobody had any empathy for
the miserable old bastard. The firm launched an investigation
but never officially nailed down who had lit the newspaper on
fire. But they all knew who had done the dirty deed. A short
time later, he was out for drinks on a Friday evening with some
traders at the firm and they ran into the bond trader at a small
bar where they liked to hang out. The bond trader had been
there since the early afternoon, drinking shots and was very
drunk already. The guy was trying to pick up some Japanese
girls but was getting blown off and seemed to be getting very
upset at their lack of interest. The bond trader stood up in a fit
of anger and punched a very fancy lamp on the bar, knocking
it to the floor and shattering it. The bartender got quite upset
at this and suggested to the bond trader in stilted English that
the man would have to pay for the lamp and then should go
home and get some sleep. The bond trader loudly told him to
fuck off and demanded another round of shots while pounding both fists on the bar. Within two minutes, three grey uniformed Tokyo Policemen walked briskly into the bar. He had
a feeling that the arrogant, drunken asshole was going to do
something stupid and he carefully watched events unfold with
great interest. One of the cops chatted in Japanese to the bartender for a few minutes and then addressed the drunken bond
trader in perfect English. The cop told him that he had acted

in a very impolite manner. The value of the lamp was 120,000 Yen (around one thousand U.S. dollars) and a credit card was immediately required to pay for this. Then they would escort the guy outside and into a taxicab. The cop further admonished the bond trader that guests in a foreign country should not act so impolitely. The arrogant fool stood up and started arguing loudly to the cop that the fucking lamp wasn't worth a hundred dollars, let alone a thousand dollars, and this was an illegal shakedown. The bond trader was waving his hands around and bellowing into the cop's face, and then struck the officer in the nose and knocked the man's glasses to the floor. It was probably an accident but no matter. The other two cops quickly subdued the bond trader and cuffed him and marched out of the bar with their prisoner. Nobody heard anything about the bond trader's fate until late the following Tuesday afternoon. The police called the Japanese head of the firm and notified them that the bond trader's visa had been rescinded. They would release the man from jail when a representative of the firm showed up with the bond trader's passport and a one-way plane ticket out of Japan. The firm was also required to pay the bar for the lamp as well as the police for the bond trader's room and board while in custody. The firm was also required to write letters of apology to both the bartender and the Police. Later, they learned that after the foolish bond trader had been taken to the Police Station, a bunch of Japanese cops had put on rubber gloves and efficiently beat the living shit out of the guy. They had then left the arrogant fool lay there in agonizing pain until the man got his one way trip out of Tokyo on the following Wednesday morning.

SILVIO SANTINI

His family went back to the United States without him every summer. Tokyo was actually a pretty miserable city in July
and August, as it was very hot and humid and the air was significantly polluted. He had vowed to behave himself in his family's absence. One Friday night in the summer he was out with
friends getting drunk at a bar. They had been buying drinks
for these pretty Japanese girls that didn't seem to speak much
English. He had no intention of trying to pick up one of these
girls. They were just having fun as far as he was concerned. He
realized he was too drunk to ride his scooter home and it was
always difficult to catch a cab late at night in Tokyo. He saw a
cab drop someone off in front of the bar and made a snap decision to grab it. He ran out of the bar and got into the cab. To
his amazement, one the girls from the bar ran after him quick
as a cat and jumped into the back of the cab with him before
the door of the cab closed automatically as they did in Tokyo.
When he looked back upon it, he thought this crazy situation
was almost like the scene near the end of the movie "Animal
House". A young boy is reading a Playboy magazine and suddenly a gorgeous, scantily clad young lady flies into the kid's
bed through the open window after her parade float crashes
and she is flung into the air. The boy looks up to heaven and
says, "Thank You God." After literally flying into the backseat
of the cab, the Japanese woman then proceeded to jump all
over him on the short ride home. He remembered taking her
up into his apartment and tearing off her clothes and fucking her right on the living room carpet. It became a bit hazy
after that but it went on for some time. He woke up hung-
over on the couch the next morning and the girl was already
gone. He immediately wondered if she had ripped him off. He

had heard a number of stories back in NYC from friends who had hooked up with strange women in bars, only to wake up the next morning and discover the girl long gone along with their rings, watch and all the money out of their wallets. One dude he knew had banged a chick that had literally stolen his fucking TV. The guy often wondered how the girl had been strong enough to get the TV out of the apartment. He walked into the kitchen and to his amazement it had been spotlessly cleaned. He was not a neat person and with the family gone there had been several weeks' worth of dirty dishes piled up in the kitchen and the floors and counters had been filthy as well. She had washed all the dishes and perfectly cleaned the floors and countertops. She had even cleaned the refrigerator and the stove. Needless to say, nothing was missing. She had left him a note in Japanese with her phone number on it and a heart drawn in red lipstick. He threw that letter out. Nothing good could come from keeping that around. Somehow he didn't think too many dudes in NYC who hooked up with some random woman in a bar, woke up to see their kitchen cleaned perfectly, a nice love note and nothing stolen.

After his first full year in Tokyo he was granted annual leave. They went to Hawaii for a week and then it was on to Pittsburgh to spend the Christmas holidays with family. They arrived in Pittsburgh on the evening of December 23. When he got to his parents house he could not wait to hand his old man one of his business cards. His title was Vice President, which did not really mean that much. In those days it was a pretty common title at Wall Street firms. But he had to admit he had been proud to be named a Vice President of the firm nonetheless. It was a cool business card because it was written in English on one side and in Japanese on the other. He handed his old man his card and after studying it for a few minutes the old man asked, "What the fuck are you the Vice President of, bullshit?" In his father's world, Vice Presidents were old dudes that had been with the company a long time. He laughed it off, but it probably hurt his feelings a little bit. He got up very early the next morning due to jet lag. His father would typically cook on all the holidays and start prepping very early. For Christmas Eve, the old man would prepare a spectacular fresh seafood dinner, which was an Italian tradition. Christmas Day dinner was always Prime Rib. Then the old man would host a big party with tons of lavish food and plenty of booze, several days after Christmas. The old man had been forced into early retirement that year but he had not given the matter much thought. He came downstairs early that morning and found the old man sitting at the kitchen table, smoking a cigarette, drinking a cup of coffee and looking glum. He addressed his father, "Hey dad you are not looking too happy this morning. It's Christmas Eve for God's sake. I thought you would be busy cooking already. I was hoping to get some snitches. (When he was a kid and his father was cooking, a snitch was when the old man gave you a taste of something while it was still cooking. He had always loved snitches.) What's the matter Pop?" The old man looked at him sadly, "You know I lost my job this year and I cannot find another one. I am very worried about how your mother and I will survive in retirement. I have not saved enough money. I cannot spend money like I used to. I cannot afford to do Christmas the right way any longer. Dinner tonight will be pasta with tuna and tomorrow we are just going to have baked ham for dinner. I am not having my party this year." He could not believe what he was hearing. He was traveling with a lot of cash so he went back to his room and then came back downstairs with a thousand dollars in the form of ten crisp C-Notes. He handed the money to his old man and said, "I cannot believe my fucking ears. Since when do you whine like a little girl when facing a challenge? After the holidays, you are going to snap out of this funk and find another job. I am sure of it. I don't want to hear any more stupid shit about how Christmas is getting scaled back this year. You are planning pasta with tuna for dinner tonight? Get the fuck out of here. You know as well as I do we need seven different kinds of seafood. There is going to be clams, crab, lobster, squid, tuna, shrimps and scallops for sure. Your grandson's love scallops. We will need a lot of scallops. As far as Christmas Dinner goes, fuck ham. We are not having shitty, fucking ham on Christmas day. Are you out of you fucking mind? You think I flew with my family half way across the world to listen to this stupid bullshit? Christmas is back on. In fact this year will be the best one ever. Get your fucking coat and let's go. We need to get down to the strip district to get the seafood for tonight, the prime rib for tomorrow and everything we need for your party. On the way home we will stop at Kaufman's, so you can buy mom something nice for Christmas. I will be your assistant in the kitchen when we get back since you will be stretched for time." The old man started to blubber and cry and then hugged and kissed him and declared, "You are the finest son a man could have. I don't deserve a son like you." He pushed the old man away and told him to shut the fuck up. He felt a great sense of satisfaction making the rounds and loading up the car with his father that morning. This pudgy, aging man didn't seem like the vicious tyrant that had brutalized the entire family all those years ago. The old man was a fantastic grandfather to his sons and doted on them, especially because the man only saw them several times a year. His boys dearly loved their Pap-Pap, as they called him. He wondered if he could forgive his father and forget all about the atrocities the old man had committed. He came to the conclusion that some things could never truly be forgiven or forgotten. He determined to try his best to forget about the past and enjoy the good times they were now enjoying. When they left Pittsburgh, his father demanded as many of his business cards as he could possibly spare. He gave his dad the whole stack he had brought along. His mother later told him how the old man delighted in passing them out while bragging about his successful son. His father died several years later.

In his second summer in Tokyo he joined the firm's baseball team that played in the Japanese bank league. It was unofficially a league only for the locals. But he had befriended the middle aged administrative Japanese man who managed the team and convinced the guy to let him join the team. During his time in Japan, he made a point to befriend as many of the local staff as possible, unlike most of the other ex-patriots in the office who thought they were better than the Japanese natives. The Japanese took their baseball very seriously. The team had full baseball uniforms and everyone on the team was expected to arrive several hours early for each game so that they could warm up properly. He had been a pretty good baseball player in his youth, but had not touched a bat or glove in over 10 years. He foolishly expected it would all just come right back to him. On opening day, the manager started him at second base and batted him fourth in the lineup. The manager was obviously expecting good things. He was rusty and played a terrible game. He made several errors in the field and struck out four times in a row. It was a pitiful performance and he was humiliated. Everyone on the team was very supportive regardless of his bad showing. They really had a good team spirit. After the game, they went to a local restaurant near the baseball field where they sat on mats around a low table and drank Saki and shared all these great Japanese dishes family style. This was a tradition after every game and the manager was able to expense it to the firm. Tokyo was full of batting cages where they played loud music, had a bunch of loud video games and lots of kids were always hanging out. With his family gone again for the summer he was determined to restore his honor on the ball field. He started driving his scooter to the batting cage every night. Within a few weeks he had found his stroke again and was consistently pounding the ball on the highest speed. He also spent a lot of time throwing a hard rubber ball against the back wall of his building so he could practice throwing, fielding fly balls and grounders, and get back the smooth side to side movements essential to play the infield properly. He knew he was ready to play again but for the next six Saturdays in a row he rode the bench. He could not blame the manager for making him ride pine after the shitty way he had played in the opener. He stayed positive and did not complain. He cheered the team and really enjoyed the games and the meals they shared afterwards. Halfway through the season, a number of players were on vacation so he was back in the starting lineup by necessity. This was an important game for the manager. An old colleague of their manager managed the other team and this was a heated rivalry. They played their games on a college baseball field and the fences were pretty deep for a bunch of amateur ball players. He had not seen one home run hit over the fence all year. He hit three home runs in a row over the left field fence and ended the game 5 for 5 with 11 RBIs. He also turned several double plays and made a number of other good plays in the field. It was a dominating performance and he led the team to a smashing victory. He could tell the manager and the rest of the team were awe struck by his display of pure power. After the game, the other team's players came over one by one and bowed to him. He felt like the king. At the meal afterwards, the manager toasted him warmly for the greatest home run display in the history of the team. For the rest of that summer and the next season as well, he started every game and established himself as the best hitter on the team. Years later, he looked back on that afternoon he hit three home runs in the Japanese bank baseball league as one of the greatest days of his life.

Chapter 7

There were three basic types of ex-patriots in Tokyo. The first group hated the experience and did everything they could to get out of there as soon as possible, regardless of negative effect on their careers. The second group enjoyed the experience well enough, but was glad to leave Japan once their two or three year stints were over. The third group became Japanophiles and wanted to stay indefinitely. He fell into the second camp. He had enjoyed living in Japan but was ready to come home when his three years was over. He came back to a completely different firm. The C.E.O. had been ousted a year before he returned and the firm had undergone significant upheavals. Most of the senior managers with ties to the old C.E.O. had been purged and the firm was essentially under new management. He did not recognize his old department. The White Rabbit, the Chief FX Dealer and the Head Options Trader that had sent him over to Tokyo were all gone. In reality, it was quite common for ex-patriots in his industry to return to home office as outsiders instead of receiving a hero's welcome and promotion as was usually advertised when you accepted the assignment. His new boss, the recently named new Head of FX Options had spent some time with him in Tokyo before his return to NYC. He was none too impressed. The guy actually came from a pure Fixed Income background and did not seem too knowledgeable concerning the FX market. Never mind the fact that he had been carrying the department on his back for three years on a P&L basis while building the firm's presence in Tokyo, and he had not even got a look from the new senior management of the firm for the top position in FX Options. He deduced that the new boys would inevitably bring in their own people and a leftover from the old regime like himself probably had the life expectancy of a housefly. Moreover, he felt he had been stiffed on his bonus for the past year. The new options desk manager warmly welcomed him back and assured him he had a bright future with the firm, but he was not convinced. It was his intention to get the fuck out of there as soon as possible. Within a few months of his return, he was contacted about an opportunity to start the FX Options desk at a smaller investment bank that did not have a strong FX market presence, but was now committed to building up the business. His interviews went so well that they offered to bring him in to launch a global FX Options group and manage their spot FX trading desk. He was now a Chief FX Dealer himself.

He realized that he was no longer just a trader but had also become a manager and he took his new responsibilities seriously. He had to evaluate existing staff at his new firm and make the tough decisions about who needed to be let go. He also needed to get involved in the recruiting of new traders and sales people to build the department. His input was required to assist in the development of option-trading systems at the firm and he also needed to work with operations staff to integrate the new systems into the firm's risk-management and accounting processes. He was busier than hell during his first couple of years at the firm, but he later realized it was probably the most satisfying work experience of his life. His dream to become both a producer and a manager at a major Wall Street firm had come together. During his years as a trading manager on Wall Street he often repeated several quotes from his late father. Despite the bad memories of abuse, the influence of the old man never left him for long. Whenever a trader under him indicated that they hoped that their losing position would come back, he would admonish them with, "Why don't you shit in one hand and hope in the other and see which one fills up first." If a trader or sales person started making excuses about where a trade had gone sour he would reply, "Yes, and if the dog had not stopped to take a shit he would have caught the rabbit!" These sayings were pretty applicable to most problems that might occur on a trading desk and he used them so often it probably got boring after a while. There was some ineffective staff that had been hanging around for years at his new firm not doing much and it was not difficult to work with human resources to send them packing. There was a middle-aged Italian salesman named Luigi that he felt some empathy for. Luigi should have been the first to go, but instead the man made the first cut. Luigi wore a worn suit and tie into work every day and most of his shirts seemed to be stained. The man always reeked of body odor in that old school European way. The firm was not paying Luigi much and he had to admit he felt sorry for the man for some reason. Pity is definitely not an effective tool for a manager on a Wall Street trading desk. It is probably not a very good tool for professional management of any kind. Luigi would sit at the desk all day long, staring at screens and not say much to anyone. At exactly ten minutes before three PM each day the man would pick up the phone and start speaking about the markets loudly in Italian. Right before three o'clock each day Luigi would forcefully ask for a price in dollar/mark (U.S. Dollar vs. Deutsche Mark) in five with a heavy Italian accent. For a week or two the dollar/mark trader would make the standard five-pip spread and Luigi would repeat it into the phone before passing on the price. After he had observed this process for a little while, he instructed the dollar/mark trader to trim the spread to just three pips to try and entice Luigi's client to deal. He was curious who this client could be and wanted to see a trade print. The tighter spread did not seem to matter and Luigi continued to pass on the price each day. Finally, he told the dollar/mark trader to make Luigi a choice price. This meant they were willing to buy or sell the dollar/mark at the same price for no spread. They were offering to accommodate the client in the exact middle of the market. Any client that had a legitimate spot trade to execute would trade on a choice price nine times out of ten. Still Luigi continued to pass in the same fashion. The next day he tapped into Luigi's phone line and waited for the phone call. There was no one on the line. Luigi was speaking into an empty earpiece for ten minutes, asking for a price in five dollar/mark and then passing. It was comical but also quite sad. He knew he had to get rid of Luigi and he did the dirty deed. When he fired Luigi the man went into a long rambling speech in broken English discussing in great detail all the troubles and poverty in his extended family. Eventually, Luigi began to cry and beg for his job. He had been advised to always have a human resources representative to attend the meeting, every time he sacked somebody. But he had foolishly made an exception this time because of his feelings of pity for the man. After Luigi finally shuffled out the door for the last time, he felt like crying himself. It was pretty pathetic. He began to wonder if he was too soft-hearted to make much of a desk manager on Wall Street.

He was excited about having spot FX traders report to him. It was the early 90s and it would be several more years until electronic dealing systems effectively put the interbank spot FX voice brokers out of business. Interestingly enough, due to the complicated details involved with options trading, the voice brokers in FX options survive to this day. The market has not been able to develop electronic dealing systems sophisticated enough to replace the voice brokers in FX Options in any convincing fashion. From the mid 70s to the mid 90s the money market brokerage firms had a great business in spot FX voice broking. Every spot trader on an FX trading desk would have five or six voice boxes with brokers spouting a steady stream of prices. When the markets were fast it seemed impossible that these brokers could effectively manage the flow. The spot FX brokers sat around large round tables in their offices and displayed their prices in front of them as they haggled on the phones with their list of spot traders. Some of these spot voice brokers learned how to write rapidly backwards so they could efficiently display their prices to the other brokers. The voice brokers traded with each other all day long on behalf of their spot trading clients. When the FX market was running fast and furious it was a melee for these guys to maintain orderly markets and keep straight who had done what. The dirty little secret of the spot FX voicing broking market was a sort of informal barter system known mostly as Points for Cash. There were constantly out-trades, mismatches and trades that some banks refused to honor. All the trading was done on taped phone lines but in fast markets it was often difficult to determine where an error occurred and to identify what had really happened. Points for Cash was the spot FX voice broker's mechanism to resolve trade issues most of the time. Basically, they would identify spot FX dealers who would be willing to accept trades they had not done and thereby generally accept losses that did not belong to them. In exchange, at a later date the FX spot traders involved would receive profitable trades they had not done to pay them back. Points for Cash kept track of all these secret ledgers between the voice brokers and the spot FX traders who were playing the game. FX spot traders were rewarded for this hidden service by lavish entertainment and also cash kickbacks in many instances. Nobody would ever talk about the Points for Cash but everyone knew it was there. Some of the best FX spot traders in the market were the money market voice brokers that often ran intraday positions quite profitably. When the markets were slow in the afternoons, the spot FX traders would frequently banter back and forth with their brokers. There was one broker in particular who had a booming voice and was very amusing to listen to. His spot traders set up dinner with this broker and some colleagues at Peter Lugers, the quintessential NYC steakhouse. It was located just across the Manhattan Bridge in Brooklyn. It was and still is quite simply the best damn steak you will ever eat. The brokers picked them up in an enormous stretch limousine and the six of them made their way over to Peter Lugers. The voice broker that had intrigued him was one of the fattest men he had seen in a long time. The guy wore a rumpled suit and wouldn't stop cracking jokes in a loud voice on the way to the restaurant. The big, fat voice broker was pretty fucking funny and they all could not stop laughing. Peter Lugers was known for Porterhouse steak served family style and the portions were enormous. The fat broker insisted on ordering steak for eight even though there were only six of them, as well as many different side orders. The good red wine flowed freely and the conversations were amusing. But he found his eyes drawn to the fat man. He had never seen anyone eat so much heavy rich food, with so much vigor and gusto. Halfway through the dinner, the fat broker called over the waiter and ordered steak for two to go. The fat broker could talk loudly while eating massive quantities of food and guzzling large dollops of red wine all at the same time. There was not one little spec of dinner left on any plate and while the rest of them were stuffed and passed on desert, Big Boy polished off two orders of pecan pie slathered in homemade whipped cream known as schlag. It was an impressive display of pure gluttony. When they got back in the limousine for the return ride to Manhattan, the fat broker was sitting next to him and meat juice started to drip on his shoe from the bag that contained the steak. One of the other brokers loudly proclaimed, "You disgusting, greedy fat bastard. Look at you. You are ruining our client's shoes." With that the insatiably hungry broker grabbed the bag of steak and greedily glugged down the meat juice as it dribbled down his tie and onto his rumpled shirt. Big Boy then pulled out ten dollars and tried to hand it to him for a shoeshine the next day but he politely refused.

One of the spot traders he hired was dating a woman who was a reporter for Reuters News Television. Back in the early 1990s, Reuters was the dominant player in the information services industry for the FX market. The spot trader mentioned to him that Reuters News was always looking for traders to interview in dealing rooms who could provide interesting commentary on the FX market. It sounded to him like a good opportunity to gain some exposure for his department and the firm. He instructed his spot trader to arrange a date for Reuters to interview him on the trading desk. Several days later the spot trader's girlfriend came onto the trading floor with a cameraman and a soundman and he gave an impromptu interview to Reuters right on the FX desk. He expounded his market views and insights in colorful fashion and felt he had done an outstanding job. A number of people he knew in the market contacted him to let him know they had seen him on television and he had done a great job. He was feeling very proud of himself when he was called into the office to speak with his boss. He reported directly to the head of the division. The man was known in the dealing room as the Sheriff. The Sheriff had been born in the South and was a very impressive individual. The man spoke in a low, slow, southern drawl and was tall and lean. The Sheriff was always impeccably dressed and never seemed to lose his temper or show any signs of stress. The man could be a hard-nosed bastard when it was called for and the entire floor had complete respect for the Sheriff. He had hit it off quite well with the man during the interview process. He smiled as he sat down in the Sheriff's office expecting to be praised for the fine effort he had done promoting the firm on television earlier that day. The Sheriff looked at him quizzically and spoke, "Where did you get the idea that you could bring a television crew into the dealing room and spout your market views to the whole world as a representative of the firm? Do you have any idea of the shit storm you have stirred up? We have an Economics Research Department here that represents the firm's views to the investment public, under the strict control of the Marketing Department of the firm. We have heavy-duty lawyers doing big time oversight on all public relations issues. The powers that be are blowing a gasket today. They are breaking my balls in fact, and want to know who the hell you are and did I know anything about this? I obviously did not, or it would not have occurred." He sat back in a state of shock that he could have made such a serious blunder in such a careless fashion. He apologized profusely and declared that nothing like this would ever happen again. The Sheriff smiled and shook his hand and told him not to worry about it. The man indicated he would work it out on his end, but in the future please make the effort to clear any kind of action he was not sure about. This was his first and last television exposure in the industry.

He had to make a number of trips to London to develop an FX options trading team there and to help the firm integrate the new options risk trading system. The firm processed all of their FX trading out of London. On his first trip over to London with the new firm he attended a big meeting with all the operations and support staff that worked on the FX business. They were quite concerned about the implementation of a proper options trading system. Prior to his arrival with the firm, they had only backed to back options. This meant the trading desk would exactly cover every option they traded with a client with an interbank counterparty. They would entice a client to cross the bid-ask spread with them, but then go out and cross the best spread they could find on the Street in order to lock in a small profit. This was a very limited way to manage the business and had a quite a detrimental effect on the profitability of the firm's option's trading activity. With an options risk management system you could inventory client trades and manage the aggregate risk of your entire options book. This could enable you to keep most of the edges you earned trading with clients. It was a long, painful meeting to say the least. The head of the operations group for the firm in London was a short, round man with a mop of blonde hair that he nicknamed Barney Rubble. There was no doubt the man was conscientious and hard working. But Barney Rubble was clueless when it came to options. Barney Rubble was very nervous about the new responsibilities and the man could not stop talking over people in the meeting. He had prepared a detailed list of everything that needed to be accomplished, but was finding it very difficult to communicate in any effective way with the rabble of bureaucrats, led by the boisterous Barney Rubble. There was one quiet chap at the end of the table with long, shaggy hair and granny glasses that intrigued him. A couple of times the man started to say something quite sensible before beating shouted over by Barney Rubble. The meeting was starting to spiral down into a series of petty arguments that had nothing to do with the business at end. It was becoming a zoo-like atmosphere and he found himself exploding in impatience and frustration. Suddenly he stood up and barked out in a loud voice, "Will everyone please shut the fuck up!" The sharp, harsh words and tone startled the proper Brits into complete silence. He continued, "This fucking meeting is going nowhere and we have been in here all morning. I need you all too please do your best to just listen attentively for a few moments. I have prepared a list of the important issues, which need to be identified and resolved. Let me sit down with this gentleman on the end and go over them please." The all sat there silently in a state of shock. He pulled his chair around to other end of the table and sat down next to the quiet, shaggy haired fellow. He took out his list and started reading out the items one by one. His new friend understood each issue perfectly and succinctly responded with broad, effective ideas to ensure proper implementation. He knew he had identified the only guy from operations who knew what the fuck was going on in the whole meeting. When he finished going over the list with the guy it was lunchtime. He suggested they adjourn the meeting and he invited Barney Rubble to lunch to make amends for being so brusque and vulgar. He also wanted to ensure that his new friend would be listened to when it came to getting the work done on their end. After Barney Rubble ascertained that he was willing to pound beers heavily at lunch, they got along just fine. He learned that the shaggy haired fellow was a consultant they had just brought in because they needed some options expertise. He pushed Barney Rubble hard to hire the man full time and put him in charge of the system installation and integration. After the systems were up and running he helped the man get promoted and transferred to New York to shore up FX desk operations there. He nicknamed the man Lord Bean, as in the Lord of the Bean Counters. They became extremely, close personal friends and remain so to this day. One thing he learned about Brits was that those bastards could drink. He rarely met a Brit who couldn't drink him under the table and he was definitely a heavy drinker. He stayed in the pub all afternoon with Barney Rubble and got extremely drunk by late afternoon.

He stumbled his way back to his hotel and passed out thereby missing an important client dinner that evening. Later in the week some OTC options voice brokers he knew in the London market invited him out to dinner. They were naturally quite excited about a new options desk starting up in London and he had a reputation in the market as an active trader and a fair man to deal with. After dinner the brokers suggested they go somewhere special for some drinks. Theoretically, the bars in London all closed early. But this was in fact a facade. There were numerous so-called private clubs that stayed open all night long where you could drink or find whatever else you were looking for. They went to a bar in a private club that was loaded with beautiful girls from Eastern European countries in sexy dresses and slinky negligees. The game was pretty simple. You chatted around with different girls and then when you found the one who tickled your fancy you paid a fee to take her home. His brokers were of course picking up the tab. He avoided going to dinners with those brokers again on his many future trips to London. The best way to stay out of trouble in life is to avoid temptation.

His firm also had a large FX Sales Desk in Paris and he made a number of business trips there as well. The firm's office was on the Avenue des Champs-Elysees, the famous street in Paris renowned for its specialty high-end shops and wonderful cafes. The office was near the Arc de Triumphe, the magnificent monument that honors those French patriots who fought and died in the French Revolution and the subsequent Napoleonic Wars. The traffic circle around the Arc de Triumphe was the most chaotic and frightening traffic pattern he had observed in his life. Cars moved in and out of this huge, unmarked traffic circle at high speeds in what seemed like over ten lanes in each direction with no lights or traffic cops. There seemed to be no rhyme or reason in driving through this traffic circle except trying to slice your way through the scrum without getting hit by another car. He remarked to his cab driver that there must be an accident every minute. The cab driver politely responded in perfect English that was a pretty good estimate. Apparently, the long established rules for all accidents in this traffic circle was that everyone was responsible for their own damage. The French Police knew it was impossible to determine fault. In his opinion, Paris was the most beautiful city in the world hands down. Contrary to conventional wisdom, he also found most French people to be quite courteous and gracious. Before he joined the firm, the Paris sales force had been in constant conflict with the London option traders because they made options prices wide and slowly. All FX sales personnel desire a quick, tight price to help them win competitive business. Under his leadership, pricing improved dramatically and the Paris sales force began doing a lot more business. He got along quite well with the Paris staff and always enjoyed his visits there. He sometimes found it incredible the amounts of extra commission or markup that the French sales staff could add on to most deals. Later he learned that kick backs were a very common business practice in France and this extra commission was often split with the clients in an obvious win win fashion. He cast no moral judgment on business flows that his desk could profit from. These days were long before all the anti-money laundering compliance procedures were instituted in the fight against terrorism. When in Paris he stayed at the famed Ritz hotel, which was a real treat. For a few brief years he considered himself a "Ritz Man". One evening he was having a few cocktails at the hotel bar with local staff when four of the most gorgeous women he had ever seen in his life walked into the bar followed by two older, paunchy Arab sheiks. What made this group of women so striking was the assortment. There was a blonde, a brunette, a redhead and a black woman, one more spectacular than the next. Apparently, if you had enough cash in Paris you could even hire designer escorts. He befriended a rough and tumble salesman at the office named Henri. The man had been a soldier in the French Special Forces some years earlier. Henri was a very aggressive salesman and was very charming but also quite intimidating at times. All of the woman support staff in the Paris office were very attractive. There was one particularly lovely receptionist named Alisanne who was rumored to be having an illicit affair with Henri. One New York morning he was on the phone with his option trader in Paris and he heard a loud commotion in the background. He heard screaming and things being broken. It seemed that Henri and Alisanne were having a loud lovers quarrel in the middle of the Dealing Room. Alisanne had been cursing Henri and throwing china at the man. Apparently, their affair had consisted of waiting around till no one else was in the office and then Henri would fuck Alisanne from behind in the men's toilet before going home to dinner with his wife and three children. She had requested that he take her to a romantic dinner and then to a hotel to make love to her like a woman and Henri had flatly refused, telling her that it was only possible for them to have sex in the toilette at work. Henri had made it clear to Alisanne this was the only way she could get some. The conflict was resolved the French way. Alisanne moved on and became the mistress of the married manager of the office who apparently treated her much better than Henri

His first full year at the new firm went incredibly well. He assembled a solid options team in London and worked effectively with the operations side of the firm to get the options risk-management system operational and seamlessly integrated with the firm's processing and accounting systems. At this firm he began to understand how powerful the operational managers at these investment banks actually were. They were the nuts and bolts that held these firms together. Traders and salesmen came and went but the senior operational managers tended to stay with the same firm for a long time and they wielded significant influence. He nicknamed the operations side of the firm the Evil Empire. But he did his best to treat them with courtesy and respect at all times and generally maintained good relations. He had also helped recruit new spot FX traders and sales people in NY. Client business volumes increased significantly, he traded like a champion and overall group revenues were significantly better than had been budgeted. Early in the New Year he was invited to a fancy offsite meeting for senior managers in the Capital Markets Division at an upscale, luxury resort. He even chatted for a while at one of the cocktail parties with the Head of the Capital Markets division who was the number three man in the whole firm. They shared a mutual interest in music and he felt like he had hit it off well with the man. He began to think he had a real future with this new firm and could eventually work his way into senior management. His one major issue was his big mouth and lack of personal discipline on the trading desk. He had a tendency to yell and scream in the heat of battle during the day when markets were moving wildly. He also had a propensity to drop a significant number of F-bombs and other vulgarities right out loud on the dealing desk throughout the course of any given day. He had grown up with a father who used profanity constantly and he had started swearing at a young age. He had even founded the Swearing Club at his catholic grade school where he initiated his young classmates into the fine art of profanity. His three years working in Tokyo had probably exacerbated the problem. He could rant and rave and drop F-Bombs with his voice brokers in Tokyo all day long and nobody gave a flying fuck. Indeed, they all found it quite amusing. After all, the voice brokers in Tokyo were all getting paid to speak to him. He could talk to them anyway he wanted. His desk in Tokyo had been off in a corner of the big dealing room and colleagues in his old firm had rarely paid any mind to his foul vocal shenanigans on the trading desk. But here back in NYC at his new firm he faced an entirely different situation. The FX desk was in the middle of a very large dealing room full of many other trading desks that made up the division. There were hundreds of traders, sales people and support staff within close proximity of each other. He was the leader of the FX trading desk and the face of the department to the rest of the division. His many loud tirades and usage of profanity was unprofessional and likely disruptive to others. He knew it was a problem but the reality of the situation was that he could not control himself. He tried not to yell and scream and swear but as soon as things got hot and heavy he could not stop. He heard through the grapevine that the bond traders at the firm, whose desk was next to the FX Trading Desk, had nicknamed him

Sam the Man in reference to Yosemite Sam, the crazy character with the vile temper in the old *Bugs Bunny* cartoons. This was not the correct image to develop for a man with senior management aspirations. Near the end of his second full year running the FX desk, profits were once again considerably well past budget, and he was very proud of the job he was doing. In the back of his mind, he knew that he was handling the important responsibilities of the position extremely well and allowing his lack of self-discipline to senselessly damage his reputation at the firm. He had befriended an elderly secretary that sat near his desk. She had somehow reminded him of his mother and he went out of his way to be nice to her. He would occasionally bring her back lunch as well as little presents of candy. On Valentines Day he would buy her a huge bouquet of flowers. She took him aside one day and tried to talk some sense into him. She began, "When I first heard you on that desk yelling and swearing I was horrified. I thought you must be an extremely awful person. Now that I have gotten to know you, I realize what a sweet, kind man you truly are. Why can you not control your tongue? Did your mother not teach you any manners? You are starting to make a fool out of yourself. They all laugh at you behind your back. Meanwhile, I hear about how impressive the performance of your trading desk is. They had never succeeded at FX at this firm before. Please try and get a hold of yourself. I do not want to see you ruin your career by such senseless foolishness." He was aghast as he listened to her well-meaning advice and vowed to her that he would try harder to limit his outbursts and act more professionally at all times. The Sheriff had started to take a special interest in him and they had several lunches together in the firm's Executive Dining room. The Sheriff would praise him for the desk performance and direction the FX business was heading in. But the man would also admonish him for his, loud, senseless outbursts and constant stream of profanities on the desk, right in the middle of the big trading floor. He remembered how one lunch had ended quite clearly. The Sheriff had smiled and said, "Damn son, I just don't know what to do with you sometimes. You are one of the smartest guys I have hired in a long time and certainly are one of the best traders. You are doing a heckuva job on that FX desk and you are the kind of guy I would like to see move up the ladder and get more responsibility. But I can't have you yelling and screaming like a wild man day in and day out. We all drop an F-bomb now again. After all we are in a tough, competitive business and it gets a little crazy out there sometimes on that trading floor. But it cannot become such a frequent occurrence as you have made it. We need talented senior managers that possess self-discipline. Do you not understand that you are a leader out there and represent the firm? We expect our managers to present a good example to the rest of the staff. What kind of image do you think the firm needs to present to our clients?" He assured the Sheriff that he would learn to tone it down. He told the Sheriff how much he loved working at the firm and how eager he was for more opportunity and responsibility. He vowed to himself that he would behave like a total gentleman moving forward.

After that last lunch, he realized that the Sheriff's tone had the sound of a final warning to calm down and rectify his unprofessional behavior. He started putting post-it notes on his screens that said things like "shut up" and "no swearing". He tried to remember to maintain composure and keep his voice down. For several months he avoided any major outbursts on the desk and felt he was slowly but surely overcoming his somewhat obnoxious image at the firm. Near the end of the year, there came a morning with a sharp, unexpected movement in the FX market and he started calling around for prices on the Reuters dealing system for a short-dated option he had in his book that he wanted to unload. He called Grossman Zachs and to his delight they made a huge bid for the option. It was way too high for current market conditions and he happily sold it to them. The trade was worth at least one hundred thousand dollars of profit for his book and that was pretty excessive in reality for a single pick-off trade of that principal amount. His number two man, as well as the junior options trader on the desk were both a little intimidated by the mighty Grossman Zachs, like many traders in the market. He on the other hand, was not intimidated one bit by the bastards at Grossman Zachs. He held a deep personal grudge towards Grossman Zachs and was very fired up by the opportunity to stick it to them. Number Two nervously suggested that perhaps he should inform the Grossman Zachs trader that the price was off the market and give the man a chance to re-price the option. After all, surely they did not want to create problems with Grossman Zachs. The junior options trader piped up that maintaining liquidity from Grossman Zachs might be worth more than the pick-off trade over the long haul. He ordered them both to shut the fuck up. He fully expected the Grossman trader to start whining and wiggle out of the deal. But he certainly wasn't going to make it easy for the son of a bitch. To his amazement, the Grossman trader readily confirmed details, thanked him for the call and ended the dealing session. The trade was now booked, the money was in the bin and he was extremely pleased. Three hours later in the early afternoon, the Grossman Zachs trader called him back on the Reuters dealing system to complain about the trade. It was too late by this time and the dude knew it. Not much had happened in the FX market since the trade and the man had probably just got around to realizing it had been a pretty bad stuffing. However, if there had been a big move in the FX market the option buy might have turned out reasonable for Grossman despite the high price paid. Clearly, both of their positions had included the trade during the last three critical hours since the deal had been confirmed. The trader from Grossman Zachs was out of luck and the man knew it. Most likely, the Grossman trader had called back to bitch and moan to let off steam, while realizing the trade was not going to get canceled or re-priced at this juncture. Personally, when the shoe was on the other foot and he had been picked off (an extremely rare occurrence) he never called back. He always took his lumps like a man while waiting patiently to return the favor with interest at a later time to the offending bank. There was an old Sicilian saying that said, "Revenge is a dish that tastes best when served cold." He knew how to ask for several seemingly random option prices from a bank that were actually designed to determine their tendencies and biases in their option pricing across currency-pair, time to expiration, delta (sensitivity of the option price relative to changes in the price of the underlying currency-pair) and other factors. He could then use this information to stuff them on an option that they were likely to misprice, particularly if he called them for the price during a brief outburst of market turbulence. In any event, he responded to the Grossman trader in a polite but firm manner. There was no fucking way that bastard from Grossman Zachs was going to get back the hundred thousand dollars. That money was now in the bank. His bank. The trader from Grossman became more pedantic as the whining continued unabated and it was starting to become annoying. His number two man and the junior options trader were reading the discussion on the dealing machine over his shoulder and started to break his balls. They were loudly agreeing with the drivel being spouted by the Grossman trader, which he found embarrassing and extremely irritating. It had become a quiet afternoon and everyone on the FX desk had become aware of the situation and was listening intently. His erstwhile options team was saying things out loud like, "He really crossed the line this time, and he really fucked Grossman Zachs on this one." The stupid bastards were ruining his triumph and he became extremely angry. He was so mad he could have kicked both of their asses at that moment. Suddenly, he snapped and began yelling at them loudly. The whole dealing room was so quiet that his loud voice was probably heard across the vast arena. He began, "You fucking guys are starting to make me sick. Whose fucking side are you on anyhow? Is that fucker from Grossman going to pay you boys a fucking bonus? Did I fuck Grossman Zachs? Of course I fucked them you stupid sons of bitches. I hate those fuckers at Grossman. I'm glad I fucked them. My only fucking regret is that I didn't fuck them harder. Stop looking over my shoulder and getting involved in my business or I will beat the shit out of both of you. You two losers can shut the fuck up right now and get on your own dealing machines and start calling around for prices and try to fuck somebody yourselves, so I don't have to make all the fucking money around here all the time!" He was probably red-faced by now and was already starting to regret his loud, obnoxious, foolish outburst in the middle of that quiet afternoon in that large dealing room. He looked at Number Two and the man's face looked pale and ashen. He knew it was not because of the outburst. They were old friends and Number Two knew his bark was worse than his bite. Usually, Number Two would be laughing by now and agreeing with him. He looked past Number Two and his own face froze in horror at what he saw. The Sheriff and the Head of Capital Markets were standing less than ten feet away and had witnessed the loud, profane, disgusting tirade up close and personal. The Head of Capital Markets was a very stiff, formal man and looked literally sick to his stomach and totally disgusted. The Sheriff smiled wanly and spoke, "Never in my career have I heard words such as these spoken so powerfully and with such feeling in the middle of a Wall Street trading floor about our true mission in this fine industry. How bold that you use such colorful language in such a loud voice on a quiet afternoon like this. How compelling it is that the presence of so many women nearby cannot deter your passion." The Sheriff then rolled his eyes and nodded his head towards the secretaries seated close by. The Sheriff and the Head of Capital Markets then walked off without further comment. The bond traders on the desk next to them all jumped to their feet and started high-fiving each other as they gave him a standing ovation. They were actually chanting "Sam the Man" and heaping praise on him and bowing in mock subservience. He slumped back into his chair like a crumpled, wet washcloth. He knew he had just blown his promising future with the firm into little bits. He wasn't even angry with his guys any longer. They had been out of line. But he could have quietly called them off the trading desk and spoken to them like a professional in the sanctity of his office. "Why am I such a fucking idiot?" He painfully lamented to himself. He got up out of his chair and left the office without a word to anyone and walked around the block to Rosie O'Grady's Pub. He sat on a bar stool until late that evening and drank himself into a state of oblivion.

Chapter 8

In retrospect, the Sheriff had probably done as much as possible for him. Early in the New Year, he received his bonus and it was very fair. In fact, it was far and away his best year for personal compensation in his life. For the first time, he made over a million dollars in a single year. This was a big milestone for him and he found it very exciting. He had always dreamed of making over a million dollars a year and he had accomplished this in his early thirties. They say that hope springs eternal. He began to think that perhaps he could overcome that fucking meltdown late last year when he was ranting and raving like a madman in front of the Sheriff and the Head of Capital Markets after picking off Grossman Zachs. His hopes were quickly dashed. As usual, the old man's saying that you can shit in one hand and hope in the other and see which one fills up first, had been proven correct. He had run his mouth too often and dropped too many F-bombs over too many incidents in the middle of the dealing room. The infamous Grossman meltdown had been the nail in the coffin. Several weeks after the bonuses were paid at the firm, the Sheriff called him into the office. The Sheriff introduced him to this fat bastard with thick glasses who was now the Chief FX Dealer of the spot FX desk. Ostensibly, this would relieve him of the distraction of managing spot traders and sales staff, so that he could put all his focus on managing the global FX options desk and improving the profitability in his own trad ing. He didn't buy that line of bullshit for a moment. The message was clear. You are a fucking animal and we want you to have as little management responsibility as possible. But you can stay here and make us more money despite your personal humiliation at being demoted, even though your performance was outstanding. His petty dreams of moving into senior management on the divisional level had been crushed once and for all. He was now heading backwards at this firm. He did his best to act professional and behave nice as pie about this stinging slap in the face. He firmly shook the Sheriff's hand as well as Fat Boy's and promised his full cooperation to make it a smooth transition. When he left the meeting there was only one thought burning through his brain. "I need to get the fuck out of here as soon as possible."

Within several weeks, he was contacted out of nowhere by the secretary of the White Rabbit at the man's new firm. The dapper Rabbit had landed on his feet as dudes at his level on Wall Street usually did back in the go-go 90s. The women was calling to set up dinner with himself, the White Rabbit and the Global Head of FX at the new firm where the Rabbit was now top dog in the Division. It was a fantastic dinner. The White Rabbit was as effusive and charming as always in extolling the virtues of the new firm and the grand opportunity they were extending to him to run their Global FX options business. The Global Head of FX was a tall, lanky Englishman who loved to party and had a wicked sense of humor. They hit it off immediately. In reality, it was a lateral move. He would be in charge of all FX options trading at the firm. But he would have zero responsibility where the spot FX trading business was concerned. He didn't really care. He needed a fresh start.

They offered a decent one-year contract with a guaranteed bonus for the first year and he verbally accepted. It was a done
deal that night and a few days later when he got the paperwork
he went to see the Sheriff in his office to resign. He tried to
stay positive in resigning to the Sheriff. It would make no sense
to burn a bridge with a hitter of this level. He expressed appreciation for the opportunity he had been given at the firm,
he noted how proud he was of his efforts in building up the
FX business, and he wished the firm continued success. The
Sheriff actually looked kind of sad and began to speak, "Well I
am not surprised that you have found another job so quickly.
But it sounds like a lateral move at best. Would you re-consider
if I could match or beat their offer for next year's guaranteed
bonus?" He shook his head and responded, "I am sorry but I
have already made up my mind and committed to my new
firm. I have given them my word and would never go back on
it." The Sheriff went on, "Well you have some legacy here for
just a few years. You really put FX on the map in the division
and helped us build up the right way." The Sheriff then paused
for a moment before continuing, "Please do not take offense.
But perhaps you should consider some counseling to figure
out why you have these loud uncontrollable outbursts on the
trading desk. They don't put you in a favorable light. There is
no good reason why a bright young man like you shouldn't
be able to get a handle on an issue like this." He stared at the
Sheriff blankly. The son of a bitch had brought in Fat Boy and
taken away his spot desk after a great year and now the man
was suggesting he should go see a fucking shrink. All this just
because he got a little worked up when the melon-heads on
the desk irritated him with their incredible stupidity in hectic

market situations. He simply stood up and walked out of the office without saying another word. He was angry and didn't trust himself to stay calm if he spoke to the Sheriff any longer. As he walked out of that dealing room for the last time all that he could think was. "Fuck that guy. He can go and fuck himself."

It turned out that 1995 was a good year to be moving to a new shop. You always wanted to have a good first year when you went to trade at a new firm. Wall Street is all about money. You needed to make money to establish yourself at any firm. You would have had to been a moron to not make money trading FX options in 1995. The market was full of opportunity for the astute option trader. It was an exciting year with his favorite currency to trade the Japanese Yen at the center of the action. He understood the psychology of the Japanese Yen market from his years in Tokyo. He also kept his own candlestick charts for the yen and many yen crosses (yen vs. other currency pairs besides the Dollar). These personally maintained charts were a competitive advantage prior to improved technology and easy access to on-demand computer based charting for all market participants, which was probably readily accessible by the year 2000. He had last switched firms in 1992, which had been another banner year to trade currencies. The FX market had really moved to the front pages of Wall Street in 1992. That was the year when the FX market, led by powerful hedge fund traders broke the will and the pocket book of the Bank of England and forced the British Pound to devalue rapidly vs. the Deutsche Mark and the rest of the European currencies that made up the ERM (European Exchange Rate Mechanism). The ERM had been introduced in March 1979 to reduce exchange rate volatility and achieve monetary stability in Europe. The system was nicknamed the Snake. The currencies could only move within bands of each other (for example plus or minus 6%) and then the band was reached and the European Central Banks would be required to intervene to maintain the band. In typical European fashion they would generally revalue the middle of the band between two currencies when pressures occurred rather than fight a potentially costly intervention war to protect the band. The ERM was the precursor to the euro, the single European currency introduced in January 1999. The collapse of the British Pound in the fall of 1992 had been a lay-up (easily identified opportunity) trade leading to extensive volatility and huge profits in the FX Market at the expense of the Central Banks. He had done exceedingly well playing limit long volatility during this period. He also made significant arbitrage profits spread trading out of line option prices from incompetent market makers at other banks. The Central Banks were not caught holding the bag very often in the FX Market, but 1992 had been an exception. After the fireworks of 1992, the next two years had been much more stable years in the financial markets. The U.S. Dollar had rebounded and then fairly stable, predictable ranges had developed. On balance, short volatility positions had favored the game in FX options during 1993 and 1994. He had been well on top of these moves during his great run at his last firm. However, 1995 was a year when financial markets kicked back into a highly volatile environment and he found it easy to make consistent money staying long options volatility. He had also developed his own tools to analyze relative value between option tenors and the FX market was deep and liquid for this type of systematic trading. Moreover, he had also stumbled upon an options arbitrage strategy that he came to call the Money Spigot in the second half of the 1990s. There were two types of expiration categories for FX options. Most of the market traded so-called European style option expiration, which meant you could only exercise an in the money option at the exact date and time of expiration. But there was another type of expiration category that was termed American style option expiration. This meant you could exercise the option at any time prior to the actual exercise date if you chose to. This feature became significant when there was a large interest rate differential between the two currencies that comprised the currency-pair for the option. When this was true, American style options often had higher valuations than the comparable European style options. At his prior firm, he had several clients that insisted on trading the American style expirations and so he had learned all the nuances involved. He discovered that clients as well as many large banks in the FX market did not understand how to properly trade this special expiration style. To make it simple, if you were short an American style option to a counterparty that should early exercise but chose not to, you could make free money if you understood the correct hedging trades to execute to earn the unclaimed interest rate differential from the long option holder. Conversely, you had to always early exercise your own long American style expiration options correctly. The game was all about selling as many American Style options to counterparties that were not likely to handle the early exercise feature properly. In this fashion, you received significantly more premium upfront than if you had been selling standard European style options. The Japanese Yen was the main currency where he focused on this expiration style arbitrage strategy. The Japanese Yen FX options market was deep and liquid. The yen had a huge interest rate differential with the U.S. Dollar and most other major currencies. Most currencies had interest rates much higher than yen interest rates. He developed systems to identify options that had hidden value in this area. These options were often quite close to an inflection point where the interest rate differential characteristic of the option required early exercise, but standard bank option pricing models were not able to detect this. He would then sell as many of these types of options as possible in a specially hedged portfolio. In its heyday, his positions were making one hundred thousand dollars a day just on this component. The Japanese Yen started 1995 in a quiet range above the psychological support level of 100 yen/dollar. In the first quarter, it surged dramatically to its post WW2 high of below 80 yen/dollar. Remember that when the amount of yen it takes to buy a dollar decreases it means the yen is strengthening. In the third quarter of 1995, the yen violently collapsed back above 100 yen/dollar. There were many option miss-pricings available and opportunities for great trades in FX options that year. In addition to outstanding market conditions, his new firm had a strong, active sales force in NYC as well as several European centers and they were hungry for aggressive options pricing. Under his management, the options desk provided the right kind of competitive pricing in London and NYC to the sales force, and trading volumes as well as profits exploded relative to prior years. The firm was also on track to open an FX trading desk at the firm's branch in Hong Kong that year and he would play an important role in that development. It was a great situation for him and he had the three best years of his career between 1995 and 1997 at that firm.

He immediately had a problem with the FX options trader who was already at the firm. The hold over trader was an arrogant, obnoxious, tall, thin English dude named Hollingsworth. When the White Rabbit and the Global Head of FX had the recruiting dinner with him they had mentioned that they wanted to retain their current FX option trader in NY. He could bring in new traders in London but they wanted him to try and work with Hollingsworth. He figured out pretty quickly that the dude was a useless, destructive, negative prick. Hollingsworth had been some kind of chess champion in London in years past and had been hired by a major bank in a high profile attempt several years earlier to bring in professional gamblers and top level players from games of intellect and risk into the world of financial markets trading. The program had been a complete bust. Hollingsworth had been sacked by that bank and then another bank before getting hired by the White Rabbit as a two-time loser. He somewhat understood why the Rabbit liked the man. The prissy English dude was obviously highly intelligent and had an acerbic wit. Hollingsworth wrote a weekly synopsis of the FX market and distributed it at the firm and apparently the White Rabbit read it religiously. He could grudgingly admit it was well written and quite amusing at times. The problem was that Hollingsworth was a terrible trader and useless on a trading desk, but somehow had retained a big ego. Under the control of Hollingsworth, the FX options pricing at the firm had been terrible and they had done very little business. The man had also consistently lost money in his own proprietary trading. The White Rabbit and the Global

Head of FX had known they needed a significant upgrade, but the Rabbit wanted to keep the guy around in the hopes some leadership might get Hollingsworth back on track. He clashed with the man immediately. He refused to let Hollingsworth have any involvement in pricing options for the sales force. Under his pricing, the firm became extremely competitive and sales volumes soared and the sales force loved him right away. When the business had been small at the firm, Hollingsworth had helped the spot desk get prices when they did big deals with clients. The man continued to get involved in this after his arrival. The head of the spot desk quietly asked him to get Hollingsworth to stop getting involved in spot trading. It had become annoying and distracting. The head of the spot desk had asked Hollingsworth to stop but the man did not seem to understand how to comply with simple requests. Hollingsworth continued to get involved in the spot price call outs even after he told him to stop. The dude was very dismissive of customer business and would sometimes mock him during the day when he would work hard with the sales force to try and get business done. It all came to a head with Hollingsworth after he had been at the firm about three months. Early in the day, Hollingsworth got involved in a spot desk call out and made a twenty five thousand dollar error. The head of the spot desk got very fired up but he defused the situation by agreeing that the options desk would take the loss. It was also worth noting that Hollingsworth had lost money all three months in a row in the man's segregated trading book. The FX options desk was still off to a great start but he was getting irritated with the obnoxious bastard costing him money and aggravating him on a daily basis. He went to talk to the Global Head of FX about the situation off the desk in the man's office. It seems the Global Head had no great fondness for Hollingsworth either. The incompetent, arrogant bastard was the White Rabbit's little pet but enough was now enough. After their discussion, he had human resources prepare a letter of warning to Hollingsworth about his bad behavior and poor performance. It was the classic way to start to build up a paper trail to help you fire somebody in the industry and avoid lawsuit risk. Later in the morning, he spoke with Hollingsworth in his office and presented him the formal letter of warning. Hollingsworth signed the document but was very dismissive and did not seem to grasp the reality of the situation.

A little while later, he was involved in a long trade negotiation over the Reuters dealing machine with Rosalyn, a senior sales lady out of the London office. Rosalyn was very attractive and it was widely rumored that she was having an affair with the White Rabbit. Hollingsworth was standing and looking over his shoulder as he typed back and forth with Roslyn on the Reuters dealing machine. He decided to leave Hollingsworth alone since the guy had already been issued a letter of warning that would make it easy to fire him in about a month. He made a number of suggestions to Rosalyn concerning her client's requirements and did a lot of pricing of strips of options on his computer. He also did scenario analysis of the different option structures and rapidly typed all this information back to Rosalyn. She loved to deal this way as she could make suggestions to the clients and price them immediately and present scenario analysis. They beat the competition time and again. He could price options quickly and was a piano player and could type as fast as any secretary. After more than one hour the deal was finally consummated. It was around twenty different options across three currency pairs with different strike prices, amounts and expirations. He knew how to price these big strip trades very efficiently. Rosalyn added $75,000 of markup to the trade; she would receive a percentage of that commission. The trades were easily worth another $75,000 in his book but she didn't have to know that. He was happy to make the effort to make 150 grand. It was certainly nothing to sneeze at for an hour and a half. More importantly, it was his job. He knew the White Rabbit insisted client activity be the focus and priority of all trading desks in the division. He closed out the deal with some friendly banter with Rosalyn. When he finished, Hollingsworth suddenly exploded in a loud voice, "That was totally pathetic! You are such a fucking pathetic loser! You make me fucking sick!" It somewhat reminded him of his own outburst in the prior year at his old firm on that day he fucked Grossman. Hollingsworth had shattered the relative quiet of that huge dealing room with a vile outburst. Thank God he was not the culprit this time around. At least in the Grossman situation, he had been on the side of making money for the firm when he was bellowing obnoxiously on the open floor. Never mind that he had been in the position of power on that desk instead of being a losing trader, that had just been written up by the new boss, and already had one foot out the door. Hollingsworth was clearly a fool despite the man's arrogance. The FX department at his new firm was also housed in a large, cavernous trading floor with many different businesses represented. He had no interest in making any kind of waves like this at his new firm. He had been acting much calmer; he made sure he kept his mouth shut for a few moments after anything pissed him off by surprise. It was helping him overcome his problem. He was aghast at Hollingsworth's outburst. How could that fucking moron think making 150 grand with zero risk, by working with a sales woman for an hour and a half on a quiet afternoon was pathetic? This was Wall Street and the purpose was to make money. Preferably doing business with clients so the firm was not taking much risk to make the money. The guy had no clue about business. Hollingsworth still thought he was some kind of champion. The man was convinced his speculative talents were great despite consistently losing money. Hollingsworth was a dip shit that did not know his asshole from a hole in the ground when it came to trading FX. He glared at Hollingsworth and growled in a low voice, "I would shut my mouth right now if I were you. I do not appreciate being called a loser in such a profane, public fashion. I don't know what your problem is and I don't care either. My advise to you is to be quiet." Hollingsworth actually started laughing loudly and squealed in a high-pitched voice, "Come on man. You know what you did. You sat there kissing her ass for over an hour. If that's what it takes to make money then I don't care anymore!" He started to become enraged and by sheer force of will kept his mouth shut for a moment. The Global Head of FX had been on the spot desk and had heard and observed the whole affair. His boss shouted at Hollingsworth, " My God man, have you lost your mind? You need to take a walk." With that Hollingsworth got red-faced and then walked off the desk without a word. The man was moving in the direction of the big escalator that went from the large second floor trading room down to the main lobby of the firm. He sat there for about thirty seconds and the whole desk was silent. Then he bolted out of his chair and began walking very briskly in the direction Hollingsworth had gone. He caught up to the son of a bitch as the guy was getting on the escalator and he got on two steps above him. There was no one on that escalator in either direction. He reached down and forcibly grabbed the back of Hollingsworth's neck roughly. He barked at him loudly, "You fucking pussy! You have crossed the line. I tried to be nice. Now I am going to beat the fuck out of you!" The pathetic, arrogant fool literally started crying. He could see the tears streaming down the man's cheeks. Hollingsworth squealed, "You can't touch me! You can't touch me! I will call security! I will call security!" The escalator was now halfway to the bottom and he suddenly remembered the big security desk in the lobby below. He let go of Hollingsworth immediately and spoke calmly, "I don't know what you are talking about. I never touched you." This remark left Hollingsworth speechless. They got to the bottom and he turned right around and took the escalator right back up and went back to his desk. He knew it was now the showdown at the OK Corral. He had to get Hollingsworth fired immediately. He waited patiently at his desk for the rest of the afternoon. Hollingsworth did not return to the trading desk. He was called for a meeting in the White Rabbit's office around four that afternoon. He sat there surrounded by Mahogany magnificence with the Rabbit and the Global Head of FX. The White Rabbit even had his miniature classic cars back. The White Rabbit began the meeting in a deep baritone, "I have heard about the disturbance on the trading desk today. Hollingsworth has claimed that you assaulted him on the escalator. We had security cameras searched but observed nothing. I would like to hear your side of the

≈ 170 ≈

story." Once again it was crunch time and he felt very relaxed and confident, "When I accepted this position you gentlemen requested that I do my best to give things with Hollingsworth a chance. I have done that to the best of my ability. Unfortunately, the situation between Hollingsworth and I has become untenable. The man is an incompetent options trader and a very destructive personality on the desk. Hollingsworth is worse than useless. The guy is very distracting and is losing a lot of money for the firm. In three months of proprietary trading Hollingsworth has lost slightly more than the maximum monthly loss limit I imposed of three hundred thousand dollars a month. This poor track is recorded in the firm's ledger. Hollingsworth has lost about one million dollars speculating so far this year. The man is completely insubordinate and virtually unmanageable. Hollingsworth listens to no one, least of all me. At the request of the head of the spot desk, I specifically instructed Hollingsworth to no longer involved himself in spot desk call outs but the guy has persisted to do so creating confusion. Today, Hollingsworth lost the firm twenty five thousand dollars on a spot trading error. I ate the loss in my P&L to defuse tension from the situation. This afternoon took the cake. I spent a fair amount of time working with Rosalyn on the Reuters dealer working on a big deal and Hollingsworth stood there the whole time looking over my shoulder." The mention of Rosalyn brought a smile to the White Rabbit's face and the great man interjected with a question, "Did we get the deal?" He responded to the interruption, "Yes in fact we did. After a number of iterations we closed over twenty options. Rosalyn booked 75 thousand dollars of mark up and was very pleased. The deal was well hedged in our books and we will make additional trading revenue from the transaction. After the deal was done, Hollingsworth started yelling and screaming at me how pathetic the deal was and how disgusting doing profitable business with clients is to him. The man's outburst was very unprofessional, embarrassing and completely uncalled for. Frankly, I think Hollingsworth requires counseling. In regards to the claim that I physically assaulted him, I will not dignify that scurrilous allegation with a response." The White Rabbit smiled broadly and shook his hand warmly and spoke again, "I am sorry to have troubled you on this matter but we have to do things by the book. Do not worry about a thing. We will handle this on our end now." He went back to the desk and by five that afternoon he had the satisfaction of seeing two security guards with boxes come over to Hollingsworth's desk and pack the dude's stuff up so that it could be shipped. The man had obviously been sacked and subsequently escorted off the premises by security.

He certainly had not considered the possibility of surveillance cameras catching him grab Hollingsworth by the back of the neck on the escalator. If they had found that on film things might not have worked out so well for him. He never intended to do anything other than intimidate Hollingsworth a bit. The man had got in his face yelling and screaming and had embarrassed him in front of the whole trading floor. Hollingsworth needed to learn that there could be negative consequences to aggressive action. In any event, he was glad that obnoxious bastard was gone. The Global Head of FX encouraged him to find a reasonably low priced guy to fill the trading slot in NY. His boss felt it was always better to develop talent and having more junior staff also helped keep more of the bonus pool at the top of the food chain. It was good advice but he became obsessed with hiring this dude he knew in the market named Chester. He had met Chester back in 1988 on this riverboat dinner cruise that one of the FX Options money market brokers used to hold on an annual basis. They had smoked pot on the deck and pounded whiskey and had hit it off pretty well. Down through the years he had loosely stayed in touch with Chester and they had chatted about the markets once in awhile on the Reuters dealing system. He had always thought Chester was a very sharp trader with good market views. The man had been the Global Head of FX Options at a decent bank the past few years but had been out of work for a couple of months. He got the idea of hiring Chester to run the London desk and bringing one of their existing traders in that office back to New York. He arranged lunch for himself and the Global Head of FX to talk with Chester. It was a little disappointing. Chester did not show that much interest in the firm or seem keen to discuss their strategy. The man did not seem all that interested in the kinds of business they were doing in London and how they expected a guy like him to increase their flows and profitability. Chester made a point to mention that there were two other banks in the chase for his services and his decision was going to be based on who paid him the most money. The Global Head of FX was not very impressed with Chester. Afterwards when they discussed the situation, his boss basically said his buddy Chester came across as an arrogant self-absorbed bastard. Chester kind of reminded the man of Hollingsworth on steroids. The Global Head of FX was not excited about getting into a bidding war to hire Chester, but he was very persistent. He pushed for the best possible contract with guaranteed bonus that he could offer Chester and his boss acquiesced. It was a pretty decent offer for midway through the year. When he verbally presented the offer to Chester the man was somewhat dismissive. Chester indicated one of the competing banks had made a better offer and he would have to come up with more guaranteed money if he was serious. For some reason, he remained convinced that bringing Chester in to run London was a good idea. He thought it over and decided to offer Chester an additional one hundred fifty thousand dollars in guaranteed bonus without getting approval. He figured this was as high as he could possible go, and this way he could avoid the embarrassment of fighting for approval only to see Chester turn him down. He called Chester with the higher offer on Friday afternoon of that week. The offer was almost equivalent to what he had been paid to become the Global Head of FX Options over three months ago. Almost to his surprise, Chester accepted. Now he had to actually deliver the offer, but that could wait for Monday. He had his man and now he was going to have a top guy trading for him in London. Chester called him at home early on Sunday morning. Chester didn't even say hello but started right in on the purpose of the call, "I needed to mention some small additional requirements for my contract. I have rented a summer place out in the Hamptons this summer. I will need the firm to pay for my summer rental as well as provide six roundtrip business class flights so that I can get back for some weekends. I will need to make all of these trips three-day weekends. Considering that I have accepted an offer below my target level and the sacrifice I am making to go and work in London I am sure this will not be a problem. You need to understand that these additional small requirements are not negotiable. I am really looking forward to being your partner.

We are going to make a great team." He was flabbergasted by this phone call. First of all, Chester had accepted the offer on Friday. Now the man was calling on Sunday morning to make new demands. Never mind that these were the kind of prima donna requirements that the White Rabbit would never approve of. He was certain of that. He would never humiliate himself even asking for perks of this nature. He also did not like the way Chester referred to him as partner. He was looking to hire Chester to run FX Options trading in London but report to him, not be his partner. He replied, "Well Chester. I thought we had a deal. Now you are making new demands. I will get back to you tomorrow on this." He hung up the phone as Chester was starting to speak again. Chester called back multiple times that Sunday but he did not take the call. He had seen the light. This Chester dude was an arrogant, greedy, aggressive prick, especially for a man who was currently out of work. He began to wonder if there really were two other banks in the running for Chester's service, or was the man just playing him for the maximum possible contract? He felt sweet relief that he had realized how foolish he was to be kissing this guy's ass and making big commitments from his bonus pool to bring in another uncontrollable, egotistical bastard. The next morning he had a chat with the Global Head of FX and told him he had decided to take the man's advice and forget about trying to hire Chester. He mentioned that he was very positive on a junior guy from his old firm that possessed strong excel skills, as well as Fixed Income experience. The guy would not cost much and would be very helpful in their development of structured note business. Structured notes were fixed income notes that had imbedded currency options that could provide interesting yields if certain market scenarios played out. You could create these notes to reflect the client's long-term market views and the products were very lucrative during this time. The Global Head of FX was very pleased with this decision. Chester called the desk several times that day but he did not take the calls. He had decided to make the greedy son of a bitch wait until the end of the day to learn that the game was over. Chester called again around five PM and he took the call. He jumped right in, "Hi Chester, hey that last set of demands you made yesterday morning has caused me to rescind your offer. We have decided to go in another direction. Good luck man, take it easy." Chester had the nerve to get angry in his reply, "What do you mean you have decided to go in another direction? We had a deal with your offer on Friday. That is my stop-loss contract with your firm. You cannot pull your offer, that would not be ethical. I was trying to get a bit more from you guys, its called negotiation. It is how highly skilled professionals do business you see. I am a reasonable man. I can cut down the number of business class trips this summer from London to New York from six to three. That will save you guys some money. Obviously, I will still need my summer rental in the Hamptons covered." He had begun to lose patience with Chester and so his response was terse and not so friendly, "Chester, what makes you think you have a stop-loss to exercise at your discretion? I have just told you that we are going in another direction. I can do whatever the fuck I want. You specifically stated yesterday that your new demands were not negotiable. Fair enough. Our final answer is no. That's it. Negotiations on our end are over. You still have those other two banks that are hot to trot to hire you so you will have to squeeze one of them for your summer rental, travel expenses, and three-day weekends, we are out of the running." Chester started blathering loudly into the phone and so he just hung up. He had his fill of that asshole at this stage of the game. Chester tried to call him dozens of times at home and at the office over the next several weeks but he avoided the man like the plague. Chester actually showed up several times at the firm and tried to get through security to see him but he specifically refused to allow him access. As near as he could ascertain, Chester never landed another senior trading position in the industry. The man had clearly been bluffing about the other two offers. The last he heard, Chester was pounding the phones working as a headhunter for a small-time recruiting firm. As the old saying goes, the greedy become the needy.

They opened an FX department in Hong Kong later that summer. He went to Hong Kong for two weeks with the Global Head of FX and the Head of FX sales, an attractive middle-aged woman named Susan. It was very exciting for them to add Hong Kong to their trading operations in London and New York, to complete the global coverage of FX markets for the firm. It was two years before the historic British handover of sovereignty of Hong Kong to the Peoples Republic of China, but there was a buzz in the air and trepidation about what changes Chinese hegemony might bring. They were bringing a number of ex-patriots over to staff the office combined with local hires from the new Treasurer for the firm in Hong Kong, Mr. Chan and his jovial number two man, the chubby Mr. Wong. The first day was actually exhilarating. The got a fully operational FX trading room up and running seamlessly with a staff of almost twenty along with effective integration with the firm's risk systems in New York and local accounting operations. In the evening of that first day he was in Mr. Chan's office along with the Global Head of FX and Mr. Wong. Mr. Chan had put out four bottles of Snake Wine onto his desk. The Snake Wine was in long, slender bottles with a small green snake pickled in beautiful green liquid. Mr. Chan began to extol the virtues of Snake Wine as a celebratory drink for all-important occasions in Hong Kong. Snake Wine was made in an ancient fashion and had many wonderful attributes. Snake Wine could make you think clearly and feel stronger. Snake Wine could make you hard like a rock as well. The Global Head of FX looked at Mr. Chan and declared that there was no way he was going to drink any wine with a snake in it. He grabbed two bottles of Snake Wine and handed one to the Global Head of FX and began to persuade his boss to drink the Snake Wine with him, "Come on man, we have to show these guys how committed we really are. Mr. Chan says it gives you a real lift and is important for ceremonial occasions and that should be good enough for us. Let's go, bottoms up, are you going to let an American out drink a Brit?" The Global Head of FX acquiesced and they both held their bottles of Snake Wine out to Mr. Chan to be opened. They chugged down the vile, noxious liquid quickly in unison leaving the snake in each of their otherwise empty bottles. The stuff was horrible beyond description. The Global Head of FX looked ready to collapse and he did not feel well himself. They stood there in silence for a moment and then Mr. Chan smiled and said, "Hey, you guys have to eat the snake now, that is the best part. You eat that snake, make you strong, make you hard!" He was starting to figure out he had been played for a fool and got impatient for Mr. Chan and Mr. Wong to drink their Snake Wine. "What the fuck!" he loudly blurted out, "It's time for you guys to finish the celebration and chug down your Snake Wine. Come on now, let's go." Mr. Chan and the jovial Mr. Wong looked at each other and then started laughing uproariously. Mr. Chan finally got himself under some control and started mocking them in his thick Chinese accent, "I tell you something. You fucking guys are crazy. First, crazy guys I ever see drink the Snake Wine. You guys so crazy I really cannot believe it. Don't you know I was just kidding about drinking the Snake Wine? Nobody drinks the Snake Wine for real. It just sits on the counter for decoration. Who knows what the hell is in the Snake Wine? Hey you gentlemen like Snake Wine so much how about you each have one more nice drink?" With that the smiling Mr. Chan tried to hand them the other two bottles of Snake Wine. The Global Head of FX ran out of the office to the men's room and apparently puked his guts out, which was probably all for the best. He stood in the office and stared at the laughing and giggling Mr. Chan and Mr. Wong and felt himself getting a bit angry at how he had been played. He spoke, "How about I stick these last two bottles of Snake Wine up both your asses?" They both became silent for a moment. Then Mr. Chan spoke again, "Oh, you are such a funny guy. You really make me laugh. I never know you options guys are so funny. You sure you don't want some more Snake Wine?" With this the two of them began laughing loudly and uncontrollably again and he beat a hasty retreat out of that office. He felt nauseous for twenty-four hours and his shit was green for the next three days.

In the second week of that trip to Hong Kong, he flew with Susan to Beijing, China to meet with a number of prospective clients. They were visiting banks and treasury departments at large industrial concerns. These were all state owned entities in one form or another. Their firm's representative in China met them at the airport. The man's name was Lee and the dude was driving a very sharp German Sedan. Lee seemed about his own age and was very well groomed and spoke perfect English. The guy apparently represented a number of foreign brokerage firms in China and was doing extremely well by all appearances. He was not very impressed with Beijing relative to other Asian cities like Hong Kong or Tokyo. The city was very drab and crowded with mostly forgettable buildings. He knew the Chinese always liked printed material that they could pore over at their convenience later. So he had prepared a number of copies of his own ten-page outline of important concepts in FX options complete with some specific trade examples. They spent two days visiting over ten potential clients and the meetings were quite cordial and productive, at least according to Mr. Lee who did some translation in many of the meetings when the clients lacked decent English skills. The Chinese liked to sell options; it was as simple as that. They liked the fact they got paid the premium upfront and if things went bad down the line they always could try to stiff you instead of honoring the contract. A number of western banks had taken losses when state-owned Chinese concerns refused to honor the assignment of option contracts they were short that had gone well into the money. The Chinese had claimed that rogue traders had executed the transactions without proper authorization. Therefore, the Chinese concerns could not be expected to honor the option contracts. This scam had worked a few times for the Chinese in high profile cases, but now financial trading agreements with Chinese companies dictated that they were responsible for internal risk-management. You always needed to pay attention carefully to all details when doing business with the Chinese. If you are careless when dealing with the Chinese you will get fucked. They had client dinners the first two nights at two of the top restaurants in Beijing. The prices were equivalent to what you would have paid in New York City for comparable quality. After dinner on the second night, Susan took a cab back to the hotel early. Lee then insisted that they go out on the town. He was shocked at the level of decadence in the Beijing red-light district. There were loud bars, gambling, raunchy strip clubs, live-sex shows and brothels galore. Everywhere they went seemed to be packed with hustling Chinese having a blast. It was not a scene he would have expected to see in a communist country. Lee insisted that the Chinese were a free people except you were not permitted to criticize the government. Business was free, open and competitive and Lee was obviously making a lot of money. It was a long, crazy night. If anyone claims he did not behave like a total gentleman that night he would take exception to the remark. The next day, Lee showed up bright and early to their hotel to drive them to the Great Wall of China at Badaling. Lee did not seem in the least bit hung-over and was very chatty on the drive. They drove about fifty miles north of Beijing on a very new, modern highway with very few cars in either direction. Once you got away from the city the terrain became very severe, barren and mountainous. The ruins of the Great Wall slithered along the mountain ranges like a giant snake. When they were close to Badaling, Lee got off the expressway and got lost driving through the small villages on dirt roads.

Susan was sitting in the back and noticed that a large black sedan with tinted windows was following them very closely. She expressed concern but Lee told her not to worry. Lee drove under an underpass and the road ended abruptly and they were in a large, rocky field. The black sedan drove up behind them and stopped and then four Chinese men got out. They were all in suits and wearing dark sunglasses. They certainly looked like Chinese gangsters. Susan screamed in terror, "Oh my God! They are going to kill us! We are all going to die!" The thought passed through his mind that she might be right but Lee got right out of the car and walked up to the four dudes. They were laughing and joking with Lee so it appeared that Susan had overreacted. Lee got back in the car and spoke, "Hey Susan, I think you need a vacation when you get back to the states, you seem a little high strung. Those guys noticed I seemed to be lost so they wanted to give me directions." When they got to the Great Wall at Badaling, he separated from Susan and Lee. After last night's shared debauchery, Lee probably figured they had bonded enough, and so the guy wanted to spend some time with Susan, which was fine with him. They agreed to meet back in four hours. He basically walked in one direction on the Wall for two hours. He got away from the tourist areas and into the barren parts where maintenance was not being done so the walking was much more difficult. Eventually he was completely by himself. It felt quite exhilarating to be alone in such a starkly, beautiful mountainous area in the most highly populated nation on earth. He thought about the looming transfer of sovereignty over Hong Kong from Britain to China. Mr. Chan and Mr. Wong from his office had both bought property in Canada as a personal hedge if things went wrong after Chinese control started. In this way, they were guaranteed Canadian citizenship and could emigrate there with their families. Based on his experiences the past couple of days in Beijing, he was convinced the transfer would go as smooth as silk. He was proved correct in this belief. Once the Chinese took over, great rivers of money and capital flowed in and out of China through Hong Kong and the city became even more prosperous. Today it was the most expensive city in the world. On the ride back to Beijing they stopped in a village to have dinner in a small, rural restaurant that Lee knew about. They probably ate over seven or eight courses of outstanding, authentic Chinese food including fresh steamed fish taken right out a tank in the restaurant, dumplings, vegetables, noodles and various pork dishes. It was incredibly delicious food, much better than the pricey meals they had partaken of with clients in Beijing. He insisted that he wanted to pay. Lee agreed but instructed him to just give them five U.S. dollars and they would be very happy. He was aghast. How could all three of them eat so much great food and only pay five dollars. Lee insisted there was nothing to worry about, they would be happy with five U.S. dollars, which were in great demand in the black market in China. He got a bit belligerent and insisted he wanted to pay them twenty dollars. Lee looked at him and said sternly, " Listen, if you give them twenty dollars you will fuck me and then I will always have to pay them twenty. If it makes you happy then give them ten and that is the maximum. They think all Americans are rich anyhow." He paid them ten dollars and they seemed extremely pleased. They developed strong dealing relationships with a number of the Chinese concerns during his tenor at the firm.

There was a woman in the IT department of the firm that he found charming when he first met her. She was a very pretty, black woman from some island who looked and sounded exactly like Downtown Judy Brown, a popular MTV VJ at the time. He flirted shamelessly with her when she was doing an extensive IT upgrade on his trading desk and was around quite frequently for several weeks. One evening he was on the desk late alone and when she finished up she asked if he would like to go out for a cocktail. He was a bit surprised by the invitation, but readily accepted. They went to the Royalton Hotel, which was a very hip midtown venue and got pounded on many massive, fancy Martinis. They were there a long time and he was keeping her laughing. When they were extremely plastered she suggested he take her home. He went back to her apartment and they had unmemorable sex and then she passed out and began to snore loudly. He began to feel foolish and got the hell out of there. His head was starting to clear and the whole thing didn't feel quite right. He had remembered the words of his late father. The old man had always admonished him to stay the fuck away from the office pussy. The old man would rant and rave that there was fucking pussy everywhere and why were so many men so stupid to fuck around with office pussy. It could only lead to trouble. The old man had seen many of his friends fuck up their marriages and/or their jobs by fucking around with office pussy. His father had surely been right on this count. He knew it. Fortunately, Downtown Judy Brown had finished up her assignment on his desk and he didn't see her for a few days. One morning he was waiting in line in the firm's lunch cafeteria behind a bond trader at the firm he did not know well. The dude looked at him and quietly said,

"It's none of my business but you seem to have gotten quite friendly with Downtown Judy Brown. A word to the wise amigo, be a little careful with that one. That girl is nothing but trouble, trust me." He thanked the guy for his unsolicited advice and began to admonish himself internally for being so reckless that traders on other desks had even noticed. She came around a few times, but he was not so warm and friendly and he tried to make it clear that he was quite busy. Several weeks later, she caught him alone on the desk in the early evening and insisted he go out for a drink with her. He selected a dirty, little dive bar nearby. He did not want this to be a pleasant time. His goal was to encourage her to leave him alone now. They sat down at the bar and ordered drinks and she began to ask what was wrong, why he was being so unfriendly, and did he not want to get together again? He told her she was a nice, fun girl but that he thought their little fling had been a mistake and they should keep the relationship professional here on out. She smiled and started talking about the great time they had the last time around. She reached out and began to stroke his thigh lightly. Then she told him that she was launching a fashion consultant business on the side and needed to borrow ten thousand dollars for some start up expenses. She was sure the business would take off and she would be able to pay him back in no time at all. He began to understand her modus operandi. She would fuck a senior married trader on the side a few times and then shake him down for some cash. He had probably disrupted the normal program by playing hard to get after only fucking her once and now she was scrambling. He remembered the little chat with the bond trader in the cafeteria and the long ago words of the old man also burned in his brain. He began to find her pithy little accent quite annoying. He was starting to get angry so he forced himself to stay silent for a few minutes. He was learning much better control both on and off the trading desk by forcing himself to stay silent for a few minutes when something suddenly annoyed him and made him angry. He knew he needed to be a little careful. He shifted in the bar stool to move away from her caressing fingers and then he spoke, "You are a very smart woman with an obvious gift for fashion and so I am sure your business venture will be a big success. I would encourage you to work out a detailed budget and a professional business plan and then look for appropriate financing at that juncture. Unfortunately, I cannot advance you a loan. I have found that when money gets involved it can ruin friendships and lead to hard feelings." She stopped smiling and lowered her voice a bit; "It is hard to believe a successful trader like you cannot afford to make a small ten thousand dollar loan to a good friend like me. It would shock me if you could not trust someone that knows you as well as I know you. I will tell you what. A loan of five thousand dollars would still be very helpful. You seem very successful at the firm. I am sure you would not want to have embarrassing allegations create problems for you. That just would not make any sense at all to me." He paused for a moment to size up the situation. He had a tiger by the tail and this was no time to show weakness. He then answered her quite forcefully, " I think it is a bit of a reach to say that we are good friends and that you know me well. Let's be honest, we barely know each other. What exactly are you threatening me with? Are you suggesting that if I do not extend you a loan, you will make our relationship public at the firm? Well you are an IT wiz. Why don't you send an email to the whole firm that says you did some work on my trading desk, we became friendly, you invited me out for a drink, and then after we got drunk you invited me back to your apartment and we fucked. You then asked me for a ten thousand dollar loan and got angry when I refused. How about something like that? Go ahead and send the fucking email. I don't give a flying fuck. I wonder how your senior management in IT would feel about that little story? Frankly, I do not think my management would care all that much. You do not report to me. I have no involvement in your management or compensation at the firm. It is common knowledge that the head of my division is banging a senior sales woman in the London office. They are both married to other people and nobody around here seems to give two fucks about it. I am having a great year, so they are not looking for any problems with me." She did not look one bit happy with this answer from him. After a moment she replied, "You don't have to get so nasty. I am not threatening you in any way. I just can't believe that you are so cheap that you cannot make a small loan to me but fine, I don't need a loan from you anyhow. You traders get such huge bonuses, while IT departments pay meager bonuses. We do all the real work at the firm if you ask me. The bonus system on Wall Street is so unfair it makes me fucking sick. Do you really think the system is fair?" Her petulant, whining tone told him that she had given up. There was no point to kick the hornet's nest again. He decided to pretend it really had been a friend asking for a business loan instead of a sleazy attempt at petty extortion. He tried to be as nice as possible given the circumstances, "Do I think the system is fair? No fucking way. Of course the system is not fair. Life is not fair. Nobody ever said it was. I have lent money to friends in the past and the result has always been the same. I get stiffed. I never get paid back a penny. I have two sons to put through college and that is not cheap these days. I am sorry but I cannot help you out here." He put some money on the bar to pay for the drinks and got up off the bar stool, "I apologize, but I have to run. Please have a lovely evening." He quickly walked out of the bar. He wanted to get the fuck away from her as fast as possible. Downtown Judy Brown never spoke to him again. When they passed each other by chance at the firm they would both look away and not say anything. He was fine with that arrangement. In the future, when his desk required some IT work they sent somebody else. He was cool with that as well.

His last full year in that firm was his best year in the industry; there was no question about it. The customer business had gotten bigger and more lucrative and he was on fire in his proprietary trading as well. His budget had increased each year, but he was well past his annual budget by April of 1997 and on his way to a fabulous year. He was making a lot more money than the White Rabbit had ever dreamed possible. He loved it when the Rabbit would come by the desk in the afternoon and ask in a deep baritone how they were doing that day and he would always reply, "Still sitting at the table Sir, it is not yet time to count the chips." He got the idea to expand into trading energy derivatives for the firm. He knew that this was the time he had the leverage to push to expand his fiefdom. Futures and options trading in oil and natural gas were growing rapidly and the deregulation of the market for electricity was also creating new trading opportunities. He began to do the legwork to plan the expansion of his business. He got his boss, the Global

Head of FX on board. They had become fast friends by this time. He attended an energy derivates conference in Houston, Texas sponsored by Enron. It was a fantastic event full of high energy and many innovative ideas and concepts. The dudes from Enron were extremely impressive. Many of the concepts and structures from the FX market were being used to model these new markets in energy derivatives. He thought about moving to Houston some day if he could land a senior trading role with Enron. It was truly remarkable to see this seemingly unstoppable energy trading juggernaut collapse into bankruptcy only four short years later. He had lunch in the executive dining room of the firm in August of that year with the President of the firm, the Global Head of FX, and the White Rabbit. The President of the firm was highly complimentary of his track record at the firm of consistently high profitability. The man was very supportive of his idea to expand into energy derivatives and promised him his full support in getting all necessary resources to make it happen. Once again he was sure he was on the inside track to a big job at a great firm and his future was assured. Once again it did not take long until he was slapped back down into reality. Several weeks later, the parent company of his firm announced a merger agreement had been reached with another major brokerage firm. Shockingly, the President of the firm resigned under auspicious circumstances shortly thereafter. At the time, this guy was considered one of the rising stars in the industry. The man has subsequently come back stronger than ever and is now considered one of the Top Titans on Wall Street. He often considered contacting the man in the past decade when his career was languishing, but never got the energy and/or the balls to do so. In any event, it quickly became clear that the newly acquired firm would be running the FX department of the combined entity. The White Rabbit was moved over to another division. Both he and the Global Head of FX were informed that they were no longer the global heads of anything. They were just senior guys at the new firm. This was particularly bad timing for his bonus for that year. They paid you a lot when you produced and they were convinced you could keep doing it for them so they needed to retain you. Because all of his senior managers at the firm were being pushed aside for the merger they had no incentive to make sure he got paid properly for his record year. Instead their incentive was to keep as much of the bonus pool for themselves as possible since this was the last year they were going to be calling the shots. He ended the best year of his career depressed about how the merger had fucked up his plans, and cost him a ton of money. He was convinced he needed to get the hell out of there and find a new job as soon as possible.

Chapter 9

In his opinion, 1998 was the last really great year for the FX market. It was the final year before the start of the euro, the single European currency that was launched on January 1, 1999. The FX market lost dozens of interesting currency pairs and a significant amount of trade volume and corporate activity with this grand European experiment. It was the first attempt in history to put monetary unity before political confederation. It was also the year the Fed was forced to engineer a bail out of Long Term Capital Management (LTCM), a large hedge fund that had borrowed extensively from most major Wall Street banks to massively leverage its positions. Market reaction to the Russian debt crisis had stressed LTCM's positions to the point where they lacked the necessary capital to maintain their margin balances with their many lenders, even at the extremely advantageous terms they had negotiated. The Fed pressured major Wall Street firms to provide their own capital to avoid a forced liquidation of LTCM's massive portfolio. It was feared this could lead to contagion and a major global financial market meltdown. It was also a year when the Japanese Yen experienced wild swings, creating huge trading opportunities in the FX market. This year also marked the beginning of a period of large mergers and consolidation in the global banking industry, which began to significantly decrease the number of major financial institutions with large FX trading businesses. It seemed to him that 1998 was the year when the golden era of the FX market began to wane.

FX had certainly been an interesting business to be involved with in the 80s and 90s. He had traveled extensively in Asia and Europe and made some memorable friends all over the world. One of his brokers in Tokyo, known as Uncle Jimmy in the FX options market, was a man he could never forget. The guy had long hair like a rock star and drove around Tokyo on a Harley Davidson motorcycle, wearing an authentic Nazi crash helmet with the swastikas crudely etched out. The Japanese loved Harley Davidson motorcycles. Uncle Jimmy was on his fourth marriage and his wife had a very attractive daughter who apparently was a groupie on the Tokyo rock and roll scene. One night, Uncle Jimmy woke up around two am and went into his kitchen to get a drink of water. Incredibly, there was a legendary rock guitarist sitting at the kitchen table in his boxer shorts, smoking a cigarette and drinking a glass of whiskey. Uncle Jimmy was not bothered in the least by his young stepdaughter's bedding of this aging rocker in his apartment. Instead, the man poured himself a glass of whiskey and sat down next to him to shoot the breeze, thereby crossing a major item off his bucket list. Uncle Jimmy tried to convince the guitarist to let him wake up his wife to take their picture together, but the man politely refused. Another memorable friend he made in the market was a German Countess who was a spot dollar/mark dealer for a bank in Australia. He wondered how European royalty could end up as a spot FX trader in Sydney? She was tall, attractive, and blonde, but the lady was no dummy. He found her short-term directional calls in the spot market to be much more consistently on target than those of any of the senior spot dealers he worked with. She had a no-nonsense approach to business along with a good sense of humor. He enjoyed trading FX with her at night for many years. Working in the FX markets during that era gave you the chance to meet interesting people from all over the world, which was a pretty exceptional opportunity in the pre-internet days. Today, the world has certainly gotten much smaller with the Internet and efficient social networks that make it easy for people to connect. The money market brokers were providing big-time entertainment to FX traders in the 80s and 90s. He focused on getting free Knicks and Yankee tickets in order to take his sons to the games. If a bank trader was doing significant amounts of business, the sky was really the limit for the kind of freebies that could be demanded. He knew one major FX option broker that kept a two-bedroom apartment in the city on the side. The man apparently took out special clients and hired escorts so that they could enjoy stress free servicing before returning home to their wives and children. He also had brokers that organized all-expense paid golf weekends in Florida for clients. In the past decade, as the FX market has consolidated, the banks have gotten a lot stricter in terms of monitoring any potential conflicts of interest for traders such as lavish broker entertainment. The brokers have tightened up their purse strings as well.

In any event, he started 1998 as a senior FX options dealer at the newly merged firm. He had been paid the biggest bonus of his Wall Street career but felt bitter about being shafted. His ego was bruised over losing the battle he had waged to be named Global Head of FX Options for the merged firm. It was interesting to observe that his new management seemed to have a much bigger risk appetite than he had ever experienced. They also seemed to have very different ideas about how to manage the customer business. The new firm was much more focused on doing large deals with hedge funds or investment banking clients as opposed to soliciting a wide variety of business with mutual funds, smaller banks, corporate accounts and other diverse client groups. These new dudes believed in taking aggressive risk and were willing to accept wide P&L swings to make money. He was accustomed to working at firms where senior management focused on consistent profitability and minimal swings in P&L, which necessitated a diverse client driven strategy. Despite his ruffled feathers over losing his official management role, he was intrigued by the opportunity to take much more significant trading risk with his own proprietary positions. During his first week at the combined firm, he looked on as FX options traders from the new firm mispriced an option to a major fund and got picked off for several hundred thousand dollars. Almost immediately, the trader at the fund wanted to increase the ticket size (amount of transaction) and those dudes were happy to do more at the wrong price. He knew that particular hedge fund trader from past conflicts. The man was an aggressive bastard that loved to bulldoze banks, just because they wanted to do business with the famous hedge fund. He had gotten into a number of loud arguments at his prior firms with the sales people that covered that son of a bitch. He could not help himself and exploded in a rage that the price was wrong and the firm was getting screwed. They all looked at him like he was from Mars, but he did manage to stop the firm from losing more money on that deal. Before too long, he had gotten control of quoting all the FX options to clients of the new firm. Senior management had quickly ascertained that he and his team were much better at making money from clients than the traders from the other firm. As a result, he was given the responsibility to manage a separate client book with his crew, but he did not have any official title. That book became the biggest earner at the new firm and his boys got paid great bonuses for that year, although he had moved on by then. He sat next to a Japanese trader named Taki. The guy seemed to have some gravy job as a proprietary trader. Taki did not seem to do much except talk on the phone in Japanese and go for long walks off the desk. The man would come in around 9:30 AM and leave by three PM each day, except on Fridays when Taki would never come in at all. Around 2:45 PM each afternoon, the fastidious little man would spray copious amounts of Windex all over his desk and screens, clean the space thoroughly, and then leave. He had tried to make small talk and discuss markets with Taki, but the man was not at all interested. Anytime he spoke to Taki, the man would look annoyed and answer with terse, one word responses, so he let it go. So much for his years living in Japan helping him connect with a Japanese ex-patriot in NYC. In February of that year, with great fanfare in the room, Taki went long dollar/yen around 123. He did some digging and learned that Taki's father happened to be a senior official with the Bank of Japan (BOJ). Within several days, all of the top guys from the new firm had sold Japanese Yen one way or the other. They were short Japanese Yen vs. the Dollar and other major currencies and they had the positions through options, forwards and spot. But the bottom line was that they had gotten the tip off from Taki and they were all short the Japanese Yen. He put on an options put structure to get short Japanese Yen vs. the Dollar. The big position worked tremendously well. From the lows of the year in February, the dollar/yen rallied consistently until it peaked above 147 by August. The BOJ had surprised the market with extremely accommodative action and unexpected interest rate cuts all throughout the spring of that year.

He had figured out the modus operandi of the dudes that ran the newly merged firm. They did not have interest or ability to grind out consistent profits by executing customer business. They were happy to quote large amounts to serious hedge funds in order to see the flows and make or lose a bundle on each transaction. They were interested in acquiring information before the market did and positioning aggressively. It was his strong belief that most so-called market geniuses on Wall Street either had some type of non-public information, or they were making money buying cheap or selling rich to suckers. It was all pretty much as simple as that. This new firm had a strong reputation as an aggressive trading operation. However, most of what they did in the market was hit or miss except for making huge profits on market movements based on non-public Central Bank strategy they were privy too. When they had the inside scoop on a particular currency, they put on big positions in their proprietary accounts and waited patiently for the chickens to come home to roost. The top options trader from the new firm was a Greek dude he nicknamed Marcellus Wallace, a reference to a character in the movie "Pulp Fiction." Marcellus Wallace had been the force that had kept him from being named the Global Head of FX Options trading at the newly merged firm. He watched Marcellus Wallace's positions closely. For several months the man didn't seem to do much of anything, but suddenly, Marcellus started shorting the Greek Drachma vs. the Deutsche Mark through some clever option structures. Within a few days, all the top guys at the new firm were loading the boat short the Greek Drachma vs. all the major currencies. In that last year before the rise of the euro, there were many rumors about which currencies might experience a serious devaluation before the final conversion to euro. It certainly wasn't a big surprise to see the Greek Drachma get revalued lower. Everyone knew the Greeks had fudged the numbers in the first place, to pretend to meet euro criteria. He learned that Marcellus' father was a senior trader for the Bank of Greece. In the words of Yogi Berra, it was déjà vu all over again. He threw caution to the wind and went long a big position of call options for the Deutsche Mark/ Greek Drachma. This made him short Greek Drachma vs. the Deutsche Mark. Within several weeks, rumors were swirling that Greek Drachma devaluation was imminent and implied volatilities soared for that currency. His option positions were exploding in value, even before the move. One morning, he came into work early and was surprised to learn that his Deutsche Mark/Greek Drachma call options had been taken out of his ledger at the firm. He had a videoconference from London with the Global Head of FX at the newly merged firm, who politely informed him that he was not authorized to trade in the Greek Drachma and so his options had been taken away. About a week later, a 15% devaluation of the Greek Drachma was announced. His positions would have made around thirty million dollars, which was significantly more than he had ever made on any one speculative trade in his career. He became quite bitter over this shafting, and came to the obvious conclusion that it was a rigged game with these new guys and he didn't have much of a future working for these arrogant bastards.

In the spring of that year, the former Chief FX Dealer from his first post MBA firm contacted him. The man was now the manager of the FX Division at a mid-sized U.S. investment bank and was looking for a new Head of FX options for the firm. The FX Division at the new firm had small, separate FX Option teams in New York. London and Hong Kong. They had decided to develop a global book in FX options, as most competitors in the market had already done. It was a nice opportunity to start over and build a business at a solid firm. They had dinner together and worked out a deal for him to move on once again. Besides a very good guaranteed bonus for the first year he was being brought in as a Managing Director (MD), which was a big deal. MD as a title was somewhat equivalent to Partner for the investment banks, which had gone public and were no longer private partnerships. It was a difficult title to attain even if you were a big producer. It was back to basics for him at this new firm. The main strategy was to make money from client business and/or engage in low-risk arbitrage trading strategies. They were looking for steady profitability, not wild swings in P&L. Any speculative losses had better be covered by existing profits. There was no budget for losing money on risk taking activities unless you were using money you had made through customer activity or arbitrage. The prior FX option trader in NY had been sacked for losing money after several years of gravy from clients had dried up. The firm had a multi-structured sales strategy in the New York office. There were sales people in the FX dealing room that dealt only with firm traders. But they also had a separate sales force that operated out of a different Dealing Room. This separate sales force was an agency only sales desk. This meant they assured their clients that they would execute all of their trades on a best efforts basis and never principal (take the other side) of any transaction. They would charge a commission for each trade and work only for commission, or so they told their clients. In reality, they took every penny they could from their clients, every chance they got. But they did have authority to deal with any bank on the street to cover all their business and they never took proprietary risk positions. He got burned a few times trying to win the business of this internal sales group and eventually, he did his best to avoid trading with them. The agency sales operation had no qualms about running over the firm's own traders.

He took an immediate dislike to the Chief FX Dealer at the new firm. The guy was a short, pudgy, foul-tempered little man with a beard who was known behind his back as the Poison Dwarf. The Poison Dwarf liked to yell and scream on a daily basis, while berating his staff. The Dwarf got away with this obnoxious behavior because the FX Department was in a separate soundproof dealing room with limited access to the rest of the firm's trading operations. The Poison Dwarf had been running the spot desk with consistent profitability over ten years, and so had deep seniority at the firm. The man seemed impossible to please, despite the consistent money being churned out by the FX traders. The Poison Dwarf's father had apparently been some kind of human rights hero in Latin America, but the man himself was a despicable human being. The Dwarf was especially cruel on a daily basis to his trading assistant. Fortunately, he did not report to the Poison Dwarf, but the man had several big option clients, so they traded to-gether every day. The Poison Dwarf would haggle down his spread on every trade so that there was very little edge left for him in all their deals. It was very time-consuming busi-ness without much upside for him. After each deal, the Poison Dwarf would stick on a big commission after the fact and get paid a nice percentage on every deal without having to manage the risk of the positions. It turned his stomach having to listen to the Poison Dwarf constantly rant and rave. It made him glad he had toned his own act down to the point where he rarely even raised his voice in the Dealing room, regardless of how active the market was. Earlier in his career, even when he had been unable to control an occasional outburst on the trading desk, he had never engaged in the kind of insulting blather that the Poison Dwarf constantly hammered his staff with. He took it upon himself to agitate the Poison Dwarf as much as possible while staying calm and professional at all times. He could tell how much the FX staff that reported to the little prick enjoyed the spectacle of him arguing calmly but force-fully with the Poison Dwarf. The pudgy mean-spirited little fellow paced back and forth, angrily shouting, so the whole room could hear the pitiful whining for a few more thousand dollars on each and every deal. It was a daily experience he actually grew to somewhat enjoy. He had to think of clever new methods of slyly showing complete and utter contempt for the Poison Dwarf in an improvisational style that could not actually be construed as insults. He quickly achieved rock star status with a number of the FX staff because he was the only one in the room that did not have to shut up and take the insults from the little prick. He could tell that it twisted the Poison Dwarf badly that he did not report to the man. The last option trader had reported to the Dwarf, so he was sure that the greedy bastard hated having to deal with him. The firm had a huge clearing business (processing trades for clients and other financial institutions) and the FX trading to support this activity was extremely lucrative. The Poison Dwarf traded spastically all day long, and loudly proclaimed his prowess as a great trader because of the profit in his ledger every day. The reality of the situation was that the Dwarf would use the clearing activity as his own little piggy bank and shift some of that P&L into his own ledger at the firm, thereby ensuring no losses. By 2011, the Attorney General of the State of New York had started filing lawsuits against a number of major clearing banks due to their egregious gouging of customers in all their internal FX transactions. That shit had been going on for over thirty years by then.

His first few months at the new firm were a bit of a struggle. Client activity was low and markets were range-bound. He had to make several long trips overseas and it was difficult to focus on trading strategies. The arbitrage in the FX options market on American style option expirations had really started to dry up and he had nothing available to ensure consistent profitability. In reality, nothing much was happening that summer except that the pressure was silently building in the global financial markets. Market participants had jumped into risk aggressively that year. The whole market was wildly short Japanese Yen and had done fantastically well. The yen was being used as a global funding currency, and it had been a money machine to borrow in yen at the low interest rates, invest in U.S. dollar, European or Emerging Market assets, and then profit on both ends of the deal. Money had been pouring into Russian debt for several years, but it was becoming clear that widespread fraud had been involved and now the Russian lenders were struggling to stay solvent. With yen depreciating so steadily, market participants on all these yen loans had made enormous profits. At least on paper, there were big profits for the borrowers of short-term Japanese Yen loans. The Japanese economy thrived on exports and a weakening yen had been critical in helping their economy attempt recovery. In 1995 the yen had hit a post WW2 high below 80 and by the summer of 1998 was trading a calm range between 145 and 147. Remember that the Japanese Yen is quoted in so-called European terms, meaning currency per U.S. dollar. The less yen it takes to buy a dollar, the stronger the yen. That summer the Japanese corporate exporters had started buying yen forward in a quiet steady fashion. The Japanese knew the gig was close to being up, but they were trying to be patient and accumulate long-term hedges under the radar. The Russian debt crisis was building in fits and stops, with rumors and denials and more rumors and denials in the normal fashion that these global economic dramas usually played out. He knew the shit was going to hit the fan and the dollar/yen rate would tank (the yen would appreciate sharply) and the implied volatility would explode. But with the market quiet and lackluster, he had to build his position slowly as well and was showing some losses his management was not looking for. The Poison Dwarf had begun to publicly dress him down in the dealing room as a loser since the man was privy to all the division's P&Ls. The Dwarf was a pincher and a poacher and a short-term trader only. The Poison Dwarf was also about as subtle as a sledgehammer with his insults. Even when his positions were still losing, he always got the best of the

Dwarf in their verbal sparring matches in front of the rest of the room. He had already discussed his strategy concerning the yen in great detail with his boss, the Division Manager. He was determined to stay long Japanese Yen delta (short U.S. dollars) and long volatility in Japanese Yen. He would keep a base position and begin to build only when the position was showing strong profitability. It was a more patient and long-term strategy than his boss was used to, but with client activity low, the man was on board with the idea. By September, the market had started to heat up and his positions had made back all losses and now were nicely in the black. He began to increase his delta and he bought more volatility as well. He increased his position several times that month until he was well in the money, but was near the risk limits he had agreed to upon being hired. Near the end of the month, he had a long meeting with his boss. The Division Manager was well pleased with the profits he had made on his yen positions and was urging him to close out. However, he was sure the crisis had not yet peaked. He held his ground and maintained his positions. In early October, the yen bubble finally burst once and for all. Panic stop-loss buying of yen across all major currencies fueled a very sharp collapse of the dollar/yen rate. It broke through the psychological support level of 130 and then several days later crashed below the long-term support level of 120. It was an enormous move in a very short period of time, and volatility in the Japanese Yen option markets soared to heights never seen before. On the day the yen broke below 120, he efficiently closed out his entire line of yen options at enormous profits. That day he personally made over five million in additional P&L, which was an incredible sum relative to the size of his positions. He realized he could have taken a much bigger position at his old firm under the new management, but would he have played a bigger risk bet with the same patience and brilliant timing? He was not sure. It was a big score at his new firm; that was for sure. Late in the afternoon of his big day, the Division Manager held a meeting with the entire department. His boss informed the whole group that it had been a record day in FX trading at the firm. The global business had made eight million dollars, a princely sum that had generated a congratulatory phone call from the famous Chairman of the firm to the Division Manager. He silently wondered if his boss had informed the Chairman that one man had made over 60 percent of the booty. He kept his mouth shut and stared intently at the Poison Dwarf. The little fucker looked glum and despondent. The Dwarf knew who had been proven right and had made the real money on the move.

His department ended up making close to twenty million dollars his first year at the new firm, even though he only traded the last five months of the year. It was a lot more than that firm had ever made in FX options for a whole year even when they had large, profitable clients. His Japanese Yen position had made over fifteen million dollars and he was getting the team more organized in trading global volatility arbitrage strategies. That area had also produced nicely in the final quarter of 1998. His boss did the right thing and paid him additional bonus for the year on top of his contractual agreement. The client business was growing very slowly and was not very profitable. In reality, the business had gotten more competitive and there was less gravy to go around.

January 1, 1999 saw the launch of the euro at the rate of 1.1800 U.S. Dollars/Euro. He was sure that the euro had been vastly overvalued for the launch and was certain that it would come under pressure after the initial honeymoon stage was over. The euro traded in American terms, which meant it was denominated in U.S. Dollars/Euro. So as the rate dropped and it took less dollars to buy a euro, it meant the euro was weakening. He liked to say the euro was like a cake made of shit batter, but exquisitely decorated with lovely, white French icing. Everyone knew that the so-called "PIIGS", Portugal, Ireland, Italy, Greece and Spain had fudged the numbers so as to gain admittance. There was no chance their shaky economies could meet the stringent euro requirements. Many market participants even speculated that France was playing jiggery poker with the data to show adherence to the economic requirements. The reality was that only the northern European countries, led by Germany, had strong currencies and vibrant, well-managed economies that easily met all the euro requirements. By 2012, many Germans would be wondering how they had gotten themselves into a position of being forced to subsidize the deficit economies of the lazy southern European peasants. He determined that the euro would experience a long, slow decline as it slowly sank from its own weight. He assumed that the new European Central Bank (ECB) would smooth the decline of the euro. For the next several years he did his best to stay short euro delta and he was an aggressive seller of euro volatility on any spikes. It was a good central strategy, and his next two full years at the firm went well.

One afternoon early in the New Year he was chatting on the Reuters dealing system with a colleague from his last firm and they were laughing about one of their old clients that they had made several millions trading with. It was a small German bank that had burst onto the FX options scene several years earlier, and had become a direct client of his desk. They had often wondered what viable strategy the Germans could possibly have been running. It had recently been discovered that the FX Options traders at the German bank had been hiding several hundred million dollars in losses over a period of several years. The Division Manager read over his shoulder and understood what he had been laughing about. His boss had recently become an avid skeet shooter and so was probably thinking about guns on a regular basis. The Division Manager loudly told him in front of the whole dealing room, "Please understand that if you lose me several hundred million dollars, I am not just going to fire you. I am going to kill you. I will bring my Browning shotgun in here and blow your brains out." He laughed at the obnoxious joke and then replied. "Well Boss, if you come at me with your shotgun my advice is don't miss. I have guns too, and know how to use them quite well." After the Division Manager walked away, one of the spot dealers in the room came over to him and excitedly asked, "Are you crazy? Did you hear that correctly? The Division Manager has just threatened to shoot you if you lose money trading. You are set for life. You can sue these guys and get paid ten million dollars. I am sure of it." The firm had hired this particular spot dealer several years earlier with great fanfare from Grossman Zachs. Not surprisingly, the man was a very poor trader and had become the Poison Dwarf's favorite whipping boy. Effective traders rarely left Grossman to join lesser Wall Street firms. They could most likely take more risk and get paid more money at Grossman Zachs than any other Wall Street firm. Top traders from Grossman would leave the firm to launch their own hedge funds. But only the losers at Grossman would peel off to a less prestigious firm. He never understood how senior management at the various firms he had worked at never seemed to understand this. They would consistently overpay for mediocre talent out of Grossman Zachs. He ignored the advice the man had given him about filing a lawsuit. Several months later, the spot trader quit the firm and filed a lawsuit for long-term disability, based on the battering his eyes and hands had taken from his years as a trader. The lawsuit was obviously a crock of shit. But back in those years the Wall Street firms were usually willing to pony up to settle lawsuits. Apparently, the guy managed to secure a settlement of several hundred thousand dollars. Years later he heard that the man was living in a studio apartment in some little town in upstate New York, eking out a living peddling real estate. Not long after the terrible tragedy that was the Columbine High School massacre, the Poison Dwarf got angry after a deal. The Dwarf loudly proclaimed to him, "If anyone is going to go postal in here it will be you. I know you are crazy enough to be a killer!" He responded, "Yes my friend, you are correct. But please rest assured that the day I come in here with guns, you will be shot first and also get the most. But first I will slap you around a bit just for fun." His response set the Poison Dwarf off and the man stormed out of the dealing room in a rage. He was called into a tense meeting with his boss several hours later. His boss admonished him; "The Poison Dwarf has stated that you threatened him with violence in front of the room. There are some corroborating witnesses. The man has threatened to discuss the situation with Human Resources. This could be a serious problem." He snapped back, "Are you kidding me? The

Poison Dwarf started the whole thing by publicly declaring me a killer. I was only agreeing with him in jest. I distinctly recall that you jokingly threatened to shoot me earlier this year in front of the whole room if I lost a bundle. Did I run around and make a stink about your comment that had obviously been meant to be humorous?" The Division Manager got very quiet after being reminded of his own public gun comments in the Dealing Room not that long ago. Then the man spoke, "This situation will stay internal within the FX Department, but I am tired of the constant bickering between the two of you. You guys are my leaders in the room and your never-ending conflict sets a poor example to the rest of the staff. You gentlemen will meet this afternoon and settle your issues once and for all." It was the most bizarre meeting of his life. The Poison Dwarf passionately blathered on and on for over an hour. He said nothing. He just sat there and listened but could not even recall what the man had said. When the guy was finally spent and paused for a moment he stuck out his hand and warmly shook the hand of the Poison Dwarf. He smiled and said, "I am glad we have finally worked things out. I feel much better and I am sure you do as well." He then walked out of the man's office without another word. The bickering stopped for a couple of weeks and then slowly got back to normal before too long. The Poison Dwarf just could not help himself.

He became good friends with an Emerging Market (EM) trader at the firm. When he joined the firm his boss had mentioned to him how this young kid had made a million dollar bonus the prior year. The EM trader was probably ten years younger than him, but they hit it off quite well. The guy had been a good college athlete and was now an active motocross

rider on weekends. The EM trader liked to talk about accu-
mulating three million dollars in cash and then quitting the
business to buy a ranch in Montana and become a full-time
motocross rider. The man had several good years in a row
while they were working together and was also doing extremely well in the stock market. Many firms on Wall Street
established stringent restrictions on the personal trading activities of staff. But this particular firm had a very loose policy
as long as you traded through them and paid their exorbitant
commissions. The Internet bubble was in full froth and the
EM trader was scoring on a regular basis. It turned out that
the guy had befriended a tech geek at the firm, who was tip-
ping the EM trader off about new companies that had recently
gone public and were set to take off. He got into the loop
with the EM trader and made several hundred thousand dollars quite quickly, which he used to help buy a beach house.
The EM trader was pushing his luck for all it was worth and
did not take many profits. One night when they were having
a beer, the EM trader told him that his margin account at the
firm now represented ten million dollars worth of stock. This
meant the man had five million dollars in equity and had borrowed another five million from the firm to hold the stock
portfolio. He was incredulous his friend had done so well and
encouraged him to lock in some of the money, "Dude, you
told me you were shooting to make three million bucks to buy
a ranch in Montana and become a full-time motocross rider.
This Internet bubble has to burst soon, I think we can all agree
there. For God's sake, at least take three million dollars out of
the account and set it aside so you can fall back on your dream
when this crazy ride ends." His friend's reply made it clear the

man had the fever and did not want to listen to reason, "My man, this party is a long way from over. I am going to make fifty million dollars for myself and then start my own hedge fund and make billions. I will buy the fucking state of Montana when I am ready." Sadly, it did not end well for his friend. Most of the high-flying Internet stocks of that era never even made money. The stock prices had raced higher on speculative fever while the actual companies were simply burning through all the cash they had raised at a rapid pace. Old school market legends that had predicted the collapse of over-valued Internet stocks and been subject to public derision, had eventually been proven correct. The EM trader got caught like a deer in head-lights, and could not exit his stocks on the way down even though the man was a professional trader. In the end, the firm force liquidated the EM trader's portfolio and the man had less than one hundred thousand dollars left to his name when the dust finally settled. Apparently, the EM trader almost got fired for the reckless personal trading. Over a decade later, the EM trader was broke and attempting to scrounge out a living to support his family by day trading futures at a fly-by-night bucket shop. These types of firms were cropping up in the new era of pure electronic trading, as the major Wall Street firms slowly imploded. The man's dreams of owning a ranch in Montana and becoming a professional motocross rider were long gone. In general, the public makes a lot of money on pa-per during speculative bubbles but rarely cashes out, regard-less of trading experience.

He liked to have dinner sitting at the bar at old school NYC restaurants. One night at Billy's, he was enjoying a glass of wine after finishing his meal. Three very pretty ladies came in and sat down at the bar next to him. They looked to be in their late twenties and must have been partying for some time since they were quite loud and boisterous. He began joking around a little bit with the woman that sat next to him. At one stage, she seemed to have gotten into a heated argument with her friends and they stalked out of the bar. At this juncture, she focused her attention on him. She was an airline stewardess from Minnesota on a layover in NYC and she was looking to have a good time. He bought her a couple of drinks and she insisted they do several shots of Tequila as well. His apartment was right around the corner, and he suggested they go back there to get high. She got very excited when she heard he had good pot and readily accepted his invitation. He was going through a divorce and had been quite depressed during that period and was not dating. But he was pretty excited that such a sexy young lady was going home with him. However, when they left the bar, she started stumbling badly and he could tell she was extremely wasted. He tried to convince her to let him get her a cab back to her hotel, but she was insistent about going back to his apartment to get high. When they got back to his apartment, he went into his bedroom to get some pot. By the time he came back out to the living room, she was kneeling down on his plush, white living room rug, puking her guts out. It was a pretty disgusting spectacle to observe and the smell was terrible. When she finished heaving, she literally rolled over and passed out on the rug next to the big mess. His evening had certainly taken a turn for the worse. He got a bucket and cleaning materials and did his best to clean up the rug while the woman lay there sleeping soundly. He propped her head up on a pillow to make sure her throat was clear and that she could breath easily. He then fired up a joint and got high by himself. He wondered if she would sleep through the whole night on the floor like that. Not long after he had finished smoking the joint, she started to flatulate loudly and this was followed by explosive diarrhea that was gushing down her skirt all over her legs and pooling onto his rug. It was horrifying. Something this awful did not seem possible. He wondered how much had she been drinking or whether she was on some kind of drugs and was experiencing a bad reaction? Anything was possible. In reality, he had no idea who this person. Then a bad thought crept into his mind. Maybe she had just died and this was her sphincter emptying out her bowels in death. He started to wonder if perhaps he had actually sold his soul to the Devil for sex with that hooker in Singapore all those years ago and now the check was going to come due. She finally stopped farting and shitting and the smell in the room was now a vile mixture of feces, vomit and pot. He found the will to go check on her and to his amazement she was breathing fine and sleeping like a baby in a pool of her own excrement. The awful mess and the realization he needed to deal with it tempered his relief at her still being alive. "What a fucking debacle!" he thought to himself. It seemed impossible that bringing this woman back to his apartment could turn into such a revolting spectacle. He decided he needed to try and clean her up as best he could. He got a bucket of clean water, soap and a bunch of towels. He pulled off her clothes and did his best to wash her as she lay there sleeping soundly. It seemed like this woman could sleep through anything. He covered his couch in towels and then picked her up and put her on the couch, once again propping her head on a pillow to make sure her air passages stayed open. He covered her naked body with a towel and then surveyed the carnage. He put the woman's clothes and the towels that seemed salvageable into a laundry basket. Then he put the balance of the shit and puke soaked towels onto the defiled rug and rolled it up. He took the rug to the elevator and threw it out in the large garbage bin in the basement of his building. He went back for the laundry basket full of the towels and the woman's clothes and brought them down to the laundry room. After rinsing them off as best, he could he washed them all in hot water with plenty of soap. It did not matter much to him that he might be ruining the woman's top and skirt, as he was giving her something to wear when she left. When he returned to the apartment he opened all the windows, sprayed about half a can of air freshener and began to clean furiously. After the clothes were dry he dressed the woman as she still lay sleeping soundly on his couch. It still seemed that nothing could wake up this woman. He put her purse right next to her on the couch and resisted the temptation to look inside it to see who this lovely, shitting, puking machine really was. He had forgotten her first name after the long ordeal or maybe had never got it in the first place. At this juncture, he didn't really know or care. He just wanted her gone, preferably without any police involvement. He began to consider the possibility that she might wake up and freak out and the cops could get called in. He briefly considered dumping the rest of his pot down the toilet just in case, but resisted the temptation to panic. Finally, he just took a long, hot shower and scrubbed himself over and over. By the time he dried off and got dressed it was now 3:30 AM. Princess was still sleeping like a baby. He lay down on his bed and must have fallen asleep immediately. He was awakened by the sound of the door to his apartment opening and closing. He looked at the clock and saw that it was 6:30

AM. God had been merciful in the end. She must have woken up, grabbed her purse and gotten the fuck out of there. She had done the right thing. He wondered what, if anything, she actually remembered about their lovely evening together. But in reality that didn't matter much anyhow. He never picked up a random woman in a bar again. Ever.

His career began to take a turn for the worse in the year 2001. He had managed to produce three strong years in a row at that firm despite the mediocre levels of client activity. He had scored with the yen in 1998 and done well with the euro in 1999 and 2000. But in 2001, the euro began to bottom out and form a base after repeatedly testing the lows near .8200 (82 cents to the euro). Lorenzo, his strong trader in London, quit the firm, leaving a gaping hole in the operation. Volatility arbitrage had also became much more difficult. In the aftermath of the stock market crash, as the Internet bubble unraveled, activity in financial markets had slowed down. Halfway through the year, his department was well behind budget, the first time he had found himself in that uncomfortable position since he had become a trading desk manager almost a decade earlier. Midway through the summer, the euro finally broke out of its trading range and burst higher rapidly causing a sharp move higher in implied volatility as well. He was positioned the wrong way and instead of cutting his losses as he normally did, he increased his losing bets without discipline. He repeatedly sold rallies in euro, and went short increasing amounts of euro volatility as the implied volatility rallied in tandem with the rising currency. It was the exact opposite of his successful yen operation of 1998. Then he had made a strong analysis of underlying conditions and put on a core position that he could patiently maintain until the move began to occur. He could systematically add to the position as it was going his way. This time, he was just fading the tape and losing money pretty consistently. He wasn't even analyzing underlying conditions very well. The Fed, under then Chairman Alan Greenspan, had turned very accommodative and had pushed U.S. interest rates down to extremely low levels, while flooding the money markets with cash. The U.S. economy was in a state of shock as all the seemingly unstoppable Internet juggernauts were rapidly imploding. Europe had become a better story and interest rate differentials now favored the euro as it moved into a long-term bull phase. He was fighting the move recklessly and foolishly. In later years, Greenspan's overly accommodative policies were blamed as one of the catalysts for the credit crisis that started in 2007 and still lingers on today. In the span of one month, he lost around five million dollars. It was not that significant an amount relative to the sixty million his department had made in his first three years with the firm. But he had wiped out most of his department's gains for the current year. Now it was no longer a question of being behind budget. He was in danger of going negative for the year and was starting to feel the heat from the Division Manager. He finally closed out all his losing positions. It seemed that he was floundering on the professional level in tandem with the upheaval in his personal life.

Out of nowhere, an old friend in the market contacted him. The man had recently become the trading manager for a hedge fund operation that was owned by a legendary market figure. More than a decade earlier, the hedge fund manager had been one of the highest profile traders on Wall Street. After trading successfully for several major banks, the man launched his own hedge fund with much fanfare. Ten years later the guy was still in business but no longer had a good market reputation or strong market profile. Regardless, his old friend was very enthusiastic about the opportunity at this hedge fund. Apparently, the fund had just raised significant new capital and the owner of the fund had decided to step back from day-to-day trading and bring in some fresh talent. He felt humiliated at his firm after his bad run, and was desperate for any alternative, so he accepted the position and hoped for the best. At this juncture, he had averaged around a million dollars a year in personal income over the past seven years. When you considered where he had been almost twenty years earlier, broke with a wife and two young children, it had been a damn good run. However, it was chicken shit relative to real hitters on Wall Street. For example, divisional managers like the White Rabbit or the Sheriff surely made ten million dollars in good years. The investment bankers at major Wall Street firms, the guys that were generating fee income for advice on Mergers and Acquisitions (M&A) or corporate restructuring, could earn twenty million dollars a year or more. Senior investment bankers often earned more than the C.E.O.s at major Wall Street firms. But the hedge fund dudes had taken the game to a whole new level. Hedge funds had originally started as offshore funds that could sell stocks short more efficiently since they were outside of domestic regulation. The early hedge funds were essentially short hedge vehicles for large money managers holding long-term stock portfolios, in the era before deep, liquid derivative markets that now provide that capability efficiently. But in the late 1980s, the hedge funds burst onto the scene on Wall Street in a big way. Major hedge funds grew rapidly into the 1990s and some of the top guys had literally made billions of dollars for themselves. He reasoned that he had hit the wall at his current job on Wall Street and jumping over to the hedge fund side was his best chance to reinvigorate his career. Despite the current bad run he had been on, his boss actually tried to change his mind. After he resigned to the Division Manager, the man replied; "I think you are making a very bad decision to leave your position as an MD here to join this particular fund. First of all, you are going through a divorce and having a bad run in the markets. It is a stressful time in your life and may not be the best time to jump into a new challenge. We go back almost fifteen years and you have more than established your credibility with me. Of course, you will have to tone down your risk and this will not be a great year for your department, but these things happen. The important thing is that you just calm down and trade with discipline, as you have always done until recently. You have a great future with this firm. It is not easy to become an MD on Wall Street and if you walk away you may never get another chance at this level. I can understand the appeal of trading for a quality hedge fund. But I think going to work for this particular fund manager would be a big mistake. Trust me when I say that the reputation of this man has not been good for a long time, and it is my understanding there have been a number of lawsuits filed by disgruntled investors over the past several years. If you leave your position as MD here to join this shady investment firm, you stand the risk of permanently derailing your career and becoming just another Wall Street Journeyman." Once again he was getting good advice at a critical juncture in his career, but this time he decided to ignore it. He thanked his boss for his kind words, but proceeded to resign nonetheless. He figured that if it didn't work out he could land another big job back on the Street. In reality, he would never again work for an investment bank, let alone get another shot as an MD. He would never manage people again. He would never come close to earning the same kind of money he had been making. He thought he was off to a fresh new challenge where bigger and better things awaited him. Little did he suspect he had jumped on that southbound express train to career mediocrity, last stop Palookaville.

Chapter 10

He quickly realized how right the Division Manager had been. He had made a big mistake. He should have never left his position as an MD in charge of Global FX Options Trading at that major Wall Street firm to become a so-called Portfolio Manager (PM) at the fly by night bucket shop. His old friend that had recruited him, the erstwhile Trading Manager at the firm, had sold him a bill of goods. His old buddy was not really in charge of anything. The founder of the fund was still very active and a very hands-on manager as well. The man could be very articulate and charming but had distinct lizard like features. The dude literally seemed to slide into a room. They all called him Slimer behind his back and it was a nickname well earned. Slimer was an old-fashioned snake oil salesman and bucket shop operator in the truest sense of the word. Slimer had organized his business similarly to most hedge funds. Slimer owned 100 percent of the Delaware LLC holding company for the operation. Underneath the holding company was the trading company, which had all the dealing lines with the banks. All FX trades flowed through the trading company to the various funds. It was a genius set up. The trading company would charge the funds a commission for each trade executed which meant that Slimer was skimming off the top. Slimer's investors all paid the "2 and 20" commission rate with quarterly redemption that was standard for hedge funds at that time. This meant they paid 2 percent a year on the money invested as well as 20 percent of all profits. It also meant they could only redeem their money on a quarterly basis. But all money that any fund paid to Slimer's trading company in trade commissions was pure profit. For any investor astute enough to make an inquiry concerning one internal firm controlling all the market activities, the hedge funds would insist that this arrangement was more efficient and would ultimately save money. In reality, it was a simple way to skim the cream off the top. He had thought he would be allocated a defined amount of capital to manage in a specific fund. This would give him a true track record as a PM, which would enable him to move on to a better opportunity at a bigger hedge fund where he could make more money. His track record of profitability at various investment banks did not mean that much to serious hedge fund operators. When analyzing the potential of interbank FX traders, it was difficult for them to ascertain how much of the profits a trader had made were due to commercial activity, and how much came from directional trading. It was also impossible to determine an actual annualized percentage return for profits made by bank traders since they were operating through the bank's credit lines instead of trading a pre-defined amount of capital under well-defined risk limits. Risk allocations at banks did not transfer in any discernable way to capital under management and a verifiable track record. Slimer had organized the trading department at the firm similarly to proprietary trading operations at major banks. These are the departments that do not engage in commercial activity and only implement directional trading strategies with the bank's capital. These departments are becoming largely eliminated on Wall Street due to the Dodd-Frank Congressional Act. Slimer was not going to let any trader at the firm establish his own legitimate track record. Each trader had a verifiable P&L record but not a Return on Capital (ROC) track record. Staff at the firm had all signed documents pledging to not discuss any firm business outside of the office or represent the firm in any way shape or form. It was the Slimer show. It was as simple as that. Each trader at the firm had his own P&L, adjusted for commissions paid to the internal trading company. However, none of the traders knew which fund their particular trades were being allocated to. It seemed that Slimer had over five funds running at any given time. The funds all had fancy names and were marketed as separate, sophisticated options strategies. In reality, all that the different funds consisted of was the FX spot, forward and options trades of Slimer, the Trading Manager and all of the Portfolio Managers. There was no coherent strategy for any of the funds, which was in direct contrast with the glossy marketing material that Slimer's sales staff churned out. On any given day, trades were allocated based on where Slimer wanted the winners and losers to land. This type of trade processing is known as post-trade allocation and is illegal. Trades should have been allocated to a specific fund before they even were executed. Obviously, each trader working for Slimer should have been assigned to a specific fund and should have been executing trades that fit the strategy of that particular fund as described in marketing documents. It did not take him all that long to figure out how the operation functioned in all its glory.

Slimer had a big ego. The man had been an outstanding college golfer and had some success for several years on the European Professional Golf Circuit, or so Slimer often told anyone who would listen. Slimer claimed to be a close,

personal friend of the late Mark McCormack, the founder of
International Management Group (IMG), a very famous international management organization that handles the commercial activities of major sports figures and celebrities. Slimer
was small in stature but talked such a big game, both personally and professionally, that you really did not know what to
believe. It was indisputable that Slimer made a lot of money
and lived an opulent lifestyle. The man owned a personal jet
as well as his own luxury yacht complete with private crew.
Slimer had a mansion in the richest town in New Jersey, a
massive apartment in the city, and various high-end vacation
properties. The guy owned farms and a number of retail businesses, all on borrowed money. The man was highly leveraged.
Slimer's core activity was efficiently fleecing investors. The
man had been in business as a hedge fund operator for over a
decade and had apparently opened and closed dozens of funds
by now. There were good reasons for this. Early in his career,
Slimer was a very high profile FX trader at several major Wall
Street firms. The man had probably been a very profitable
trader in those days. But the opportunity to accumulate vast
amounts of personal wealth by separating suckers from their
money had turned Slimer into an expert in ruthlessly churning through client accounts. Let's face some hard facts about
the investment business; if your livelihood depends purely on
calling the markets correctly over a prolonged period of time,
with no inside information or specific edge, this can be a very
hit or miss proposition. This was particularly the case if you
were no longer privy to the inside dope concerning significant interbank investment flows, secret Central Bank operations, economic data releases, pending merger activity or any

other non-public information that might indicate likely market movements in advance. Most major hedge funds that have prospered with strong track records over a long period of time have access to some kind of inside dope one way or another, or they have identified and exploited arbitrage (mispricing) opportunities in the market. Computer models to generate signals and control trading activity are highly touted in the industry but statistically are very hit or miss on a random basis. These facts are indisputable. Since the dawn of civilization, moneychangers have been getting rich through access to inside information or by ripping off the investing public. Wall Street insiders and hedge fund operators are no different than the merchant class in ancient Rome. Modern technology has enabled them to play the game a whole lot more effectively. By the year 2001, no one of any repute on Wall Street would talk to Slimer anymore. There were even a number of banks that had stopped executing trades for the firm due to reputational risk even though Slimer's business was profitable for them. The man did not have access to any valuable information so he needed to satisfy his insatiable lust for wealth directly from client accounts. Slimer accomplished this efficiently through two simple methods. First, the daily bread and butter for the business were the commissions being generated by the firm's trading company on a daily basis. Slimer encouraged short-term trading with a significant number of daily transactions so that the funds under management would be paying nice commissions on a recurring basis. The man always maintained a number of different funds so that winning and losing trades could be allocated in a strategic fashion. The fund where Slimer's personal money was held always made money. The man also understood a simple fact about the investing public, if you made a sucker money for the first six months or so you could most likely bleed them for two or three more years. Fresh new money went into the fund where Slimer's personal money was held and this fund would be the recipient of the bulk of the winning short-term trades. This fund would always generate a return of 20% or more per year and was the flagship vehicle used to attract fresh, new capital. After the six-month honeymoon (sometimes less), client money would normally be shifted to one of the other funds that soaked up most of the losing trades. The purpose of these funds, besides taking the losing trades, was to generate daily commissions, and get paid the annual two percent management fee for as long as Slimer could hold onto the money. There was no chance any of these funds were going to generate any cash on the profit-sharing side of the equation. Eventually, the losing funds would have such dismal performance records that Slimer would close them and open up new funds with exciting new names and fake strategies. Many clients were under the mistaken impression for several years or longer that their money was safely in the flagship vehicle and that they were scoring nicely. It was a bitter day for these clients when they realized they had not read the fine print and had signed away authorization for Slimer to shift their money around within his investment firm's family of fine funds. The clients would attempt to redeem some of the accumulated profits they thought they had been accruing, only to find that their original investment had taken a pounding after having been transferred into one of the "Patsy" funds, and now their principal had shrunk to far less than fifty cents on the dollar. Slimer had fended off dozens of lawsuits from disgruntled investors. His full-time legal staff had their side of the game down to a science. All of Slimers shady marketing practices had been screened by his legal team in advance of future anticipated lawsuits. Slimer ran the operation like a roach motel; money checked in but it did not check out.

The marketing staff created glossy investment pitch books, screened phone calls from irate investors, and created and distributed all sorts of phony track record reports and deliberately ambiguous client statements on a monthly basis. The great man himself did all the actual fund raising personally. Earlier in his hedge fund career, Slimer had apparently raised huge sums of institutional investment. The man had a strong reputation during his Street days and could be very persuasive. But these types of funds had long since dried up for Slimer. The man had written a book about his exploits as a trader. There was a storage room in the office that literally contained thousands of copies of this book. He did not know anyone that had actually read the book but Slimer loved to give a signed copy to prospective clients. The man's current fund raising strategy seemed to be identifying middle aged women that had just divorced heavy hitters on Wall Street. These were women flush with cash and no clue what to do with it. Slimer's marketing department would find out everything they could about these women and devise ways to arrange Slimer to meet them socially. It could be at polo matches, museum events, charity balls or countless other high society type functions where Slimer fit right in. The great man would meet them by "chance", get to know them and make the pitch and often grab investments between one and five million dollars from these vulnerable recent divorcees. It was sexy for these ladies to be able to talk about their hedge fund investment with Slimer at cocktail parties and at social occasions. They represented the type of client that would not read the fine print or even look too closely at statements for several years or more. This was the most common new investor for the operation during his time working at this fine firm. Slimer would waltz them around the firm personally and blather loudly while not introducing them to anyone. Slimer's operational staff did the dirty work of post trade allocation and creating performance reports that could deceive investors without creating legal liability. The senior people in the marketing department and operational staff had been with Slimer a long time. It was likely the important ones were well taken care of. Slimer needed a number of willing accomplices in those areas to keep his scam functioning and profitable. On the other hand, the turnover among traders was extremely high. Traders were there for window dressing and to generate commissions, churning out trades while breaking even or eking out small profits. Any traders that started to lose money or became an irritant to the great man had the life expectancy of a housefly. They were gone with the wind. The other business line for the firm was executing FX Option trades for clients for the purpose of creating false losses to shield income from taxation or to shift income from countries with high taxation rates to countries with lower taxation rates. Obviously, FX Option trading for either of these purposes was technically illegal but with tax codes so complicated it was easy for these trades to work effectively while being difficult for tax authorities to catch or even understand. Slimer had developed partnerships with a number of shady management consulting firms that provided this kind of accounting advice to domestic and international clients. By 2001, the banks had stopped being willing to execute these types of transactions for clients, and so the consulting firms needed to find counterparties with interbank access and capability in this area. They had found their man with Slimer, but the great man extracted a pound of flesh and more from these shady consultants to design and execute the FX option trades they required. This was an extremely lucrative business line for the firm.

He had been offered a salary of one hundred fifty thousand dollars year, which represented a draw vs. his percentage payout on trading profits on an annual basis. After starting at the new firm he learned that his monthly risk limit was a paltry one hundred twenty five thousand dollars a month, which meant he had zero chance to make a million dollars a year in personal income as he had grown accustomed to. He had anticipated being able to take significantly more risk at this firm. He had been seduced by the offer of a high percentage payout for his net profits, but had subsequently learned that this came without being able to create a meaningful, marketable track record, as well as receiving a very small risk allocation. He had voluntarily joined a shady organization operating outside of the law, and had done so for significantly less compensation than he had been earning for years at strong, legitimate investment banks. (By 2008 we did learn that most of the investment banks were not really that strong or legitimate after all.) Slimer's firm was the kind of place you went to work after you had lost your job on Wall Street and been out of the game awhile. It was a firm to join when you were getting desperate, not somewhere you left a great job for. He had been out of his fucking mind. He had no clue what the fuck he had been thinking when he made such a stupid decision. He could have traded poorly and still milked being an MD at that investment bank for another two or three year's minimum. Plus, they would have had to give him a nice beefy, six-figure payout to make him go away. He had voluntarily jumped off the gravy train into a puddle of shit. Perhaps he had made a bad decision due to the distractions from his ongoing divorce and his poor trading performance that summer. Not that he was going to get paid a million dollars by the investment bank he had just quit in an off year. But he would have certainly had a good chance to get back to that level in the following year if he had returned to strong performance. Slimer only traded long volatility, positive gamma long options positions. The man encouraged all of his traders to follow suit. These kind of positions required frequent spot trading orders to try and make money to offset the time decay associated with such option structures. This meant there would be hundreds of deals every trading day from all the traders, that Slimer would be charging commission on. Slimer was making a lot of money every day on commissions and only needed to stay in business to keep on churning out the cash. With this kind of trading strategy you had to work very hard to eke out a small profit each month but the commission cash register at Slimer's shop would be singing night and day. But there was a very special advantage to operating in the FX market that Slimer exploited ruthlessly. For accounting purposes, every trading day in the FX market started at 5 PM NY time on the preceding day and ended at 4 PM NY time of the actual day. This meant that there were many spot and option trades executed by the traders at the firm during the Asian, London, and New York time zones long before the actual close of the day. Typically, Slimer would house the long option positions that usually lost money over time due to time decay in the "Patsy" funds. These funds would absorb the daily time decay. When implied volatility occasionally spiked, a trader or Slimer sold out the long options structure profitably. The "Patsy" funds would make back some money to make the overall downward track appear much more legitimate. All of the daily spot trades against these long option structures could be sorted efficiently between winners and losers and allocated accordingly. The special fund which housed Slimer's own money, new clients and privileged clients made consistent money on the profitable scalps vs. the long option positions without having to pay the daily time decay bill or accept the risk of being long implied volatility and having it move lower. The real strategy being implemented was to churn client money, losing as little as possible on the overall trading while slowly sucking all of the clients blood away through daily commission charges to Slimer's trading company. It was as simple as that.

He had been working at Slimer's firm for only a short while when the tragedy that was 9/11 struck the United States like a vicious left hook from Mike Tyson in his prime. He left the office in the heart of midtown NYC quickly after the first plane hit at 8:46 am of that morning. He had been trading the London hours so had been working since around three AM that morning. His divorce was still percolating but his ex-wife had gone on a long European vacation and he had agreed to stay at the marital house in New Jersey to baby-sit their two dogs in her absence. He reasoned that a plane accident at one of the Tower's might clog up NYC and so he bolted immediately that fateful morning. He did not want to get stuck in the city with nobody available to take care of his dogs, and it was a real treat to spend some time with the puppies again. He had moved out of the house and into an apartment in the city some time ago. By leaving before the second tower was struck, he was able to get his car out of the parking garage and be heading up the Westside Highway before anyone really knew what was going on. He was listening to 1010 WINS, the AM New York news radio station, and knew the second tower had been struck well before he was even able to get across the George Washington bridge. He knew something big was going on and life, as they all knew it in the U.S. was never going to be the same. He was heading south on the New Jersey Turnpike when the South Tower collapsed at 9:59 am. The New Jersey Turnpike offered a stunning view of this remarkable calamity across the desolate, industrial wastelands that surround the city from across the river in that area. He pulled his car over to the side of the road and stared in mute open-mouthed horror as the South Tower collapsed into a huge cloud of dust with smoke blotting out the morning sunshine. He later learned that Slimer had been enraged to learn he had left the office early without asking permission that morning. After the North Tower was struck, Slimer had admonished all of the traders to stay in the office and work hard to pick off the banks. The markets were in chaos and nobody knew what was happening or where anything was trading. Most of the banks continued to quote FX spot and options into the early afternoon that day and Slimer had organized all of the traders into efficiently arbitraging the banks on a number of deals. The commission cash register was ringing that day at Slimer's and it was apparently the most profitable day of the year for the great man.

Every time somebody tried to leave that morning, Slimer aggressively bullied them into staying and continuing to work. The man did not give two fucks about what was happening to America. Slimer could smell a chance to make a nice score without taking any risk and the man was not about to let that slide by or excuse the office minions from helping him collect his booty. He was so glad he had gotten the fuck out of there right away that day. Not long after he got off the expressway, the N. J. Turnpike was closed and remained that way for several days. He had been lucky to leave when he did. NYC and all of America for that matter were going into a serious lockdown that was going to take a few days to get through. He stopped at the store before heading to the house because he figured he better stock up on basics just in case. Besides a number of staples, he picked up several massive porterhouse steaks, as well as the biggest live lobster in the tank. He also bought a mixed case of fine wine including several bottles of Chateau Margaux vintage 1983. He figured that if the world was coming to an end he was going to go out like Henry the Eighth and his dogs were going to pound their way through big porterhouse steaks for dinner with him. He spent that fateful day with his dogs feasting on steak and lobster, drinking fine wine and smoking high-test pot while watching the television non-stop as the amazing, horrible saga unfolded. He had a number of friends in the market that went down that terrible day in American history. These days, it was interesting to observe that the Manhattan real estate market had weathered the storm of the credit crisis and financial market meltdown of 2008 and prices had gone even higher while most of the country was still experiencing slumping real estate markets due primarily to lack of credit from the banks. It was obvious that ten years later, NYC was still the number one target for an attack from al Qaeda or any number of other Islamic terrorists. It seems that wealthy people have a short memory concerning how extremely vulnerable they really are.

He ascertained that buying options and leaving positive gamma scale orders in either direction, as Slimer wanted all his traders to do, was a mug's game. You had very little chance to win. Slimer loved to trade during the Asian time zone from 5 pm NY until midnight. If the implied volatility went up for any trader's long option position and Slimer could take a small profit on the position in the evening when the trader was not around, the man would sell out your position without asking and just cancel all your spot orders. Slimer also took it upon himself to change the spot orders that traders left and execute them early if the man was concerned the orders might get close and miss. A seasoned options trader would leave orders that were designed to maximize profitability vs. the time decay of the position. To have somebody change your orders and execute them early on their whim made it impossible to trade the position effectively. Slimer's focus was to see many transactions in order to optimize commissions on each and every day. The man felt that if he closed out somebody's position at a small profit they could go ahead and put on a new position the next day, and be charged more commission along with the investors for the privilege. Never mind that you could never make any real money trading if you cut every profitable position quickly. Taking quick winners while allowing losing positions to move against you was a strategy guaranteed to lose money over time. Slimer was happy to have seasoned traders past their prime grubbing hard, actively trading, and churning commissions. As long as they could manage break-even or small positive, while keeping their mouths shut, they could hold onto their jobs and get their payout on what they had made for the year, after they had covered their draw. Slimer needed the commissions and decent looking resumes to put in his glossy marketing documents. Quitting was not an option even though he knew it had been an idiotic decision to take the job. He needed to sit tight and stay employed at least until he could close out his divorce. He shifted his focus while employed by Slimer to pure volatility arbitrage trading. He reasoned that the only chance he had to make any money while employed at that firm was to execute a strategy that Slimer would not be able to cover when he was not around. It was also important to minimize commissions paid if he wanted to earn anything he could consider reasonable relative to what he had so foolishly walked away from. Although the euro had started trading in 1999, many of the banks still did not understand how to price implied volatilities accurately for all the new cross options. This refers to euro vs. other currency pairs such as Scandinavian Kroner (SEK) that was a low volatility, low interest rate differential currency pair or South African Rand (ZAR) a high volatility, high interest rate differential currency pair. The banks were inconsistent and in accurate across the smile curve (implied volatility of low delta options vs. ATM options along the time curve, primarily one week through one year tenors.) This phenomenon was especially true during brief periods of market turbulence caused by surprise geo-political news or economic data releases well out of line with market expectations. He could track the correct volatilities for currency pairs across the smile curve better on his simple spreadsheets than many of the banks with multi-million dollar derivative systems. His strategy was to identify mispriced options and put on spread positions via judicious trade execution. This could be accomplished most effectively during the London time zone when the heavy hand of Slimer was not around to interfere and break balls. On a normal day Slimer would arrive to the office around 8:30 am NY and stay for several hours before heading out to play golf and then take an afternoon siesta. The great man would return to the office late in the NY afternoon to oversea the post-trade allocation process. Slimer then seemed to trade most actively in the Asian time zone before retiring for the evening. The London time zone was the period Slimer would never be around to get involved in your trading strategy or execution. As a simple example, in a particular currency pair he would sell Y amount of a 25-delta two-month expiration call option vs. buying X amount of a 35-delta three-month call option. He would generally structure these spreads to be slightly positive theta (earn time decay) and require minimal hedging in the FX spot market. The point was then to simply wait patiently for the spread to move back into line and then you could cover the spread cleanly and book your profit. Many mornings he would arrive at the office by three AM and then immediately grab three or four hours of sleep on one of the plush, comfortable couches in the office before the NY morning opened. He was cool with the London time zone trade execution guy and so the man would never rat him out to Slimer. Then he could leave around noon and go and play golf himself. Even if the banks would quote non-Asian based euro cross options during the Tokyo trading session the spreads would be extremely wide and it would be extremely difficult for Slimer to ever cover one of his spreads. He believed that his positions had piqued Slimer's interest in euro cross options. Not long after he started focusing on this strategy, Slimer scored a huge pick-off of a major investment bank on a euro cross option, around lunch time in Tokyo. A trading assistant who should never have even agreed to quote the option had seriously miss-priced the trade. The implied volatility was not just off the market; it was outside of the historical range of where an option of this delta and tenor for this particular Euro cross currency pair had ever traded historically. Then the trade somehow slipped through the investment banks system and was settled before the investment bank finally realized they had just handed Slimer five hundred thousand dollars. A half million-dollar pick off on a relatively small principal amount option was unheard of. Many banks had forced clients to sign legal agreements that required the cancelation of any trades outside a certain tolerance of the actual verifiable market rate. But these guys had been sloppy and had not gotten this type of documentation signed by Slimer so they were out of luck. They could only beg for Slimer to give them back their money. The Global Head of FX at this major investment bank came to personally see Slimer. Apparently, the Global Head told Slimer that if the trade was not reversed they would close their dealing lines with the firm. They also vowed to discredit Slimer in the marketplace. Slimer refused to cancel the trade but politely asked the Global Head if he would like to play a nice round of golf together to make amends. The Global Head angrily bolted out of that office within ten minutes of arriving. No chance they were getting their half a million dollars back from Slimer. After word of this stuffing got around the market no bank would quote Slimer Euro based cross options during the Asian time zone. His positions were safe from the greedy, grubby hands of Slimer. He made a profit the first year and was paid the one hundred fifty thousand dollar bonus he was owed. He would have most likely gotten a significantly higher bonus if he had stayed on as an MD at the investment bank he had quit to join Slimer's firm, even if his department's performance for the year had not improved. However, in many respects it was not a terrible job during this stressful period in his life. Outside of getting to the office at three AM he did not work that hard and got some sleep on the job at least two or three days a week.

Early in the New Year, he had a very interesting dinner with an old friend in the market. The man had been one of his FX option brokers in Tokyo. In fact, he had introduced this guy to another one of his brokers over there and the two brokers had subsequently become fast friends. In the mid 1990s they had started their own brokerage firm in NYC. They had offered him the chance to join them as a partner, but during that period he was making good money and his marriage was on the rocks, so it was not an opportune time to take the risk and join a start up venture. They had originally launched their firm as a so-called "SOES Bandit" brokerage shop. SOES stood for Small Order Execution System. It referred to the dealing system used by NASDAQ stock trading firms in those days when the brokerage firms openly colluded in their market making practices for these stocks. Essentially, the big broker-dealers made inside spreads to each other in these stocks and then widened the spreads substantially to retail clients. But by the mid 1990s any firm that was properly set up and licensed could access the inside pricing system and did not legally have to reciprocate or risk capital making markets in their own book of stocks. Firms set up this way could offer much lower commission rates and the inside market bid-ask spreads in NASDAQ stocks to day traders in exchange for much larger trading volumes. This basically describes the short-lived "SOES Bandit" firms and this strategy is how his friends initially started their business. When the Internet started to explode, they shifted their strategy to building an online retail brokerage business. They had hired a software whiz and had developed strong online trading account management and support systems from scratch. They played the game nicely. They raised money from private investors and then timed an Initial Public Offering (IPO) early in the bubble cycle. They had gone public at nine dollars/share and had traded as high as thirty-five dollars/share before the Internet bubble had burst. The friend that had invited him to dinner in early 2002 was President of the company and had two million shares of stock. The other old friend was C.E.O. and had close to three million shares. At the height of their brokerage firm's post IPO stock market valuation, they were rich beyond their wildest dreams. But this sudden Internet wealth could be difficult to shift from paper profits to actual cash. All of the Internet stocks traded at such huge valuations for a period because of the big speculative buzz and because the number of shares that were floated were such a small percentage of the firm's total outstanding shares. The prices of Internet stocks were driven for a time by abnormal supply/demand conditions. Typically, the Internet IPOs only sold about ten percent of the company's shares. The officers of the firm were banned from selling any shares for a whole year after the IPO. Even after that first year, if the firms were still in business, any selling of stock by officers of the company was frowned upon and there was strong moral suasion at firms not to sell. In the rare cases where an Internet company had real legs and became well established the officers could slowly start to sell out some of their stock and get access to their cash, but this took time and these situations were the exception. A lot of Internet firms initially had huge stock market valuations after their IPOs but subsequently went bust and the officers failed to cash out in any substantial way. Most of the dudes that got rich after Internet IPOs had done so by selling their companies to established mainstream firms before the stock market had crashed back to reality. The President of the online brokerage firm had invited him to dinner and had discussed the firm's history with him and was obviously angling for advice of some kind. The firm was struggling to stay afloat and had never turned a profit in all the years they had been in business. After the Internet bubble had burst, the stock price of the firm had cratered. It had hit a post IPO low close to three dollars/share, which was where the CEO had got the bright idea to borrow money against his holdings in the stock to buy more stock and increase his long position in an attempt to push the price of the stock back up. His efforts had worked nicely for the first several months due to calming conditions in the stock market and the thin market for the stock. The stock had reached around twelve dollars/share and had stabilized for a brief period. The President had many heated arguments with the CEO over the past several years about trying to find a buyer for the firm so they could all cash out to some degree and at least capture some wealth before the company potentially went bust and they lost everything. But the initial success of the IPO had clouded the CEOs reasoning power and the man had rejected any ideas about selling the company. The

President of the brokerage firm knew that the only real asset they had was the proprietary software they had developed to run an online brokerage firm. The software was extremely scalable and could save a large, established brokerage firm a lot of money in development costs if they were expanding into the online brokerage market. The President had arranged a deal for a major broker to buy them out at thirteen dollars/share not long after the stock price had been artificially propped up to twelve dollars/share by the CEO. It was a genius maneuver to pull a rabbit out of the hat and cash out despite the end of the Internet madness. The President had convinced the CEO to take the deal so they could all get their money and live happily ever after. But at the final meeting to close the deal the CEO snapped and fucked up everything. The CEO was most likely bent out of shape that the President would be given a more senior role in the acquiring firm after the buyout. The CEO also seemed to forget how the stock price had gotten back up to twelve dollars/share and how fragile that price level was. The CEO shocked the acquiring firm and demanded they increase their offer to fifteen dollars/share at the last minute. The man was overplaying his hand and had zero real leverage. The large brokerage firm became enraged and broke off all negotiations. The stock had quickly slumped down to eight dollars/share and had only stopped falling because the CEO had stepped in once again to buy more shares and support the stock price. The President asked him his advice on how to proceed at this juncture. He figured the President knew what the best strategy was, but needed to hear it from an experienced trader. He told the guy it was now a game of musical chairs as far as who might capture any of the fake equity left in the stock. He advised the man to resign from the company immediately and sell out all his stock. This action would crush the stock price and all his old colleagues at the firm would hate his guts but at least he would end up with something. This is exactly what the President did. The man quit and sold all his shares over a period of several weeks. By the time the man had finished liquidating his holdings, the stock price of the online brokerage firm was below one dollar/share never to recover. The average price of his stock market sales was around three dollars/share well below the original IPO price of nine dollars/share. But the President had grabbed the last six million dollars of equity left in the firm and stuffed it into his own pocket instead of leaving it for the market. At least the man had not stoically gone broke in tandem with the foolish, stubborn CEO and the rest of the officers of the firm.

Near the end of his second year with Slimer, they finally got into a heated argument. He had been doing a magnificent job managing Slimer's bad option positions and was systematically winding them down without much loss. He was far and away the best performer at the firm with his own operations that year trading under the strict P&L limits. Slimer contractually owed him around three hundred fifty thousand dollar in bonus based on the percentage deal he had in writing. Slimer was a nudge and the kind of man that could give a woodpecker a headache. In any disagreement, Slimer would start talking fast and loudly and try to force you into agreement. One Friday morning in early December, Slimer was in a foul mood and started making disparaging remarks to him about some great trades he had cleverly executed to save the man hundreds of thousands of dollars in losses. Slimer had been breaking his balls here and there all week and he had had enough and became annoyed. He loudly dressed Slimer down in front of the room in the same seemingly polite, clever fashion and tone he had perfected in his many verbal sparring matches with the Poison Dwarf. For once he let his guard down and let Slimer see how much he actually held him in contempt. Except Slimer clearly understood insults and did not take kindly to being embarrassed in front of all of the minions. Slimer slithered back into his office and slammed the door and that had been his cue to bolt out of the office early that day. That Saturday afternoon he went back to the office and cleaned out his desk and took home all his personal belongings. He deleted any computer programs he had created that he did not want to leave behind. He had a feeling he was not going to last long in the kingdom of Slimer. He had authority at that firm to trade directly with the banks. That Sunday night the night desk manager at the firm called to inform him that Slimer had ordered the man to contact all the banks and take away his authorization to deal. He thanked the night desk manager for the heads up and asked the man not to embarrass him with those calls to the banks. He promised the guy he would not call any bank to trade. The next morning Slimer attempted to fire him without paying any bonus. The man obviously understood there were contractual obligations involved and was trying hard to get him to sign a Letter of Indemnification for nothing. Slimer was making a number of thinly veiled legal threats while blathering on and on about this and that. Slimer had a certain natural hypnotic skill. The man had been living a lavish lifestyle plundering investors money for over ten years and semed to be able to replace the old suckers who finally fled with new ones.

Slimer could talk very rapidly and forcefully and then get you to agree to something without even knowing what you were agreeing to. It was an important skill for shysters of any kind. He had learned that in dealing with Slimer you needed to ignore everything the man said and just keep stubbornly repeating your argument. Frankly, he daydreamed during most of the repulsive little man's tirade. It was easier to stay on point that way. Every chance he got he politely told Slimer that he wanted to leave the firm amicably but he insisted on being paid the full three hundred fifty thousand dollar bonus that was owed to him. After about an hour of annoying, repetitive banter Slimer smiled and suggested that they compromise. The lizard like man reached into his desk and pulled out a prepared document for his perusal. Slimer was offering him half of what was owed or one hundred seventy five thousand dollars in exchange for the signing of an indemnification agreement. Clearly, this had been Slimer's plan all along and the past hour had just been an attempt to see if he was stupid and weak enough to go away for nothing. Besides bilking clients, Slimer had a reputation for fucking most of his employees out of money at some stage. The vicious bastard was embroiled in lawsuits and had a full-time attorney the guy met with every day. Slimer was a litigious, arrogant prick and seemed to take special pleasure in having lawsuits dismissed, which the man seemed to accomplish quite regularly. Slimer politely suggested that he have a lawyer review the documents and that it was in his best interest to accept the offer and move on. As soon as he sent back the signed Letter of Indemnification to Slimer he would receive the one hundred seventy five thousand dollar bonus. The man pointed out that this was a better deal than was usually offered to anyone in this situation. He knew for a fact that Slimer had booked all of his deals that year into the special fund where the man kept his own money. He had made Slimer millions of dollars but the man was determined to fuck him out of half of his bonus on the way out the door. At this juncture Slimer called a large, private, uniformed security officer with a big gun into the room. He was informed that it was time to go and his personal effects would be packed and shipped to him. He knew that Slimer wasn't really sacking him for the insults. The man had had about enough of him by then. He was not playing ball the way he was supposed to. Although he had far and away the best P&L among the traders at the firm he also paid the least commissions by a wide margin. His success was stirring the seeds of discontent at Slimer's shop and this could not be tolerated. A number of the other traders had been picking his brains about his strategy any chance they got. Some of them had started to push back at Slimer and express the desire to trade longer term and decrease their level of day trading. He was preaching the gospel of freedom and revolution behind Slimer's back and it was time for him to go. The public argument had given Slimer the excuse and the will to pull the trigger.

He had been dating a very lovely Italian lady and they had grown close. They had met through a mutual friend earlier that year. He had found the woman who could soothe his soul. He had been discussing with her how difficult it would be to win a lawsuit against a determined, experienced, unscrupulous master litigator like Slimer. She had lived in Queens since coming to the U.S. and had many relatives there as well. She told him that she knew an old family friend by the name of Sam who was an attorney, owned a real estate agency and was reputed to be a made man in the mafia. She suggested that Sam might be able to provide some assistance in this matter. He went to Sam's office and had a candid discussion with the man concerning the situation. He showed Sam the settlement offer, his copy of the firms accounting ledger showing his profits for the year and his signed percentage agreement from Slimer. Sam was a very polished, gracious man. After listening politely to him and then silently reviewing the documents Sam responded, " It is indeed a great pleasure to make your acquaintance and I am so pleased that my dear friend has met such a fine gentleman. Let me speak frankly about this matter and I am certain that you will hold our conversation in the highest discretion regardless of your decision on how to proceed. As I see it, Slimer legally owes you three hundred fifty thousand dollars and has offered you one hundred seventy five thousand dollars to settle this claim. Slimer has a strong legal team, significantly more money and resources than you and is well experienced in litigation. Clearly, it will not be easy to win a lawsuit for the balance owed. Never mind that an attorney will most likely want to work for forty percent of what they recover in addition to some kind of non-refundable retainer. It could take years and you may likely end up with nothing if you choose to pursue litigation. Basically, the contested one hundred seventy five thousand dollars represents about eighty seven thousand five hundred dollars after taxes have been paid in this city. If you like, I will persuade Slimer to pay you the full amount that is owed. If I did not believe your claim was fair and just I would not agree to intercede in this matter. Normally, I charge fifty percent of what is collected for this type of service but considering our dear, mutual friend, I will be glad to handle this matter for just twenty five percent, lets call it twenty two thousand dollars even. After Slimer pays you the full amount, make an appointment with my secretary to come and see me about one month later and bring me the money in cash. Does this sound fair to you?" He enthusiastically shook Sam's hand warmly and readily agreed to the man's offer. Sam exuded a quiet, deadly confidence and he was fairly certain it would not take much for a man like that to make Slimer cave in. He received a FEDEX package less than two weeks later with a signed settlement letter from Slimer and full bonus payment. Included was a personal note from Slimer thanking him for his service and wishing him the best of luck professionally moving forward. It was also politely requested that he sign and return the Letter of Indemnification since his bonus had been paid in full. It was especially sweet that Slimer had paid up first and was requesting the signed agreement after the fact. Slimer was a charlatan, a bully and a scum bag who had no problems stepping on toes or worse to get his way. But the man was no fool. Sam represented a threat Slimer was helpless against. The shyster made a good business decision and paid him what was owed. Handing Sam that envelope with twenty two thousand dollars in crisp, new hundreds was a wonderful feeling. They enjoyed a delicious lunch together at a fine local Italian restaurant and Sam insisted on paying. It was always a pleasure to do business with a true professional. By the year 2011 Slimer's funds had all long since closed and the man's business empire was in disarray. Slimer had gone through a long, costly divorce, filed for personal bankruptcy and was racked with cancer and apparently fighting to stay alive. Sometimes in life what comes around does go around.

Chapter 11

The sad reality was that it did not feel good getting sacked by Slimer. His rational mind understood that getting away from that crooked bastard should have been his highest priority, but he had settled into a fairly relaxed routine that past year at Slimer's shop. It was obvious that the man did not like to pay people and so getting paid your bonus fairly was always going to be an issue there. Never mind that if the regulators ever got a clue as to what Slimer was up to that shop could have been raided in a heartbeat. On the other hand, in later years Bernie Madoff taught the market how completely clueless and ineffective government regulation of Wall Street really is. Slimer was probably right to sneer at the possibility of getting shut down or worse by the government. He had always told his colleagues there that it would never surprise him to get off the elevator and see a yellow police line around Slimer's office. It is probably human nature that losing any job makes you question the mistakes you had made and how you should have done things differently. He was not out of the market long before he started at a small hedge fund in early January of the New Year. The fund had been launched a year earlier by an old market friend of his. He had always considered his friend a talented trader but knew the man was also a very eccentric individual. He had given the guy his first break in the business. He had gone on a recruiting trip to his business school and hired this guy for a coveted Sales and Trading summer internship at his old firm, years ago. His friend had impressed him during the interview. The man was a trained classical musician and had a sharp mathematical mind. They had stayed in touch down through the years. His friend had spent five years or so on the Street and then had landed a job as a PM at a major hedge fund. The guy had big years in 1995 and 1998, which were the right years for a good FX options trader to score. After that his friend had languished for a number of years at the big shop before launching a hedge fund himself. The man had been his client at the last investment bank he had worked at. He used to leave his office on slow days to have coffee with his client. In reality they would take a walk into Central Park and burn a joint. His friend loved getting high and this shared vice helped them get along pretty well. The man had launched the hedge fund in impressive style. His friend had raised seventy five million dollars in total capital and had been granted a two year lock on this capital at the standard "2 and 20" commission rate for hedge funds. This meant they guy had been guaranteed gross income for his firm of around 1.5 million dollars a year for two years. Plus the fund would be paid twenty percent of all net profits. Unfortunately, the man's standard long option position structures (long volatility) and delta leans had not worked well the first year, and the fund had lost around thirteen percent for the year. A year after launch, the fund had not earned any incentive fees and capital under management had dropped because of the trading losses. The fund had a very nice office in midtown Manhattan only a few minutes walk from his apartment. Several weeks after Slimer had sacked him they were getting stoned in his apartment one afternoon and they began to discuss him joining the firm. He had explained his volatility arbitrage strategy for euro cross options and his friend was very enthusiastic about having him join the firm to implement the strategy. The shook hands on a deal of one hundred fifty thousand dollars a year in salary that would count as a draw vs. a ten percent payout on his trading profits for the year. His risk limits would be structured to represent a capital allocation of twenty-five million dollars. They also talked about whether working together, or more precisely him working for his friend, might ruin the friendship if things did not go well. They both agreed that they would stay friends regardless of how things went and they set a date for him to start. It seemed like a good opportunity to establish his own track record as a PM while working in a relaxed atmosphere with a good friend.

He did not get off to a good start with his old friend. On his first morning on the new job his friend informed him that he was going to have to accept a salary of one hundred twenty thousand dollars a year instead of the previously agreed upon one hundred fifty thousand. His friend had suddenly realized that the monthly two % management fees had been declining as money was lost and assets under management (AUM) subsequently declined. For the New Year, the man was starting with only sixty five million of AUM, having lost ten million trading in the prior year. This meant the anticipated revenue from management fees had dropped from 1.5 million down to 1.3 million. Clearly, all staff at the firm was going to have to pay their fair share. Everyone would have to sacrifice; there was no other way. What a bunch of fucking bullshit. He found this news extremely annoying and clearly unacceptable. He had not bothered to look for a job in the last month since they had reached an agreement. They spent the next two hours in his friend's office arguing back and forth. Eventually, his friend agreed to keep his salary at one hundred fifty thousand dollars a year because he made it clear he would otherwise walk away. Then came the coup de grace. He was exhausted from the stress of the two-hour argument when his friend then handed him a long, twenty-page employment agreement. It was full of detailed legal speak and it was obvious his friend had copied it from his prior employer, a large, well established, and very profitable hedge fund. The agreement included a very detailed non-compete clause whereby his friend could keep him out of the market for a year after separation regardless of the reason. The only stipulation was that he would have to continue to be paid during that year. He signed the employment agreement without putting up too much of an argument. He watched where his friend put the signed document in his unlocked desk. That first day he waited around the office until everyone else had left. Then he went into his friend's office and replaced the signature page he had signed with a copied one where he had drawn a picture of a hand flipping someone the bird.

His friend had assembled a fairly bizarre staff. There were three other employees already working at the firm. He became the fifth member of the illustrious team. There was an administrator that his friend had nicknamed Girly Man behind his back. His friend had apparently been fucking Girly Man's girlfriend some years ago and had stayed in touch with the lady for the occasional poke. His friend had met Girly Man through the guy's girlfriend. Girly Man was a very effeminate little fellow with a consistently sour disposition, but the man was a bright and a competent administrator. The head of the back office operations was his friend's alcoholic older brother. His friend's brother was actually a nice guy but the poor fellow had the look of a man who had gone ten miles on a bad road. His friend's brother had apparently been a top flight golfer and a successful salesman in the early days after college but had spiraled down and been unemployed over ten years before the man's brother had hired him. The back office had been a constant problem the prior year due to Big Brother's incompetence. Shortly after he joined, he took over the back office and his friend's brother stopped coming into work on a regular basis. The last employee of his friend's hedge fund was a slimy little Russian named Boris. The man was supposed to be a researcher developing an automated pairs-trading program to be used to trade a long/short equity hedge fund. These models identify and track stocks that should have a high degree of correlation over time. Typically, they might be market competitors in the same industry group. Trade signals are executed automatically on electronic stock exchanges whenever the spread between any two stocks is deemed to be out of line. Equal dollar amounts of one stock are sold short against a long position in the correlated stock that is deemed undervalued. These programs are deployed at large hedge funds to manage many billions of dollars and were very effective on balance, prior to the global credit crisis, which started in 2007. During this period of sustained market turbulence and high volatility, liquidity became very suspect in the stock market and many of these long/short programs sustained heavy losses. His friend had dreams of cracking this market but Boris was not the answer. As near as he could tell, Boris spent his day trolling the Internet for porn. Boris seemed to be especially fond of heterosexual porn that featured men with extremely large cocks. Boris would often squeal in a high-pitched voice for his friend to come into the office he shared with Boris and his friend's brother. His friend seemed to enjoy the porn breaks and would often sit and watch the porn with Boris for fifteen minutes or longer in the middle of the day. It was extremely irritating to be in the same office with the sniveling Boris. He started making money right out of the blocks and Boris was up his ass all the time trying to pick his brain about what he was doing. He had decided to keep all his spreadsheets and his option valuation and risk management systems on his own laptop. He told Boris flat out that if the man hacked into his laptop when he was not around he was going to give him a brutal beating. His friend had some convoluted option risk management system that had probably been coded ten years ago. The man tried to insist that he load all his positions on that system as well but he refused. He had agreed to do all the back office work for the firm, which meant his trading as well as his friends. But if his friend wanted to monitor the risk of his positions on his own system he would have to load them up and run the positions all by his lonesome. He wasn't too concerned about having to put up with Boris for too long. He guessed that since Boris and the alcoholic brother had long since proved themselves useless and the firm was not prospering, they would not last long. He could tell from many conversations that his friend had started to obsess about what might occur with the investors in the hedge fund when the two-year lock-up period was over. He was also starting to figure out that his friend was a cheap bastard. His hunch proved correct and the alcoholic brother and Boris were fired within a month or so after he had joined the firm. It was now just him, his friend and Girly Man.

On balance, the first few months of his time working with his friend were pleasant enough. They took a walk to his apartment to get high almost every day and had dinner together once a week. After the first quarter he began to doubt that the fund would last. Despite getting off to a good start he was not convinced he would ever get paid a bonus. He made three million dollars in the first quarter at that firm which was a terrific start for twenty five million in capital. It represented a twelve percent annual return, which would have been a decent year. Unfortunately his friend dropped six million in the first quarter. This meant the fund had net lost three million on sixty five million and so was down close to five percent for the year. Considering the fund had dropped around thirteen percent in the first year, the investors were not happy and were putting increasing pressure on his friend. But his friend never wavered in trading conviction. His friend's positions never fundamentally changed during the year they worked together. The man had apparently run the same strategies on a consistent basis the year before. The guy was always long low delta options with three basic directional themes. His friend owned low delta calls on Swiss Franc and Japanese Yen (long puts on the U.S. Dollar vs. these currencies), low delta call options on Gold, and low delta puts on Fannie Mae and Freddie Mac. His friend would rant and rave on an almost daily basis back in 2003 about how the U.S. dollar was being debased by fraudulent activities by the FED, how the only real, hard currency left was Gold, and how Fannie Mae and Freddie Mac were a scam and were doomed for insolvency. In fairness to his friend, if the man had been running those positions with the same leverage during the credit meltdown from 2007 – 2009 the fund might have been the top performing hedge fund on the planet. His friend might have outperformed John Paulson, the hedge fund operator who rose to fame and fortune by making billions being short sub-prime credit markets. During this period of severe market turbulence, the Swiss Franc and Japanese Yen soared higher vs. the U.S Dollar, Gold exploded well beyond its all-time high and Fannie Mae and Freddie Mac collapsed into government receivership. Implied volatility in the markets reached heights never seen before, which is how long volatility positions generate huge returns. When the credit crisis finally broke wide open, all of his friends macro views were proven correct, but five years too late. Success in the investing field was about having the right view at the right time with the right positions. His friend was way too early and so his fund went bust even though his macro views were ultimately proven correct. Technically speaking, his friend had taken on a risk known in the hedge fund industry as netting risk when he was hired. He was supposed to be paid ten percent of his gross trading profits in bonus, regardless of the overall performance of the fund. He began to realize that if the overall fund performance stayed poor for the balance of year, all the investors might pull their capital after the two-year lockup had expired. The fund would be essentially insolvent and his friend would have little incentive to pay him any bonus owed except on the basis of honesty and personal integrity. Most hedge funds that got into a hole of down twenty percent or more closed. This was because of an industry concept termed the high water mark. It basically meant that you had to make back all outstanding losses before any payout of the twenty percent incentive fee on profits could be paid for any given fund. This was the variable fee that had made the leaders in the industry billionaires. A sleazy hedge fund operator like Slimer would happily close out funds with large outstanding loss balances and open fresh, new funds with clean track records where the man might get paid some incentive fees. He had not gotten any kind of written legal agreement from his friend so the payout was essentially a gentleman's agreement.

In the second quarter of that year, opportunities in his euro Cross volatility arbitrage strategy began to dry up. However, he still made another million dollars, which meant he was up four million for the year on twenty five million in capital, which represented a return of sixteen percent. Unfortunately, the markets were quiet and his friend had stubbornly dropped another six million in that quarter. So halfway through the year, the fund was down eight million dollars on sixty-five million in capital, a loss of slightly more than twelve percent. He was up four million but his friend had dropped twelve. The basic math did not add up to a happy ending for him at the fund. They had been spending a fair amount of time together between work, getting stoned at his apartment, and having dinner together. His friend liked to hear himself talk and after awhile had began to repeat himself over and over. The man's main passion, as the hedge fund he had founded slowly imploded, was exchanging long-winded romantic emails with professional women in the industry who were unavailable. Successful, older women that were either married or in long-term relationships would exchange flirty emails with his friend and he would have to listen to his friend read them out loud to him from the man's blackberry. It had gotten tedious and boring. His friend never seemed to go out on any dates or actually have sex with any of the women so he did not see what was so thrilling about exchanging all these emails. His friend had also become fixated over Snoop Dogg the famous rapper. The man learned all of the nuances of Snoop Dogg's language and would spend whole days talking like him while referring to himself in the third person as Snoop Dogg. He went on several dinners with bankers where his friend was Snoop Dogg all night and never broke character. He had to admit that the man had the whole Snoop Dogg thing down perfectly. It was a little scary that the guy could do it so well and not crack a smile or break character. Some of the bankers seemed to be a bit uncomfortable and did not get the gag, whatever it was. After a while, he found it very embarrassing and after the second or third time refused to go on any more client dinners with his friend. His friend was very dismissive of FX sales people. The man was very difficult to do business with. He could hear his friend constantly complaining loudly about every price and spending many days trying to bully the banks into price improvements, calling the FX desks back every hour on the hour to demand a better deal. The man also had no qualms about breaking a trade if a better price came in after the fact. This was considered completely unethical in the industry but his friend could care less. Despite his friends rude behavior and poor market ethics the man expected to be wined and dined on a regular basis by the female sales women that covered the firm. Then the man would pretend to be Snoop Dogg all night long and refuse to discuss business or work out trade issues. It got to be quite humiliating. He needed a break and told his friend he was taking the month of July off since markets were slow and there was very little opportunity. He emphasized how proud he was of his sixteen percent return for the year and did not want to foolishly give away profits in slow, trendless markets. He also suggested that his friend lighten up on the long directional volatility positions and shift to delta neutral (no delta lean in the options structure) to preserve capital in a slow summer. The man went berserk when he broke the news to him. His friend seemed to be extremely crazed about having to book his own back office trades. Finally, they agreed that he would teach Girly Man how to book the trades in his absence. He realized his friend had no clue how to handle any back office issues. By this stage of the game, he didn't really care if his friend fired him and he had written off actually getting paid the bonus owed so he took a month off anyhow. Interestingly enough, his friend kept him on the payroll so he came back in August to finish the year.

The first thing he realized after getting back to the firm was that there was very little opportunity in the financial markets, especially in the areas he was focusing on. His Euro Cross volatility arbitrage had gotten to be a very skinny trade and the FX markets seemed lackluster and trendless. He made up his mind that he was going to hold onto most of his trading gains for the year. It was obvious the fund was going to lose most, if not all, of its remaining capital through year-end redemptions and the firm would close sometime in the next year. He managed to make another million dollars and thereby generated a P&L of around five million for the year. He was determined to have the satisfaction of contrasting his profitable market operations vs. the man's own losing trades which now seemed destined to sink the fund. He began to push Girly Man to prepare some kind of official looking document that would verify his return vs. his capital allocation at the firm. In this way, at least he could prove his track record for his year at the firm. He had made it clear that he wanted this document on a discreet basis but Girly Man went straight to his friend with the request. Naturally, his friend hit the roof. The man made it clear there would be no track records from the firm except for the overall fund performance. Internal allocations were nobody's business outside of the firm. This was the beginning of tension slowly building between them that fall. He began to beg out of their weekly dinners as often as possible. He also told his friend that he had lost his connections to buy pot and he was taking a break from getting high until he located a new source. This enabled him to spend less time being forced to listen to the man's repetitive, boring, crazed blather. It had only been a bit more than two years since he had left his position as an MD at a prestigious investment bank to join Slimer's shop, but it seemed like an eternity. He made some efforts to find a new trading position in the industry. Several interviews for a PM position at major hedge funds went nowhere. He had lunch with his old friend Andy, from the MBA program at his first job after business school. The man had been spectacularly successful in building a large hedge fund. Andy very politely verified what he already begun to suspect. He had probably damaged his reputation pretty badly with his choice of hedge funds since leaving the sell side of the Street. Slimer was considered a criminal and a pariah in the industry in a much greater scope than he had realized. His friend that he currently worked for also had a terrible reputation as being dishonorable, unstable and ineffective. Nobody cared that he made five million dollars at both shops with a very low risk profile. This was a chicken shit amount of P&L, considering that PMs at major hedge funds were generally allocated a minimum of one hundred million dollars or more to start. His track record as a hedge fund PM was useless. Indeed, it was probably quite detrimental due to the poor reputations of the shops he had worked for since leaving the sell side of Wall Street. Andy's sincere advice was to try and get a big job back on the Street and then maybe circle back to the hedge fund side in two or three years after he had restored his reputation. It was not a very uplifting lunch, especially since Andy showed no interest in giving him a shot, which had probably been his true motivation for reaching out to the man. He turned his focus back to getting a job back in FX. His best opportunity probably would have been to contact the Division Manager at his last major investment bank. He had a long-term relationship with the man and had always performed well except for those last couple of months when he had gone through a bad patch. But pride kept him from making that phone call. The man's words when he left the firm kept running through his head, stinging his soul. It had not taken that long for him to start feeling like a Wall Street Journeyman. The irony was that he had performed quite well as a hedge fund PM considering his limited risk allocation at both shops. But he had made poor choices about which firms to work for. He was guilty by association. It seemed he had gone from having a good name and strong reputation in the FX options market to being a complete has-been fairly rapidly. Life turns on a dime and Wall Street careers are no exception. In fact, on a relative basis, Wall Street careers can probably implode a lot faster than most. The White Rabbit and the Global Head of FX at that Wall Street firm had both left the industry. The Sheriff had moved on from the old firm and prospered. The man was now the CEO at another major investment bank. If he had played his cards the right way, he might have been one of the Sheriff's long-term top lieutenants, making millions of dollars a year. But he could never get past the Sheriff's secretary and his phone calls were never returned. He had dinner with several of the sales women that covered the firm. It did not take much prodding to learn that they all actually despised his friend. They found the man to be a vicious chiseler and a creepy sexist. He did manage to get interviews at some banks but they did not go anywhere. He had been a fairly senior desk manager for almost ten years and had spent three years in Tokyo prior to that but his services as a desk manager no longer seemed in demand. Because he had been a senior manager as well as a hedge fund PM, the banks did not want to give him a chance to move back onto the Street as a line trader either. It seemed that his career on Wall Street had run out of steam.

He made the decision to buckle down and finish out the year, see if his friend would pay him something, and see if perhaps the fund might still survive. The atmosphere in the office had gotten a bit tense among the three of them. Girly Man had started pushing for his own trading limits and he listened to many long arguments between the two of them. His friend never acquiesced and let Girly Man pull the trigger on anything. In late November, he had his worst blow up yet with his friend. He was helping the man with some trade executions in what was a probably a last ditch effort to score late in the year and avert disaster for the fund. A mutual friend they had both worked with at that first firm was now a senior dealer at a bank and they traded directly with the guy. Johnny mispriced a large Swiss Franc option by around a half million dollars and his friend ordered him to deal and hold the bank to the wrong price. He refused and this resulted in a big screaming match between the two of them. He had done his share of pick-offs early in his career, but this was different. Johnny was an old friend and the price was way off. He had come to realize it was better if a bank was off by twenty or thirty grand on an option price. This would rarely create an issue. But a half a million dollars was way too much. The error would be caught and the bank would come back and fight to cancel the deal. In reality, the trade agreement with that bank contained protective language, so the deal would not have been enforceable. It was a question of when that trade would be busted, not if. Then Johnny would realize that both he and his friend were scumbags that had no qualms about pathetically trying to fuck an old friend in a desperate attempt to steal some money. He told his friend to shut the fuck up, and then he picked up the phone and informed Johnny that the options price was off the market and should be checked and corrected. His friend grabbed the phone from him and started screaming at Johnny that they were dealing and the bank had better honor the price. Naturally, Johnny knew something was up by this stage of the game and refused to confirm a deal. His friend then stormed out of the office in a rage. It was becoming a zoo-like atmosphere in that office. That afternoon he had a long conversation with Girly Man about the sad state of affairs at the firm. He learned something interesting from their discussion. It seems his friend had been expensing every single meal since the inception of the fund. That included all of the many dinners they had together that year. Meanwhile, every time they had dinner he had paid his friend cash for his half and then his friend had paid via credit card. So his friend had been reimbursed for all of their dinners and then taken his cash for pocket money. It was a telling insight into the man's true character if there had been any doubt left on that count. The next day he closed out all his trading positions and decided to hunker down until the end came. They never discussed the pick-off incident with Johnny, they started getting high together again, and the relationship was superficially friendly for a while after that.

Early in December, the fund received redemption notices that most of the capital was fleeing as of year-end. His friend announced to both him and Girly Man that starting Jan 1 there would no longer be any salaries paid at the firm. They would all have to work together for free to try and save the fund. His friend would surely abscond the last four hundred thousand dollars left in the firm's bank account in one way or another. This triggered their first real discussion about the bonus he was owed. He had decided that if he could somehow pry a hundred grand or so out of his friend, he would hang on at the firm for another three months while he looked for new employment, under the theory it was always easier to find a job when you were still working somewhere. He quickly realized that he had been engaging in wishful thinking. When the topic of his bonus came up, his friend immediately indicated that the bonus would absolutely be honored and he would surely receive his three hundred fifty thousand dollar bonus. However, he would have to take the money in shares of the firm. His friend was offering him around half a percent of the firm in lieu of his three hundred thousand fifty thousand dollar bonus which meant the man was valuing the firm at approximately seventy million dollars. This represented a ludicrous value for a firm that was clearly going bust and worth nothing. Even if the fifty five million capital left at the firm had not already been redeemed, it meant his friend was valuing the fund at over one hundred percent of AUM. This was the height of absurdity. The value of hedge funds had been a hotly debated topic around that time. At the height of the bull-run for hedge funds, some had argued that any given hedge fund might be worth as much as five percent of AUM, assuming the fund had stable management and a good long-term track record. These days, the value of established hedge funds is generally assumed to be more around two to three percent of AUM. They spent a long afternoon arguing back and forth on this issue without coming to any agreement. Finally, he decided he might kill himself if he had to spend another day in that office listening to the man's demented ravings. It was remarkable how his old friend still had delusions of grandeur despite the grim predicament his fund was in. He decided he might as well end things but he wanted something back from his friend for the money he had made the fund. He told his friend he that he was resigning but he insisted on being paid thirty-five thousand dollars or ten percent of what he was actually owed. If his friend could come up with this modest bonus then they could shake hands and part company still being friends. This was not a situation where he would have even considered asking Sam to intervene or take any other aggressive collection actions of that nature. However things had gone that year, they had been friends a long time and the conflict would stay between them. His friend readily agreed to this solution and they shook hands on the deal. They hung out a few times early in the New Year and his friend seemed eager to put the past behind them and resume the friendship. He was only putting up with the guy at this stage in the futile hope that he might get the thirty-five grand. Naturally, his friend never paid him. After a few months, he stopped returning phone calls and answering emails from his old buddy. In the end, the friendship did not survive working together. They were both millionaires so thirty-five grand should not have been the reason to end a friendship. Indeed, the money was the excuse not the reason.

Chapter 12

Early in the New Year, he ran into another old market friend by chance in a NYC bar. Salvatore had been an aggressive, successful FX salesman at several of the investment banks where he had run FX options trading back in the 90s. They had done a lot of profitable business together and had maintained a very good relationship during the years they worked together. Salvatore had started his own brokerage firm about four years ago and had contacted him to gauge his interest in becoming one of the founding partners of the firm but he had passed on the opportunity. He had lost contact with the guy after that. It turned out that Salvatore's firm had done well and was growing nicely. The firm was a boutique institutional equity brokerage firm. Salvatore became very excited when he told him that he had recently left a fund and was looking for a new employment opportunity. It seemed the entire options desk at Salvatore's firm had recently bolted abruptly, leaving the man in a bind without specialized options trading capability. Salvatore and a junior level stock trader were attempting to execute the options transactions for the firm's sales staff. But the kid was in over his head and Salvatore was neglecting his big clients and losing business. It was becoming a serious issue for the firm. His old colleague made him a job offer right on the spot to become the Head of Options. He was offered a guaranteed salary of $200,000.00 for the first year as a draw vs. a hefty percentage payout of the net revenues of the options desk that needed to be rebuilt from scratch. His immediate focus at the new firm would be to quickly learn the nuances of the equity options market and solidify the firm's stock options trading capabilities to support the existing equity sales professionals. His mandate was then to hire staff and grow the firm's business in options. He was very intrigued by the coincidence and the job offer. His attempts back in the fall to find a position as PM at a major hedge fund or a trading job in FX with a Wall Street firm had gone nowhere and had left him quite discouraged. He had not even started looking for work again. Out of the clear blue, a good job offer had fallen into his lap. The opportunity to finally work in the equity markets and learn stock options trade execution was very exciting. The downside was that this was a job offer in the brokerage industry and not really a trading position as he had always defined it. He understood that this was a sales job more than anything and to make real money he would have to learn the equity options market and develop sales skills on the fly. Moving from trading to sales was a fairly regular occurrence on Wall Street, but it was generally a one-way street. Once a trader had moved over to sales they rarely moved back to trading. Deep down he didn't think he was very well suited to becoming a salesman. The concept of licking the boots of clients for his commissions was decidedly unappealing to him. But he decided he really didn't have much to lose. If he could stick it out for a year at the new firm at least he would earn two hundred grand and not have to start living on savings. More importantly, it was a chance to learn a new market and he would still be in the game. He would not have to accept the life after Wall Street transition that a number of his old market friends had already faced. From what he could ascertain, it was a difficult evolution and involved unpleasantness like working hard to learn new job skills so that you could earn significantly less money. He had been dreading going back to the interview well and had started to think his career on Wall Street was already over and it was time to move on in life. He thought about it over a few beers with his friend and accepted the job on the spot. He was a desk manager again. He would be running the stock options desk at a small brokerage firm.

Salvatore had started the firm with a very simple business model. The firm was an executing broker only on listed exchanges. The firm executed trades for clients but then "gave up" these trades to the client's clearing broker. This meant clients did not have accounts with Salvatore's firm where the assets where being held. Instead Salvatore's firm simply executed the trades on behalf of clients and charged commissions. Executing your trades with one broker while holding your assets with another broker is a common practice in the industry. Being an executing broker not only simplified the operational side of the firm, it also meant the firm would have far less regulatory oversight, since it was not actually holding client assets. It was a business model to generate pure fee income, which has always been the premium cash to make on Wall Street. Obviously, a firm of this type needed to give clients the incentive to execute trades through them since the clearing broker wanted this business as well. The firm consisted of specialized sales desks, a stock trading group, the options desk that he had been hired to rebuild, and some back office support staff. One sales desk was made up completely of Russians and focused on doing business with funds back in their home country. The Russian funds all paid five or six times the going rate for institutional brokerage and the senior Russian salesmen were printing money for the firm and making millions of dollars a year for themselves. It was pretty obvious they were paying cash kickbacks to the Russian traders in exchange for the huge trading volumes and outrageous commissions. Bribery is a way of life for Russians. Kickbacks to clients have always been a lot more prevalent on Wall Street than anyone involved in the industry would ever care to admit. There was another sales desk comprised of slick talking French and Spanish dudes that naturally focused on business with European funds. Those clients also paid higher than normal commission rates and there were probably some kickbacks involved, but it was nowhere as egregious as on the Russian desk. There was also a desk that focused on doing business with risk arbitrage funds and equity long/short funds. This desk did a lot of business at extremely low commission rates but it was still profitable business for the firm. Stock trading for these types of funds generally involved spreading one stock vs. another in some kind of ratio. For example, an order might be to sell three shares of stock X vs. buying two shares of stock Y at a differential of twenty dollars. The stock-trading desk at the firm had become specialists in this kind of business. The firm was not highly capitalized since it was not holding client assets and was simply executing trades and then giving them up. Theoretically, the firm was not engaging in any proprietary trading for its own account. But the spread trades for risk arbitrage and/or long/short equity funds enabled the firm to generate considerable profits for its own account. This was because a spread trade in stocks was not something that could be tracked in any verifiable way by exchange records, typically known as Time and Sales. (This refers to the record of all trades for any given stock or any other exchange traded product on any given day. If your order has been placed with a brokerage firm and it should have been filled, you are guaranteed a fill. For example, if you left a bid to buy a stock lower and then the stock traded below your level after you left the order, you are guaranteed to be filled and the brokerage firm working the order is liable.) In the case of spread trades for risk arbitrage or long/short funds the firm could not be held liable for these types of orders. It behooved the firm to get as many of these orders as possible at a low commission rate. This was because the firm could make consistent trading profits under the radar working these orders. As an example, lets say the firm had a spread order to buy 50,000 shares of stock X vs. selling 30,000 shares of stock Y. Suppose that over the course of the day the firm managed to buy 30,000 shares of stock X vs. selling 18,000 shares of stock X, but then the price of the spread moved fifty cents away from the desired ratio. The firm might give the client a partial fill on 25,000 shares of stock X vs. 15,000 shares of stock Y but keep 5,000 shares of stock X vs. 3,000 shares of stock Y for themselves. The client would be pleased since they received a trade execution on a significant portion of the order, and were well in the money by days end. Meanwhile the firm could unwind the last 5,000 shares of the spread at a $2,500.00 profit and this money did not have to be paid out in commissions to any salesmen. Salvatore's stock traders were making money daily under the radar in this fashion. The last desk in the firm was a generalist sales desk catering to institutions and high net worth individuals. The one thing the sales desk all had in common was that they provided their clients with a lot of personal attention and lavish entertainment.

He could not stand Salvatore's partner who ran the stock-trading desk. The man was a loud, profane bully of the worst order. The guy had four or five young traders working under him and spent the day verbally abusing them. Somehow the desk held it together and got the job done but it was painful to watch on a daily basis. It was hard to believe, but this dude was even nastier than the Poison Dwarf. Watching this asshole humiliate his traders with his vile tirades all day long turned his stomach. He was certain that Salvatore's partner was going to get a serious, well-deserved ass-whipping some day. It caused him to spend some time recriminating about his own loudmouth antics on trading desks in years past. He consoled himself with the fact he had learned control and behaved like a gentleman at all times these days. Besides which, compared to this bastard, he had been nice as pie on his worst days. Needless to say, the stock trading operation seemed to be a revolving door, with traders quitting and new ones joining every month. He heard through the grapevine that the last head of the options desk had been able to convince the whole team to move in tandem to a new firm, due to their universal hatred of Salvatore's partner. His first order of business was to figure out how the market for stock options worked and to solidify the firm's execution capabilities in this area. The firm was only involved in trading of listed stocks and options. The major difference between the listed equity options market and the OTC FX options market was how the trades cleared. Listed products traded on an exchange where there is open price discovery. It also means there is a clearing firm that takes the other side of every trade with the member firms, and they take the other side of their customer trades. This essentially eliminated the credit risk to all concerned, provided the clearing firm stays solvent. To date no major clearing firm has failed in any of the major financial crisis' going back to the stock market crash of 1987. In the case of the interbank FX options market, the banks traded with each other and accepted each other's credit. In the aftermath of the global credit crisis of 2008, credit between independent counterparts has become consistently more difficult and trading has shifted back to exchanges in a big way. There were a number of stock exchanges where options traded including some purely electronic exchanges, which were in the early stages of growth and development in 2004. By 2012, a vast majority of exchanges had moved to electronic platforms and the majority of business had moved away from old school open outcry exchanges. You could determine the price of any listed stock option on your information screen but that price usually did not provide the necessary liquidity to execute a client trade efficiently. For example, a given call option may have a price of .50 at .70, 50 per side on the information screen that accessed the prices from all of the stock exchanges where options traded. This meant that you could buy 50 options at .70 or sell 50 options at .50. If you bid or offered for a better price or a bigger quantity on the screen it was not guaranteed that you could execute the trade immediately. Often times, posting a big order on the screen could cause the market to move rapidly away from your interest. A client might indicate they wanted to buy 2000 of this particular call option and needed to see your best offer. You would then contact all your available counterparts at the exchanges or upstairs trading desks to locate better offers in bigger size. In this example if you could show the client a .65 offer for the full 2,000 you could usually print the ticket. But the trade would still have to be executed on an actual exchange. He faced two challenges at this firm; initially, he needed to improve the option execution capability and the expertise available to existing salesmen and clients of the firm. But his broader mandate was to build a business broking equity options to the interbank market. The money market brokers that had built profitable desks broking FX options to the interbank market had applied the same business model to the listed equity options market. They had teams of guys that covered the traders at the major Wall Street firms and solicited their interests or got them to make prices on demand for options. These traders could show tighter spreads and bigger size than would usually be available from the trading screens. In return, the traders could get prices or shop their own interests with the money market brokers. All of the trades that were executed by the money brokers need to be posted and cleared on an options exchange. There were a number of exchanges that focused mainly on accommodating these types of "crossing" transactions. The traders could also expect lavish entertainment and other free perks like free tickets to major sporting events or Broadway shows. In other words, business as usual for the money brokers. They provided a necessary service for traders, but it was a service that could be duplicated with diligent effort by the competing brokerage shops. So success for the money brokers was all about developing personal relationships with the individual traders so that they would give them their interests and support them with prices. If he could build a successful interbank equity options brokerage desk at this firm, he could potentially make significantly more money than he had ever earned in the past. But he would need to become an aggressive salesman, schmoozer, and a party animal. The salesmen at this firm were out almost every night entertaining clients. Deep down he knew he did not possess the ambition, drive and will to move effectively in this direction at this stage of his life. He had taken the job because it had fallen into his lap when he was out of work, which is usually not a precursor to success. But the challenge for the first several months of the job was to improve the firm's liquidity and trade execution capabilities in stock options. This was something he could sink his teeth into and then he would have to address the larger issue of long-term business development at the firm.

The first several months at the new firm went quite well. He quickly became very proficient at stock option trade execution. Salvatore was able to immediately move back to servicing his own extensive client list and seemed quite pleased with his efforts. He mastered the firm's electronic trading platform and made an effort to get to know all of the firm's floor brokers. He figured out which guys he trusted and had access to significant upstairs liquidity. The sales desks had many options interests on a daily basis. The trade flow kept him and the junior trader hopping. He started developing option trade ideas and presenting them in document form to the sales staff so they could pitch their clients. Some of the salesmen started having him speak to their clients directly as the voice of options expertise at the firm. He definitely shored up the firm's options capability in short order. But executing trades for the clients of the salesmen at the firm did not give him any commission to be applied towards his percentage payout. He had to bring in his own clients and build a business in options or he would just be providing a trade execution service. After he had been there a couple of months one of the generalist salesmen left the firm. This firm had an extremely high turnover rate. He had talked to two of the clients of the salesman that left on a regular basis. He contacted them and requested to keep providing them coverage. Both clients agreed to work with him directly. He cleared it with Salvatore and he had his first two clients. He immediately started doing business in both stocks and options with these clients and so he started to generate some independent commissions. A few weeks later he caught a big break. Another senior salesman left the firm. One of the guy's clients was a huge hedge fund manager. The man was the kind of client that every major Wall Street firm was aggressively soliciting. The big hedge fund manager had not been that active a client of the firm, but he had recently talked to the man regarding a specific option strategy. The guy had liked his idea and gone ahead and given the firm a big order. When he had asked the salesman for a piece of that commission the prick had flatly refused. But with that salesman gone, he contacted the big hedge fund operator and made the sales pitch. Somewhat to his surprise, the dude agreed to give him a shot. He got a little lucky with his first couple of trade executions for this big client and also gave the man a couple of excellent short-term market calls. Suddenly, he was rolling in business from this heavy hitter. The guy seemed to like him a lot and did a tremendous amount of business over a stretch of three weeks. He cranked out about three hundred thousand dollars of gross commissions over that period of time. With his forty percent payout, this represented one hundred twenty thousand dollars of personal income. Including the other two clients he was up to almost one hundred fifty grand of payout. This meant he was getting close to covering his draw for the year and he would be making some real money for himself much quicker than he had anticipated. Salvatore was ecstatic with his sudden burst of independent business. He seemed to have landed what was known as a whale in the industry. A whale was that one big client that single-handedly makes a salesman's career. The truth was that the more he thought about it, he knew that building an interbank stock option broking desk was not something he had a lot of interest in. It was a very high entertainment gig and would require long days and nights of focused client attention. He had calmed down over the past few years. He was living with his Italian girlfriend now and was no longer a party animal. He had cut way back on the drinking and pot smoking and had little interest to go out on the town on work nights. Never mind that kissing the asses of a bunch of twenty-something hot shot equity option traders did not appeal in the least. He began to believe that if he could continue generating significant commissions with his own clients Salvatore might back off that plan. After a busy day he invited the big hedge fund operator to dinner on a whim. To his surprise the man readily accepted and they arranged to meet the next day at a nice restaurant. Salvatore was duly impressed. It seemed this gentleman was very private and rarely accepted dinner invitations from brokers, unlike most of the other clients of the firm that were complete whores for entertainment. He enjoyed the trade execution aspect of the job and he began to hope that he might be able to bang out a few good years at this firm. However, he seemed to have forgotten what his late father used to say about hope. Shit in one hand and hope in the other and see which one fills up first. Fate intervened to derail his progress at the firm.

His older son had always seemed to have his head on straight. The firstborn had graduated from a good school and was working hard to build a life for himself. His younger son had always been a problem child. This one was slight of build but very aggressive and charismatic. The younger son was a mathematical genius but cursed with some serious learning disabilities that were difficult for him to overcome. The kid was very headstrong and had become very wild at a young age. He had been a very indulgent father. He was very lenient with his kids, probably in response to his own abusive childhood. Instead of being an authority figure, he had gone the route of being best buddies with his boys. This works pretty well when kids are young, but becomes increasingly ineffective when they become teenagers and need guidance and control. He had always struggled with how to discipline his sons concerning drugs and alcohol, given his own lifelong proclivities. He had lectured them many times about the dangers of hard drugs and had been honest about his own involvement at a young age. But he had stressed how he had sworn off hard drugs while still in college and had never wavered. When the kids were younger, he used to kid himself that they were not aware of his own regular pot smoking and binge drinking, but he eventually figured out that the kitty got out of the bag a lot earlier than he had suspected. It is hard to keep shit from your kids. He vividly remembered receiving a call on the trading desk at his last investment bank from the principal of the high school.

His younger son had been arrested for selling pot out of his locker. The kid was so foolish and arrogant that they had it on film. If it hadn't been his own son he might have laughed as he watched the kid smile and make change for his customers. The divorce had made his younger son become very defiant and their relationship had disintegrated as the poor kid spiraled down into heavy drug usage. He spent a lot of time and money over a number of years bailing the kid out of trouble and trying to get his son some help, but nothing seemed to work for very long. Finally, they had stopped communicating. On the night before his big dinner with the hedge fund honcho he got a very disturbing phone call from one of his younger son's childhood friends. It seemed the kid was back on hard drugs in a big way and had landed in a crack house in the slums of Trenton, NJ. His son's friend feared for the kid's life. Some of them had tried to get him out of there, but it had not worked out. They felt he was the last hope to save his son. He needed to get the kid out of there before it was too late. Without hesitation he agreed to meet his son's friend in a few hours to get the specifics on the exact location of the crack house. He determined to get the kid out of there that night. He contacted a rehabilitation facility in Pennsylvania that the kid had been in and out of in the past. They insisted that his son would have to be admitted into a nearby hospital for withdrawal treatment before he could begin rehab. He felt a cold, deadly calm as he made his plans to get his son out of the crack house and into the hospital. He loaded his 20 gauge, over and under Browning shotgun and put it in the back of his SUV under a blanket. His old man had bought him and each of his brothers one of these magnificent sporting arms for their tenth birthdays. It was a beautiful dark brown walnut skeet shotgun that was very light and easily handled. The old man had paid around five hundred dollars way back when for this gun and it was now worth more than five thousand dollars. It had been a good investment if nothing else. He also grabbed his goofy cap that had a light on the visor like a coal miner's helmet. He used it to walk his dogs at night. It was after midnight by the time he found the crack house in the slums of Trenton. He put his cap on and switched on the light. He grabbed the loaded shotgun and walked up to the open door. His heart was pounding and he had no real plan except to charge in there and try and grab the kid and get him out. There was no way he was going into a crack house in the middle of the night unarmed. There was a scary looking crack head outside the door, leaning against the wall smoking a cigarette. He charged right up and stuck the shotgun in the crack head's face and barked, "There's a fucking white kid in this shit hole, looks like he's about fifteen years old. I'm his father and I'm here to get him the fuck out of here. If anybody tries to stop me I will blow their fucking head off!" The crack head glared back at him with a mixture of fear and shock and responded, "Crazy mutha fucka! You one crazy mutha fucka! You think you fuckin Rambo or some fuckin shit like dat waving dat big ass fuckin gun in my fuckin face. That little mutha fuckas here. I told that little mutha fucka get the fuck out of here, he don't belong here, but that little mutha fucka don't want to listen to nobody. You go in there waving that fucking gun around with your fuckin light in nigga's faces, some nigga gonna shank your ass you crazy mutha fucka. What good that gonna do you or your son? You get that fuckin gun outta my fuckin face maybe I help you." It struck him that the crack head

was acting a lot more like a gentleman than he was. He immediately decided upon a different course of action. He shifted
the shotgun over to his left hand and pointed it to the ground.
He then responded, "I apologize. I had no right to stick a gun
in your face out of nowhere. I am an upset father so I hope you
can understand." He then fished out his wallet with his right
hand and pulled out a hundred dollar bill and handed it to the
crack head. He continued. "Please go inside and get my son
and I will wait out here. I really don't want any trouble with
anybody here. I just want to get my son and get the fuck out
of here. Consider this payment in advance for your assistance."
The crack head smiled, "Now you gettin smart, Big Daddy
Rambo. I get that little mutha fucka outta here. He's a smart
boy doin some dumb ass shit right now. I get him outta here
no problem." The crack head was as good as his word. Within
a couple of minutes, the dude returned with his son. The kid
was a bit disheveled, but his eyes looked surprisingly clear. He
looked at his son and simply said, "It's time to go." His son just
stared back and nodded. He could tell that the kid was ready
to get the fuck out of there and get some help so it was good.
As they turned away from the crack house the man shouted
after them, "You listen to your father boy! I see you back here
I gonna whup your fuckin ass!" They walked back to the car
without speaking to each other. They drove through the night
to the hospital in Pennsylvania in silence. It kind of reminded
him of the night drives with his old man when he was a kid.
They never spoke a word on that ride. What the fuck was there
to talk about?

　　After getting his son admitted to the hospital, he sat around
the rest of the night and did some serious thinking. It had

probably been a stupid plan. He could have been killed or he could have shot somebody and ended up in jail for a long time. Instead, here he was sitting in a hospital with his son safe and getting medical help. He had been very lucky or maybe some divine power had been looking out for both of them. For the first time in many years, he silently prayed and gave thanks to God for their deliverance. He called the office the next morning but Salvatore was not there. He briefly explained the situation to his assistant and made it clear he did not know when he would return to work. He didn't give a fuck about business at this point in time and completely forgot about the dinner scheduled for that night with the hedge fund honcho. After his son spent several days at the hospital, the plan changed. He accompanied the kid to a rehabilitation facility in Phoenix, Arizona. It was probably better for his son to get as far away as possible. It took several more days to finally get the kid out there and admitted for a long stretch of rehab. During their time together, they reconnected and had a number of interesting discussions on many different subjects. He stayed away from any lecturing. What the fuck did he know about rehab anyhow? He had been barely controlling his own demons and substance abuse for most of his life. His son was brilliant, and it was a damn shame to see him waste all that talent with all this destructive activity. When he finally left his son for good, he decided to play golf the afternoon before his flight back. It was a brutally hot day in May in Phoenix and the temperature was one hundred and sixteen degrees. When he walked into the clubhouse at a golf course, the pro seemed shocked that he wanted to play in that oppressive heat. Apparently, most people out there only golf in the mornings in the summer;

it is too hot in the middle of the afternoon. After he briefly explained the situation to the pro, the man refused to accept any payment for the golf or the rental clubs. He played that round in less than ninety minutes and broke eighty for the only time in his life. His son returned some months later and went back to college and got his degree. The kid has remained off the hard stuff and stayed out of trouble for the most part since then. Over a week had elapsed before he got back to the office. He explained the situation to Salvatore as best he could. All of his momentum as a broker was gone. He had lost his whale. The hedge fund honcho would not take his calls. You usually don't get a second chance with dudes like that. He was back to executing option trades for the sales force without generating much business on his own. Shortly after his return, he was hit with another big shock. His girlfriend was diagnosed with a serious form of cancer. She faced radical surgery and then extensive chemotherapy. He marveled at her strength, poise and courage in the face of such severe adversity. During her treatment, she lost all her hair but she never lost her smile. By the grace of God she recovered and eventually they were married. They remain very happy together to this day. In any event, he completely lost interest in being a broker at this juncture and began just going through the motions. Early in June, he had a long discussion with Salvatore. The man had lost patience with the development of the options desk. Salvatore had negotiated a deal to bring in an entire interbank equity options brokerage team and he was no longer the Head of Options at the firm. He was offered the opportunity to remain with the firm as a generalist salesman, since he made some commissions and still had two clients. He politely refused and assured Salvatore that there were no hard feelings. He expressed his appreciation for the opportunity. He knew he was not cut out to be a broker. Who the fuck had he been kidding anyhow? He agreed to stay through the end of the month to ensure a smooth transition for the new team. Salvatore graciously paid him the additional fifty grand in commissions he was owed, although the man was not contractually obligated to do so.

Chapter 13

He took the rest of the summer off after leaving Salvatore's firm. As summer turned to fall, he began to feel restless. He had played a lot of golf that summer and come to realize that he would never gain any real proficiency or consistency at that addictive, impossible sport. His brief stint as an equity options broker had left a bad taste in his mouth. He did not want that experience to be the swan song of his Wall Street career. He decided to give it a shot as a market maker trading options for his own account on the floor of the big futures exchange in NYC. He had always felt he could be a great trader on the floor of an exchange. It was time to find out once and for all. He had an old friend from business school that had been scratching out a living on the futures exchange for the past fifteen years or so. His friend explained that there were a lot of ups and downs, but over time the man had averaged around two hundred thousand dollars a year trading options on the exchange. It was not really an exciting amount of money for him, but considering that all of the options trading pits were only open three to four hours a day it sounded like a good lifestyle. Also, he would be his own boss and this appealed to him since he was sick and tired of working for the man. You had to play the game and jump through some hoops to become a member of the exchange. There was a mandatory period you had to spend as a trading clerk. His friend took care of the paperwork to handle that requirement. You also had to learn all the nuances of open/outcry futures pit trading. There were even mock trading sessions and written exams to pass before you could formally become a member of the exchange. The process took several months. While he was waiting to get his exchange membership he opened an account at his friend's brokerage firm and went short ten DEC cotton futures around 51.00 (51 cents/pound) just to have some skin in the game. Cotton had been trending lower for sometime and his reading of the charts led him to believe the price would continue to head south. Each cotton futures contract represented 50,000 pounds of cotton that had to meet the exchange specifications. Futures contracts were almost exclusively closed out prior to any actual physical delivery of the commodity. But the potential for delivery and the strict requirements for deliverable grade quality were necessary to ensure the integrity of the futures market. He held the position for some time while he was working on acquiring his membership to the exchange. Cotton futures traded in increments of five tics, which represented 5/100 of a cent. Eventually he was about 700 tics or 7 cents in the money on the trade. This meant he was up around $35,000.00 on the trade on a mark to market basis. Not long before he acquired his exchange membership, he was chatting about his cotton position with a floor trader he had befriended. The floor trader remarked that the next day was First Notice day for DEC cotton so he had better roll his DEC futures position to MAR if he wanted to stay short cotton. First Notice day meant that from that day forward, all short positions could theoretically be assigned, which meant actual physical delivery would be required. He certainly did not have the capability to deliver 500,000 pounds of exchange grade cotton. But he found the roll requirement annoying because the DEC cotton was trading around 44.00 whereas MAR cotton was trading a cent lower around 43.00. As a former FX options trader, he assumed that the different contract expirations had a very consistent, linear relationship, as they did in FX. This was a bad assumption. He also assumed nobody would request delivery immediately and so he could run his DEC short at least one more day. This was an irrelevant assumption. His target had been around 42.50, so he determined to wait till the next trading session and then close out his short position and book his profit. Just to be safe he put in a GTC stop-loss buy order for DEC cotton at 45.10. This way he assumed he could lock in at least a six cents profit and would be sure to make around thirty thousand dollars on his first commodity futures trade, which would represent a good start. This was another bad assumption. The next morning he was aghast to see the DEC cotton market open limit up at 47.10 bid and apparently nothing had even traded. Meanwhile, MAR cotton had traded down another hundred tics to 42.00. His stop-loss order had not been executed since the market had opened limit up with no offers available. All of the commodity futures had daily trading limits and if these daily limit movements occurred on the opening there was simply no trading that day. The daily limit in Cotton was three hundred tics or three cents. It turned out that a certain large physical commodity broker had cornered the market on all available cotton suitable for satisfying DEC delivery requirements. He was fucked along with all the other lazy shorts that had not closed out prior to First Notice day. There was no way out until the market started trading again. His friend advised him to keep his GTC stop-loss buy order working and when the market finally became unlocked he would at least be able to close out the position. The DEC cotton market was limit up on the opening for two more days. On the fourth trading session after First Notice day, the market opened around 54.00 and his stop loss order was executed. He bought back his ten short DEC cotton futures at 54.10, thereby booking a fifteen thousand dollar loss on a position that had been more than thirty five thousand dollars in the money just a few days earlier. It was actually a good thing he had left that GTC stop-loss buy order working in the market. DEC cotton closed limit up again that day and eventually hit a high above 65.00. At that juncture MAR cotton was trading around 39.00. It was a harsh welcome for him to the wonderful world of trading commodity futures. His old friend assured him it had been a cheap lesson.

The large trading floor of the futures exchange initially seemed like an ancient bazaar to him. It was full of people in colorful jackets engaging in loud, heated commerce. There was an ebb and flow to the trading floor as different trading pits opened and closed throughout the day. The opening and the closing were always the period of the most heated trading activity in any given pit. All of the futures and options pits were still solely open/outcry trading at this time. Several years later the exchange would be sold and consolidated into a large electronic exchange and futures trading would shift to a purely electronic platform. Only the option pits still provide significant liquidity via the open/outcry system today. Options have been the most difficult product for the electronic exchanges to take over, but it seems inevitable. You could find anything you wanted on that exchange floor. He befriended a trading clerk whose real job was selling high-grade pot. The man had been bringing in product onto the floor on a daily basis for years. There were quite a few attractive female trading clerks that openly operated as independent escorts on the side. A number of them had steady gigs with the largest floor brokers for specialized client entertainment purposes. There were several large bookies brazenly running sports books all day long in tandem with their duties as phone clerks on the floor trading desks. A big market existed on the floor for all manner of designer goods knock-offs including clothes, watches, electronics, and anything else you could think of. "Free markets for free men" was the mantra they all swore by on that exchange floor.

By 2004, most of the savvy old-timers knew the days of open/ outcry futures trading were nearing the end. The future's lobby always argued that open/outcry was the most efficient method of price discovery, but his time on the floor convinced him of quite the opposite. It was no surprise to him that most futures markets have now migrated exclusively to electronic trading platforms. Options will surely follow suit within the next several years despite the technical issues involved.

He had opened an account with his friend's clearing brokerage firm and funded it with one hundred fifty thousand dollars. He had assured Mr. Bluggo, the jovial senior partner of the firm, that he was an experienced options trader and would be running a professionally hedged options book. Floor traders had tremendous leverage since they were being margined as a clearing member and not as a retail client. All positions would be marked to market at days end and the floor traders were only required to maintain appropriate variance margin. Basically this meant he could build up an extremely big book and as long as he didn't fall more than one hundred fifty thousand dollars in the hole, he would technically not have to pony up more margin. Of course, the firm could always request more margin if they didn't like the risk profile of your book and if you didn't pony up on time they could close out your positions. His last decision after becoming a member of the exchange was whether to lease a seat on the exchange or buy one. You could buy a seat for approximately two hundred fifty thousand dollars or lease a seat on a monthly basis for five hundred dollars. Leasing the seat certainly seemed to be the prudent decision from a capital allocation standpoint. His friend told him that seats had traded between a low of seventy five thousand dollars and a high of four hundred fifty thousand dollars over the past fifteen years. His friend had never bought a seat and strongly advised against it. He considered buying but opted to lease instead. Several years later when the takeover of the exchange was announced, seats briefly traded for well over one million dollars before dramatically selling off in tandem with the credit crisis. He decided to start his commodity options trading in coffee. It was a large pit with significant trading volumes. There were probably over a hundred traders and brokers in the coffee options pit. The coffee futures pit was much larger; there were probably several hundred traders and brokers there. On the opening and closing periods of the day, the noise coming from the coffee futures pit was deafening. It sounded like being directly under a large, commercial jet taking off. The lobbyists for the futures industry always claimed that the futures pits provided free competition and the most efficient pricing available for clients. This was far from the truth. The trading activity in the coffee options pit was a completely rigged activity. There were a number of major brokerage firms that had customer desks within easy access of the options pit. Their brokers controlled most of the paper (trade orders) that flowed into the pit. They worked closely and efficiently with a number of well-established option traders who had spaces in the pit within close proximity of their desks. Theoretically, they were supposed to publicly announce what option or option spreads they needed a quote for, as well as the size. Every trader in the pit was supposed to be given reasonable time to respond to the inquiry and make the price. They were supposed to compete for the best price and then execute the trade. However, the game did not actually work this way. The brokers and traders in the cartel were friends and were as thick as thieves. Most of their big interests would be quietly discussed with the traders they always did business with. In advance, the dealing prices and amounts would be agreed upon as well as the split up of the trade between the traders who were a part of the cartel. Then the brokers would quickly announce the interest, the traders involved would instantaneously quote a price and the trade would be immediately executed. Everyone else in the pit was out of luck. He was bringing trading sheets into the options pit with him every day. These sheets were generated on excel spreadsheets and printed out daily. The sheets were crammed with numbers that told him fair value prices as well as the Greeks for options based on all the variables such as futures price, type of option(s), expiration of option, and implied volatility. Most of the big interests were spreads. Even if you got close enough to hear the interest when it was announced, it would take a few seconds to locate the particular options on the sheets, compute the prices, figure out the spreads and then price an appropriate bid/ask spread. There were a number of traders who had laptop computers strapped to their chests and they could calculate any spread price faster than he could with his sheets and mental arithmetic. So even when some paper was properly announced in the middle of the pit, he could not make a price quickly enough to even compete. It was impossible to compete with traders that had already made the price and pre-agreed on the trade. The fifteen grand he already lost on cotton futures after being thirty-five grand in the money had left a bitter taste in his mouth. Before starting in the coffee pit, he had determined that he would not just pay away the spread and take outright risk positions. If this were to be his trading strategy, there would be no point to become a member of the exchange and trade on the floor. His strategy would be to make prices, earn the bid/ask spread, and then run hedged option portfolios. After his first week he had done zero trades and was quite angry about the blatant collusion that dominated trading in the coffee options pit. If he could get even a small piece of most of the big deals that went through the pit he would have a chance to make money. But he felt like he had no chance to even get a deal. His friend traded orange juice options. It was a much smaller pit and his friend had been trading in that pit for over a decade so the man was a member of the cartel there and got a split of all the juicy paper. His friend advised him to relax and be patient. He needed to accept that it would take time to get quick with the pricing, and even longer to get to know the pit brokers and long-standing traders in the pit, to possibly get a shot at the gravy deals. His buddy suggested he hang out for the rest of the year and focus on trying to get to know people in the pit. He wasn't exactly starving so what was his big hurry? They can't just let anyone compete for the pricing or the spreads would narrow too much for anybody to make money. This speech didn't exactly sound like "Free markets for free men" to him. It did not seem like such an appealing personal strategy to him. When he suggested that perhaps he should move over and try trading orange juice options his friend adamantly opposed this idea. His buddy did not want to be squeezed by him for some of the gravy that was flowing his way. The Monday of his second week in coffee options he noticed one of the leading paper brokers from the coffee options pit sitting alone in the lunchroom. He sat down across from the guy and introduced himself. He explained that he was new to the coffee options pit but he was a well-experienced professional options trader. He wondered what he needed to do to get a shot at some trades. He suggested that perhaps they needed tighter spreads on small stuff from time to time and he could help them out in that area. The pit broker stared at him for a moment and then spoke, "You know I haven't noticed you in the pit yet. It's a big pit you know. Pricing in the coffee options pit is done by open/outcry so that we always compete for the best possible price for our clients. I am not really sure why you think I can do anything for you. But I will tell you what you can do for me. My colleagues and I really enjoy going to Madison Square Garden to see the Rangers play. We especially enjoy the good seats down low so you can hear and feel the action. It so happens that we are a little light on Rangers tickets so far this season. How about you buy four tickets to four different games. Good seats. Don't buy us any shitty peanut heaven type seats. You can just slip me the tickets in an envelope nice and casual, without a word. Sometime after the last game maybe I will talk to you again. Now I have to ask you to leave, since my friends will be joining me shortly." He was incredulous. This arrogant prick thought he was going to buy them sixteen box seats to the Rangers so that maybe the man just might talk to him again some day. Those tickets would cost thousands of dollars. The scary part was that the guy seemed completely sincere. He smiled at the broker and simply replied, "Nice talking with you." He walked away in disgust.

Once again, it had not taken long for him to believe that his latest career move had been a mistake. He had anticipated there was collusion in the pits, but he had assumed that the competitive nature of open/outcry would have ensured fair access to at least some of the paper washing through the exchange floor. He could have filed a complaint with the oversight committee of the exchange, but that would have made him an instant pariah. There wasn't much to do except to keep plugging away and try to compete for deals as best as he could. By Friday of the second week he still had not done a trade and his frustration level had grown. That Friday was an expiration day for the front month coffee options contract. There was always a ton of gravy being slopped into the options pit on expiration day, since many institutional clients wanted to clean their positions and were willing to pay away edge in the process. It was options trading in its purest form. He identified a number of potential trades that were winners and tried to compete aggressively for the deals. But the option brokers never acknowledged him even when he was the best price. It was starting to get maddening. The final five minutes of the session always grew extremely loud and frantic in the pit and this effect was exaggerated on an expiration day. In the height of the closing flurry with less than a minute to go, he saw one of the big option brokers bid 15 tics for one hundred call options with a strike of 100 that were set to expire. The front month coffee futures were trading around 97.30 (which meant .9730 dollars/pound of deliverable grade coffee.) So 15 tics was .0015 dollars bid for a strike that was immediately going to be worthless. Instinctively he tried to sell the broker the 100 and to his amazement the man signaled he was done. He was shocked no one else in the pit had hit that gravy bid first. The broker then signaled .15 bid for 200 more options and he immediately sold those and was filled again. Then the broker bid for 200 more and he sold those as well. So after two long weeks of no trades he had sold 500 call options with a strike of 100 for 15 tics in a matter of seconds. Suddenly, the closing bell sounded at 12:30 PM, trading immediately halted and the pit went silent. At this juncture, the serious looking options trader with a laptop he had stood next to all week turned to him and said, "Well dude I am impressed. You got some set of balls." The man had ignored all of his earlier attempts that week to chit chat so hearing him speak had instantly put him on his guard. He replied, "The options just expired so its free money. Why does taking free money mean I have balls?" The options trader smiled wryly and then rattled his world, "Dude, did you not do your homework before jumping in here? The long option holders have until 6 PM today to decide to exercise. The Brazilian coffee report is out at four PM today. Anything can happen. You never know, you might come in Monday morning short 500 coffee futures in a rising market. If that's not balls I don't know what is. Hey, have a nice weekend dude." The man smiled and walked away and he was left standing there feeling like a fool. He had been an extremely successful professional FX options trader on Wall Street for almost twenty years and here he was jumping into the commodity options market with his own money, trading like a rank amateur. Prudence dictated that he go back to the office of his clearing firm and ascertain how he could determine after six PM if he had been assigned on any of the call options. But it was a horrible thought to even consider. He blindly went home with no way to even determine if had been assigned later on that evening. He realized that this had been a foolish, impulsive trade and his clearing firm might not be too happy. Maybe if he did not draw any attention to himself the options could expire unnoticed. After he got home, he told his girlfriend he had good news and bad news, "The good news is I finally did a deal in the coffee pit, the bad news is I might be broke by Monday morning." Needless to say, this news did not bring her a lot of joy. He refused to elaborate. He found the Brazilian coffee report on the Internet at four PM. It seemed to him that it was not a bullish event. By all accounts it sounded like a banner crop report. Surely this should not cause someone to exercise call options that had been almost three hundred points out of the money (OTM) when the futures had expired. But economic reports on the Street had always had an immediate effect on prices relative to market expectations and not to the absolute number. He realized he had absolutely no clue what market expectations for this report had been. In his own mind, he reasoned that the buyer of the options had been an institutional player cleaning up a large, short position before a big number. But in reality, it was all guess work for him on that Friday evening. Each coffee contract represented 37,500 pounds of deliverable grade coffee. This meant he had sold 18,750,000 pounds in total of one-dollar call options. So every cent or hundred tics above 100 could cost him $187,500 if he was assigned on all five hundred call options. The odds of these options being assigned seemed incredibly low, but he had no way to accurately measure the probability of this event, so he had blindly gambled. He received $28,125.00 in premium for this risk (18,750,000 pounds of coffee x $.0015 dollars/pound.) He consoled himself that it was going to be the easiest twenty-eight grand he had ever made. But he smoked a lot of pot and drank a lot of fine red wine that weekend to stay calm. It didn't feel like a very easy twenty-eight grand by Sunday night.

That Monday morning he avoided the office and went directly to the futures pit and waited for the coffee futures to open. It had been a bearish report for prices and the market opened around 92.00, which represented over 500 tics lower from Friday's close. The old saying said that it was better to be lucky than good, and this was certainly applicable to this trade. He had made the $28,125.00, but it was somewhat ominous to him that the movement had been five hundred tics lower and he had sold options less than three hundred tics OTM higher. A random event had luckily gone his way. He knew that. He didn't lie to himself. If he had been assigned the short futures and they had moved two hundred points against him, that would have represented a loss close to three hundred fifty grand, including the premium he had received. If coffee had been limit up for a number of days, like he had already seen occur in cotton, the loss could potentially have been in the millions. The probability of an outcome above 100 and full assignment was very low but this represented unquantifiable loss potential (as well as unquantifiable profit potential to the long option holder who had paid the 15 tics.) He had only deposited one hundred fifty thousand dollars with the clearing firm. He was standing next to the coffee options pit right before the opening (the options opened after the futures) when Mr. Bluggo's secretary approached him. It was the first time he had seen her on the floor so this definitely was not a good sign. She tersely informed him that Mr. Bluggo needed to see him immediately. Under no circumstances was he to execute another trade before he had spoken with Mr. Bluggo in person. He meekly followed her back to the office without saying a word. On the short walk there he racked his mind for a defensible argument to justify the trade. The issue was not the fact that he had sold 500 call options. The issue was that he had done so with only one hundred thirty-five thousand dollars on account for margin with the clearing broker. He had assured Mr. Bluggo that he was an experienced, professional options trader and would run a hedged options book. Then his first trade was to allow a futures trade that had been thirty-five thousand dollars in the money to lose fifteen thousand dollars. The problem was that he was zero for his whole commodity options futures trading career in terms of actually executing a trade with positive bid/ask spread. He seemed to have zero chance to get even one options trade like that anytime soon, let alone a whole book with steady, daily activity, which was required for consistent profitability and risk-management. Instead, his first options deal with the firm was to sell five hundred naked options. The fact that the options had expired worthless did not really matter relative to the unquantifiable risk he had taken with such a skinny margin balance. If he had been assigned all five hundred options and they had been in the money and he did not take action, the clearing broker would have been forced to cover them at the market. The clearing broker would have to cover all losses above his balance to the clearing firm immediately. Then they would have to go after him for the money. He was sure this kind of situation happened frequently and often did not work out well for the clearing broker. He thought about it logically and realized that Mr. Bluggo should close his account immediately. How could the man take a chance with a reckless bastard like him being authorized to trade whatever he wanted on the exchange floor? If he were in Mr. Bluggo's shoes, he would close the fucking account immediately and be done with it. He resolved to say as little as possible and try to exit the firm with dignity. Fuck it; at least he had made a little money. Maybe it had been stupid to sell the options but he had made the twenty-eight grand. When he sat down in the office, he could immediately tell that the normally jovial Mr. Bluggo was spitting mad. The man threw the firm's position report on the table in front of him and screamed at him angrily, "What the fuck is this? Are you fucking kidding me? What are you, the fucking Charles Manson of option traders? You lying son of a bitch! You told me how experienced and professional you were. You told me you were going to trade a hedged options book like your friend has done here for the past fifteen years. Then your first move is to get caught in the short squeeze in deliverable Cotton and dump fifteen grand on futures. Now your first options deal is to sell five hundred fucking 100 strike call options in coffee with only one hundred thirty-five grand on margin? What kind of an asshole do you think I am you son of a bitch?" He was mortified to be on the receiving end of this vile tirade. But logically he felt that Mr. Bluggo was totally justified. If the trade had gone sour they would have been the ones holding the bag for everything over one hundred thirty-five thousand dollars. He felt totally humiliated. Not much more than three years ago, he had been an MD at a premier Wall Street investment bank making an average of one million dollars per year for seven years running. Now he was getting brutally dressed down by the senior partner of a lightly capitalized, small commodity brokerage on the futures exchange. All this stress and conflict was over a measly twenty-eight grand in premium. How the mighty had fallen! He paused for a moment and then responded in a calm voice, " I had strong reasons to believe the options would expire worthless. But relative to my margin balance I should have sold no more than fifty not five hundred. I got a little carried away. I sincerely apologize for this lapse in judgment and I can assure you that it won't happen again." Mr. Bluggo looked at him incredulously and said, " What are you saying? Are you saying you have inside information on these coffee reports?" The way Mr. Bluggo asked the question he could tell that the man was considering the possibility that he did have some kind of special dope. Wall Street on all levels was full of senior managers looking for logical reasons for trades that in reality represented blind gambling. In his experience, the traders at the big Wall Street shops who made the most money were often the guys who took maximum risk and got lucky. He always remembered the words of a senior bond trader he had befriended at one of his previous employers who was probably making five million dollars a year at the time,

"Dude, I don't know why you play it so close to the vest? Game theory says roll em when it is somebody else's money." He didn't answer Mr. Bluggo's last question. He just looked him in the eye and stared at him trying to look as sincere as possible. The bottom line was that he now had one hundred sixty-three thousand dollars in his account and no positions. Mr. Bluggo softened his tone, " Look, you can trade like this if you want. We have guys that trade like this. They keep around two million dollars in their margin account at all times." He spoke, " Once again Mr. Bluggo, I can only apologize and assure you nothing like this will occur again." There was no fucking way Mr. Bluggo was going to get any more margin money from him. Fuck him. He would close his account and take his one hundred sixty-three grand back. There were a ton of shaky little clearing brokers on that exchange competing for business. Mr. Bluggo replied, " I tell you what I can do. I want you in the penalty box for two weeks. I want to see you come in here every day and get down to the floor but just observe and do not trade. Can you comply with that?" He smiled and warmly shook Mr. Bluggo's hand, "Absolutely. Thank you so much for giving me another chance. I won't let you down." The bottom line was that the risk was covered and the money had been made. There was a huge culture of no harm / no foul on Wall Street on all levels. When you made money they rarely asked a lot of questions. When you lost money they got up your ass with a microscope. That might explain why there were so many spectacular blow-ups on all levels on Wall Street. He let Mr. Bluggo have his moral victory. He was in no hurry to trade again. It seemed clear to him that he did not have the patience or will to grovel for an extended period of time just to maybe get a little taste of the action in one of those shitty commodity option pits. He decided to hang out with his friend in the orange juice pit and just shoot the breeze, while relaxing and contemplating his future. Instead of relaxing, he witnessed a savage beating administered to the locals in the orange juice options pit, courtesy of a hedge fund that understood leverage, liquidity and the effects of a sharp, short-term margin squeeze.

The thing he learned that first week of standing with his friend in the orange juice options pit was that all the locals had the 80 (eighty cents per pound of frozen orange juice concentrate) conversion on in size. With the front month futures trading around 85, they all had the locked position on in a large amount, relative to the liquidity in the pit. The conversion meant that the option market makers in the pit collectively were short the 80 strike calls, long the 80 strike puts and long the futures on a one to one to one basis. The paper in the commodity pits used to be purely hedging option structures from both producers and consumers. Now consumers dominated the flow and this created a huge skew in the options favoring OTM call options over OTM puts by a wide margin, on an implied volatility basis. Price gaps on upside surprises like a crop killing frost in Florida wreaked havoc on short-term prices for oranges and this created the upside price gap risk. Sometime ago, a hedge fund had apparently bought a large number of 80 strike call options from the pit, building up a large position when the futures were below 70. Several months later there was a large rally and the futures traded into the mid 90s. The hedge fund had apparently come back into the market and sold out 80 puts against all of their long 80 calls. The pit was glad to take the other side of these trades since theoretically it meant the bid/ask spread on both trades had been locked in. However, he had just learned that long option holders had the right to exercise up to 6 PM on Friday, long after the futures pit had closed. When he asked his friend about this small wrinkle, the man grew quite annoyed. The cartel in orange juice options had done this 80 conversion in size and had booked nice profits on the deals as far as they were concerned. Each day on the close in orange juice futures, heavy selling pressure came into the market to drive it down 100 tics after most of the day had seen quiet and lackluster trading. Friday morning orange juice futures had opened at 81.90, briefly rallied and then steadily sold off all day to close at 80.50. The next Monday morning there was chaos in the orange juice futures market. The futures were limit down and all of the local option market makers, including his friend had been fucked by the hedge fund that had traded the 80 conversions. It seemed that while all the locals had abandoned their 80 puts, the hedge fund had also abandoned their 80 calls even though the futures had closed at 80.50. The option locals had all assumed they would be assigned on their short 80 calls and thereby sell futures at 80 to close out their long positions. This had been a bad assumption on their part. So now both sides of the options trades were gone and the options locals were collectively long thousands of futures in a market with thin liquidity. Apparently, the hedge fund had come into the market on the opening selling aggressively. The hedge fund had the capital to margin their positions easily. The orange juice option locals had been sheep led to the slaughter. The locals needed to sell out their long futures or be forced to pony up significant amounts of margin cash to hold onto their positions. Many of the smug orange juice option locals that had been snubbing him as a newbie looked physically ill to learn that they were long futures and the market was limit down. They stood there in the pit all day like zombies as nothing traded. The next morning, the covering blood bath occurred and orange juice futures traded below 73 before beginning to trade back higher before the day was over. Several of the options locals had blown up, meaning they had actually lost more money than they had on account. Their clearing broker would now be after them for every penny they had, until they paid back their deficit balances. By Friday of that second week, orange juice futures had traded back above 82, just to add insult to injury to the battered orange juice options pit. His friend was very conservative relative to the other members of the orange juice options cartel and yet had lost around one hundred thousand dollars, cutting the man's profits for the year in half in one fell swoop. It was pretty absorbing to witness the carnage up close but feel the sweet relief of not being involved. His two-week penalty box period was over but he had little interest to trade commodity options. He decided to take the rest of the year off and decide what to do next year after the holidays. He did not believe for a moment that he could feasibly acquire any reasonable share of the crossed bid/ask spreads in any of the option pits anytime soon to actually have a legitimate chance to make money on a consistent basis. The trading activity in those commodity option pits was too full of collusion and underhanded deals. But as he had just witnessed in orange juice, even if you were in the cartel the potential for disaster awaited you in situations that seemed innocuous. He had serious doubts that he was ever going back to the commodity options trading floor after the holidays.

Chapter 14

Whenever his Wall Street career had seemed to hit a brick wall, another opportunity had quickly fallen into his lap without his even looking for it. This occurred once again. The first week he stopped going into the futures exchange he received a surprise phone call from Lorenzo, who had been his right-hand man at all three investment banks where he had managed the global FX options trading business in the past. Lorenzo had left the last investment bank the same year he had. The man had joined the hedge fund department of a major European bank and had moved up the ladder. Many major banks had responded to the rapid growth in hedge funds in the 90s, by launching departments focused on creating hedge fund business by leveraging the resources of the bank. These bank hedge fund departments consisted of two main business lines, Fund of Funds (FOF) and Single Strategy Funds (SSF). Lorenzo had been named the Head of Volatility strategies within the SSF group for the hedge fund department. Lorenzo had received approval to launch a global volatility arbitrage fund and needed to hire a PM to help manage the fund and run trading during the NYC time zone. He was offered a salary of two hundred thousand dollars a year along with a discretionary bonus supposedly based on performance. He accepted the job offer without hesitation. He had little interest to return to the futures exchange floor and he didn't even have a current resume at this stage of the game. He didn't see what he had to lose. He was very appreciative to get the offer and the fact that he was now reporting to a man who had worked under him for almost ten years in the past didn't bother him all that much. He had long since been knocked off his high horse. A number of guys that had reported to him at one stage or another had gone on to senior positions on Wall Street in the current decade, as his own career had languished. He certainly felt some recriminations and wondered how he had let his career decline so rapidly. But Lorenzo had always been his favorite. He loved the man like a brother. He was excited about the opportunity to help Lorenzo build a business at the European bank and started immediately.

It turned out that he was the first employee in SSF to join the hedge fund department of the bank in NY. All of the other employees in NY worked in the FOF department. This was pretty convenient since it meant he didn't report to anyone in NY. He reported directly to Lorenzo out of London. He hired a trading assistant and had his own little office away from the big FOF group. The net result was that he could come and go as he pleased and push the envelope on vacation time as long as he kept Lorenzo informed of his whereabouts and made sure the positions were always being monitored diligently. Most of the capital being managed by the department was being handled by FOF, which was a bigger business and had significantly more employees than SSF. FOF was a nice racket to be in at this time. In the late 1990s, the banks had all decided they were missing the boat and needed to be involved with hedge funds on a direct basis. So a number of major banks brought in teams to build up the businesses quickly. FOF was the easy place to start.

An FOF was essentially a portfolio of hedge funds sold as an independent hedge fund with the strategy of investing in hedge funds. The FOF were all selling themselves as the mutual fund equivalent in the hedge fund space. The FOF all claimed they had senior analysts and risk management professionals to ensure optimal performance. The FOF also claimed that they could provide better transparency and liquidity than single hedge fund investments. In reality, all FOF analysts ever did was kiss the asses of big-time hedge fund managers and chase performance. Chasing performance in funds management is similar to momentum investing in stocks. It essentially means buying something today because it went up yesterday, therefore, it must mean it will go up tomorrow. This strategy never works out in the long haul. Most of the day traders during the Internet stock boom were momentum investors and the party ended in tears for 95% of them. The buyers of Mortgage Backed Securities (MBS) that got slaughtered when the credit bubble burst in 2008 were essentially momentum buyers or performance chasers. FOF typically charged a "1 and 10" fee schedule, which meant they charged a one percent annual fee on AUM plus a ten percent share of all profits above a certain target, that was usually LIBOR (London Interbank Offered Rate.) LIBOR is the average interest rate that leading banks in London charge when lending to other banks. In late 2004 the credit markets were in full froth and banks could borrow all the money they wanted at LIBOR. At this particular European bank, the hedge fund department had initially been funded by billions of dollars that the bank had borrowed easily in the credit markets. The department had then raised a significant amount of additional capital from existing clients of the bank. Sales people at banks could always sell any product internally to captive clients when they were incentivized properly. FOF marketed themselves as an efficient method to invest in hedge funds, while diversifying risk or focusing on a specific industry strategy with a portfolio of the leading fund managers. FOF claimed that they could invest in major hedge funds that investors would not be able to access on their own. In reality it was a simple business model for the managers of the department. They were using the banks' capital to invest in hedge funds and then they were skimming off the top to compensate themselves handsomely. The bank, along with the clients, were getting reamed since they were paying the FOF "1 and 10" fee schedule on top of the standard "2 and 20" fee schedule that the FOF had to pay most hedge funds. This was also passed directly onto the investors in the FOF. The managers of the department were making millions of dollars a year even though the performance of their FOF lagged the returns on major hedge fund indices year in and year out. The Head of FOF for this European bank in NYC was a strange bird. They all called him Twinkle Toes behind his back and it was pretty easy to see how this nickname had evolved. Twinkle Toes talked a big game about womanizing in an extremely inappropriate manner in the office, but no one really believed that the man liked girls. The man told many off-color jokes and delighted in publicly insulting everyone in the office that worked under him. Twinkle Toes would laugh and giggle as he did his best to humiliate his staff on a rotating basis. The prissy little dude definitely gravitated towards being touchy feely with the men in the department that tolerated this behavior. Twinkle Toes also seemed to delight in homoerotic jokes and used gay references frequently in his constant, annoying prattle. The dude liked to hear himself talk. Twinkle Toes apparently took his personal trainer and the trainer's buff buddies out on a weekly basis for fine food and wine and expensed it all to the bank. He remembered his first meeting with Twinkle Toes. The man had initially impressed him. Twinkle Toes talked very quickly and drew a lot of circles, arrows and lines with different color markers on a big markerboard, while writing a lot of phrases in very small and illegible script. The man threw out a lot of hedge fund buzz words and phrases like portable alpha generation, blended beta synthesis, and equity market correlation gamma creation, to just name a few. After he had sat through several meetings with Twinkle Toes, he began to realize that the man was simply regurgitating the same drivel, reworked to suit the occasion, while combining the catch phrases with the same act on the markerboard. It was how Twinkle Toes handled meetings on a daily basis. The man was a pathological liar. At various times, he heard that Twinkle Toes had been a famed computer programmer and was the partner of Steve Jobs at Next. He also heard how the guy was a black belt in karate and a professional skier. Twinkle Toes was short, skinny and weak. The man actually went skiing with some sales people who promptly told everyone else in the department that the guy could not even ski. Twinkle Toes also claimed to have PhDs from M.I.T., Stanford and Oxford, at various times. These claims were checked and found to be fraudulent. The man also talked often about having been on the board of a major European bank before this current gig. He personally checked this out and found out that Twinkle Toes had been a mid-level trader who had blown up and got fired during the Russian debt crisis. Twinkle Toes claimed to be from a family with billions of dollars but nobody had ever heard of them. Lastly, the man would talk at great lengths regarding his close personal friendships with all the major hitters in the hedge fund world. By all accounts, the few that actually knew Twinkle Toes considered the man an annoying, pathetic little asshole with a big mouth. Not long after he joined the bank, a junior analyst in the FOF group verified the true ethical nature of Twinkle Toes. One of their major funds had invested in a hedge fund that had blown up, meaning the hedge fund had lost 50% in a single catastrophic month. The dramatic loss on this particular investment badly skewered the return profile of the particular FOF that was involved. Twinkle Toes had ordered the junior analyst to omit the data from this bad investment in the new marketing materials that were being developed. When the junior analyst ethically refused to go along with this "inadvertent" omission, the kid was ruthlessly sacked. A new lackey happily moved up and generated the fraudulent marketing document. Twinkle Toes figured that a strategic omission of data could always be explained away in a pinch. All this aside, Twinkle Toes managed the department in NY and was making millions of dollars a year. The man was better at playing Wall Street than he was at this stage of the game. That was probably the one bitter pill he had to swallow at this new gig. Twinkle Toes was a pathetic, bullshitting, incompetent stooge, but the man was making significantly more money than he had ever made even at the height of his career. He had always taken great pride in his prior successes on Wall Street. Realizing that a scumbag like Twinkle Toes was a highly compensated Wall Street executive, while his own career was clearly in decline, was very sobering and enlightening at the same time.

The SSF staff were all based in Europe prior to his arrival at the bank. They had launched a number of single strategy hedge funds using bank seed money. The plan had been for the funds to build up good track records and then market the funds to outside investors. The problem was that most of the SSF funds had performed badly. Lorenzo had been on the FOF side but had moved over to try to jump-start the SSF business with volatility-based funds. Lorenzo had become a disciple and true believer of the religion of back testing, which refers to analyzing past price data to develop trading strategies. Basically, back testers comb through historical market data and determine trading strategies that would have worked well based on the data for the time period analyzed. Then the back testers take the great leap of faith that the markets will repeat past price patterns in the future. They believed that the trade strategies that have been optimized based on past data will work in the future as well. Statisticians call this kind of statistical analysis data snooping. You can always figure out a trade strategy that would have worked well in the past if you have access to the data. The issue was the assumption that this would work moving forward. One old market pearl of wisdom that he had often repeated to traders that worked for him was that "old Harry Hindsight always got it right." Back testing became quite popular in the 90s as new computer technology made it much easier to get a hold of market data and conduct in-depth statistical analysis. Lorenzo had acquired a large amount of price data on liquid asset classes including equity indices, FX and fixed income. What made the man's approach somewhat unique was that the data included implied volatility historical price data along with the price data of the underlying asset. This was fairly new. Most of the back testing he had heard of in the past had involved calling directional movements in the markets themselves, not the implied volatility of the options on the markets. Lorenzo had several quantitative geek types working for him and they had accomplished a plethora of statistical analysis prior to his arrival. The new volatility arbitrage fund was to be launched on this statistical work. He knew in his heart of hearts that it was all a bunch of bullshit. He had zero confidence in any trading strategy based on back testing. In his mind, it was like working out a detailed plan to exit a complicated maze and then assuming that the same pattern would work equally well on a brand new maze. Another example might be weather forecasting. Back testing on weather would mean statistically analyzing weather patterns for past years and then using the analysis to generate future weather reports. Nobody would accept this as an accurate methodology for predicting weather, but somehow it made sense to people when it came to financial markets. It seemed obvious to him that the random nature of market movements and the constant stream of unanticipated news and events would make the analysis of past data fairly unreliable in predicting future market movements. But back testing had been used to raise a lot of money in the hedge fund industry going back to the 1980s. This fact was incontrovertible. Many people on Wall Street on both the buy side and sell side wanted to believe there was a logic to markets and that diligent analysis of past market data would create trading strategies based on sound scientific principals. Lorenzo was certainly convinced this was the only way to build a consistent strategy and the back testing results would be the core of the strategy for the new fund. His old friend was also convinced that creating marketing materials stressing the quantitative nature of their fund was their only chance to attract investors assuming the funds' returns were good, of course. He was highly skeptical but was more than willing to play ball for his 200 grand a year plus bonus. It was as simple as that. The interesting part of all this data analysis was that it led to the standard options strategy being employed at most banks; sell options to earn the premium. Lorenzo's statistical analysis showed that one-month options on liquid asset classes were overvalued on a fairly consistent basis. The strategy basically boiled down to selling options on over twenty different underlying markets. There were a lot of bells and whistles that had been worked out based on the data. These included how to weight the risk allocations across markets and how to delta-hedge and risk-manage the positions. But really it all came down to Options 101, which was to sell options and try to make more money from the premium received than the cost of managing the risk of the position. It makes intuitive sense that options appear consistently overvalued when you statistically analyze how options were priced vs. what kind of market movements subsequently occurred. Option writers perform the service of an insurance underwriter in some sense. In normal circumstances, the options writer should win. But if unexpected events occur which create sharp market reactions, then the advantage shifts to the options buyer. Indeed, there is a school of thought on Wall Street that believes options are consistently undervalued because standard options models underestimate the likelihood of unexpected market movements. The bottom line was that he wanted the fund to perform well and grow so that he had a better chance of getting paid good bonuses. He really had no choice but to diligently apply Lorenzo's strategy during the early months of the fund's launch. If performance was lagging, he could then push for his own ideas to improve the strategy.

In retrospect, the gig at the European bank with Lorenzo worked out as well as he could have possibly expected. He lasted around five years there and averaged approximately five hundred thousand dollars in total annual compensation including bonus. It kept him in the game and on the gravy train. The interesting aspect of the strategy for the first three years or so was that the selling of options across various liquid asset classes on a portfolio basis was actually a fairly low return, low volatility strategy when measured on a monthly basis. This reality was counter-intuitive to the perception that most people would have that selling options would create highly volatile return streams. You made a small amount of money on most days but in any given month there were several days where sharp market movements occurred and the fund would take a whack. But in the hedge fund world the scorecard for fund performance revolved around the monthly return profile of any given fund. Their fund steadily made small amounts of money most months and so the fund had a low volatility of return, which is considered more attractive to investors. He worked diligently with Lorenzo to improve the performance of the fund. He convinced the man to let him take some side bets via options within a proprietary pocket of the fund. He traded well on balance and helped juice the fund's returns. He also pushed Lorenzo to selectively include more option buying and they developed some signals based on his ideas that worked pretty well. Basically, down through the years he had always like buying options when deep, liquid markets became abnormally range-bound for several days or longer. Typically, after several days of tight consolidation, a breakout would occur and this would favor a well-timed option buy. It was really common sense. There were so many market participants whose livelihood depended on trading these markets that they could stay in a tight range for only so long. Eventually, the range had to break and then the short-term traders would jump in and accelerate the move. They also developed some signals that helped them decrease or cover short option positions when conditions became extremely unfavorable. Lorenzo insisted that all of the ideas he presented needed to be statistically validated. He found this somewhat annoying, but he didn't really care as long as some of his strategies were implemented and performance improved. He learned that Lorenzo and his managers enjoyed creating new funds and products, and over his five years at the bank they launched several additional funds based on similar ideas. Performance steadily improved between 2005 and 2007 and he was happy enough with the situation. The funds were performing and increasing in AUM and his compensation was steadily growing. The job certainly didn't bring him the same money or satisfaction he had enjoyed while managing global trading groups earlier in his career. But, he was making a decent living and enjoyed working with his old friend. In 2008, the global credit crisis struck with a vengeance and Wall Street would never be the same. In September of 2008 it had become clear to him that markets had shifted into a state of sustained disequilibrium. Events were starting to unfold at a very rapid, unpredictable pace. Liquidity was drying up in markets and huge price swings were starting to become the norm instead of the exception. Implied volatilities had risen dramatically and Lorenzo's models wanted to go maximum short options. He became certain that this would prove disastrous. He was determined to convince Lorenzo to override the models and after much effort he succeeded. They covered all short options positions and went

long volatility. They didn't establish long options structures as
big as he wanted, but they dramatically changed the risk profile of their funds. To him it seemed as clear as day that this
was the right strategy. He realizes now that Lorenzo was potentially taking dramatic career risk in agreeing to this subjective override of the models that were supposed to dictate fund
strategy. If markets had calmed and volatility had collapsed,
their funds would have been punished when they should have
been scoring by being short options. Their subjective override
of fund strategy was spectacularly successful. In October of
2008, he witnessed the most explosive market volatility of his
career. Indeed, that was probably the best month to be long
options in a long time. Their flagship fund generated impressive returns. Had they stuck to Lorenzo's models they would
have blown up. The funds would have all definitely gone bust.
Instead, they posted stellar returns and 2008 would prove to
be their best year by a wide margin.

Their flagship volatility arbitrage fund won a prestigious
award in London in early 2009. They had been selected the top
performing fund in their investment category due to strong
performance and low volatility of return. It was interesting for
him to note that they were the only bank-owned hedge fund
to win an award. Every other fund that won something was
a real hedge fund that was privately held. He had long since
come to the conclusion that he was not a real hedge fund PM.
He was a bank employee managing a bank product. Despite
their relatively strong five-year track record, they had never
been able to raise significant assets that did not come directly or indirectly from the bank. Serious hedge fund investors
would never put money into a bank-owned hedge fund. It was

as simple as that. Nobody would every really take them seriously. The basic assumption was that the managers of a good,
viable hedge fund strategy would never want to be a part of a
bank since compensation could never match the levels available to PMs in private hedge funds. More importantly, any
hedge fund owned by a bank would be subject to a great deal
more unwanted scrutiny than most successful hedge fund operators would be willing to tolerate. If you were a PM for a
hedge fund owned by a bank, the hedge fund community at
large considered you a hack. He had gone on a number of sales
calls in the first three years at the bank and had realized that
none of the hedge fund investors in the U.S. would ever give
them a look. He didn't really care. He was making a fine living
and not working too hard, which was good enough for him at
this stage of his life. They had a great year in 2008 when the
hedge fund community at large got pummeled. This happened
because hedge funds in general had become huge frauds by
2008. All of the major hedge fund indices had strong positive
Betas. This simply means that the performance of most of the
hedge funds was strongly correlated to the stock market as
generally defined by the S&P 500 market index. When high-
profile hedge funds were posting stellar returns in the 80s and
90s, they were making a lot of money in non-traditional asset classes such as FX and commodities. By 2008, there was
so much money stuffed into hedge funds that there was not
enough capacity in non-traditional asset classes for the big
hedge funds to put their money to work. The obvious solution was for the hedge funds to plough money into the stock
market. In the past decade there was an explosion of hedge
funds that invested almost exclusively in equities in one form

or another. The performance of these hedge funds, based on the tracking indices, consistently underperformed the S&P 500 in both directions over time. They made less money than stocks in bull markets and lost more money than stocks in bear markets. Logically, this made complete sense. The hedge funds were investing in stocks but charging outrageous fees for investors to participate in their stock picking abilities. Typically, they claimed that all of their stock picking was done through quantitative methods. If some computer model was generating your stock market bets, this must be better than throwing darts or using some other equally random methodology. At least this was conventional wisdom in the world of hedge fund investing. The big fees charged by hedge funds cost more than the value of their stock picking abilities by a wide margin. A sensible investor would always be better off in a stock market index fund or large mutual fund since the fees were significantly less and the correlation to the S&P 500 or the applicable equity market index was better. Investors that did well in hedge funds over time were lucky. It was that simple because the deck was stacked against them. A lot of major investors deluded themselves that an allocation to hedge funds was an interesting investment in a non-traditional market class that could help diversify their investment portfolio. In reality, they were paying a bunch of overpaid, arrogant bastards to gamble with their money.

The FOF industry began to implode in 2008. These investment vehicles had sold themselves as a sensible alternative to direct hedge fund investing. During the bull run in the decade prior to 2008, the performance of FOF in generally significantly underperformed hedge funds. This made logical sense due to the extra layer of fees tacked onto FOF. Most of the money invested in FOF came from the banks and other large financial institutions that had established hedge fund departments. This made the capital fairly stable until the credit market's crisis. Whenever they were pressured about their returns lagging major hedge fund indices, the managers of FOF had stressed that they were providing better transparency, liquidity and risk-management than investors could find in direct hedge fund investing. These fraudulent claims were exposed by the global credit crisis. In 2008, investors in hedge funds bitterly became aware of the concepts of "Gating" and "Side Pockets." "Gating" referred to a hedge fund no longer allowing investors to redeem their investments in the fund. In simple language, the hedge fund could declare that they would no longer allow anybody to take their money out of the fund until further notice. Most funds had provided legal indemnification for this action in their offering materials. According to hedge funds, they needed to "Gate" a fund when redemption requests became so extreme that they would force the fund to take excessive losses when liquidating the investment portfolio in order to give the clients back their cash. The hedge funds could "Gate" and then keep the money of investors who wanted out and continue to charge them normal fees. Ostensibly, the hedge funds would "Gate" to protect the investors who remained in the fund from taking losses caused by forced liquidation. It was certainly a convenient excuse to refuse to give investors back their money, while continuing to charge them fees regardless of poor performance. "Side Pockets" referred to a hedge fund setting aside illiquid investment products like MBS, EM securities, or complex derivative products. The hedge fund could declare that a fair price was no longer available for the investment products in the current market environment and so the fund would no longer attempt to mark the product to market. Instead, the hedge fund would carry the investment product in a "Side Pocket" at historical cost until a liquid market returned. In 2012, many major hedge funds are still holding "Side Pockets" created in 2008. They still haven't paid the piper on a lot of the shit. The creation of "Side Pockets" was supposedly to protect investors from unfair price swings caused by illiquidity in the markets. It was certainly a convenient way to indefinitely postpone taking losses on bad investments. Most of the assets being managed by the hedge fund department at his bank had been raised from internal bank sources or from major clients of the bank. By late 2008, the bank and the bank's clients wanted their money back from the internal FOF due to poor performance and a general cash crunch hitting the financial services industry. They were all in for a rude surprise. Most of the major hedge funds that the FOF department had invested in had "Gated" and established significant "Side Pockets." The hedge fund department could not get their money back from the hedge funds and so they could not return money to their clients. Therefore, they "Gated" their funds as well. So the bank and the major clients could not get their money back or even be assured of the value of their investments in the internal FOFs. The volatility funds he was managing with Lorenzo performed extremely well in 2008 but they suffered big redemptions from the bank as well as from their outside investors because they did not "Gate" or establish "Side Pockets." In essence, they were punished for performing well and keeping their funds liquid. He bitterly learned the reality of being a bank employee when it came to his bonus for 2008. They had managed around four hundred million dollars that year and made over one hundred million dollars. It was a tremendous performance considering global stock markets had collapsed and hedge funds were getting punished. Based on the standards of the prior years, he should have been paid a bonus of two million dollars or more. At a real hedge fund, the number would have been at least five million. It should have been his best year ever in the industry. Instead, he was paid around three hundred thousand dollars in bonus and was informed he was lucky to get that. He was particularly bitter about the shafting he had received at the hands of Twinkle Toes. A new fund launched by Twinkle Toes in 2007 had invested heavily in their flagship volatility fund as well as making managed account investments with outside managers that were getting paid monthly fees. Twinkle Toes had assured him that he would be paid directly based upon performance at the same rate as the outside managers. Instead, when push came to shove, he got stiffed and was paid nothing from Twinkle Toe's fund. He was furious over this shafting but powerless to do anything about it. In 2008, the FOF industry performed worse than major hedge fund indices (they lost even more money) and they were forced to "Gate" in the face of significant redemption requests. The FOF had not provided investors superior risk management, transparency or liquidity. Instead, FOF had underperformed direct hedge fund investing once again. Since 2008, the FOF industry has steadily declined as many major financial institutions take their lumps and close their hedge fund departments.

In 2009, his bank dismantled the hedge fund department and all the senior management left to start a private investment firm. The bank wanted to retain their award-winning volatility fund, but Lorenzo was insistent on becoming a partner in the new private firm being launched by the departing senior managers. The bank approached him about taking over the fund but he refused to stab Lorenzo in the back. Besides, the bank had proven they wouldn't pay a proper performance fee if the financial climate for the bank was difficult. A true hedge fund PM was supposed to get paid based purely upon performance, not based upon the current business climate. He resigned from the bank after the whole department was closed and determined that he would retire from the industry. Lorenzo persuaded him to join the new private investment firm. The new firm was to be modeled after the hedge fund department at the bank and contain both FOF and SSF. They had found a deep-pocketed investor to fund the new firm. He had to give them a lot of credit for that. It was not easy to find money in the fall of 2009 but these dudes had been able to pull it off. He was able to negotiate a sign-on bonus from the new firm since they were desperate to market the new volatility fund as the award-winning fund with the same management team. This made 2009 a good year for him in term of personal compensation, if nothing else. It galled him to join a firm where Twinkle Toes was a senior partner, but nobody else was offering him a good salary and benefits and a sign-on bonus to stay in the game.

Chapter 15

By the end of 2011, he had come to a stark realization. He no longer gave two fucks about the Market. The passion and excitement he had experienced from his long-term involvement with financial markets were gone. The Wall Street environment now sucked in general and he hated his current job. He was beginning to forget what he had found so compelling about trading in the first place outside of the money. He was hanging on in the game for the money and no other reason. His two years at the private investment firm had been personally boring despite the wild swings in the financial markets during that period. Lorenzo had insisted at the new firm that the volatility fund be managed purely quantitatively. This meant that he could no longer do any creative trading to improve fund performance and keep the game interesting. Their fantastic performance in 2008 had been directly based on overriding Lorenzo's models and making subjective trading decisions to go long volatility across various asset classes. His experience and instincts had saved the day for that fund. But Lorenzo had seemed to come to the wrong conclusions about the fund's success. The man seemed more than ever convinced that the models were robust and were the keys to strong performance and the raising of capital. It had become obvious to him that it was fine to use the concept of models to raise money from investors, but the actual trading of the fund would be better served through a bigger focus on qualitative decision making. If they had followed the models in 2008 they would have blown up instead of posting great returns and winning an award. That was reality. Never mind that it made the game a lot more fun and interesting if you were making some subjective decisions. In fairness to Lorenzo, more and more investors no longer wanted actual living, breathing traders to make the decisions. They all believed that computer generated trading signals was the answer. Never mind that most of that stuff was not working very well in the new, random illiquid market environment. They were all kidding themselves. They were trying to hold onto the new dream. He had begun to realize that there was a lot of luck involved with success on Wall Street. But some said luck was where opportunity and preparation meet. They were both very experienced option traders and he had almost always had good instincts when market crisis were building during his long career. But for any number of reasons, including pressure from his partners, Lorenzo had determined the fund at the new private firm would be based 100% on the models. This meant he had essentially become more of a trade execution professional and less of an actual PM. The fund was traded purely using the signals from the model with no management overrides. The performance of the fund was lousy and they struggled to raise AUM at the new firm. For the first year, it had stressed him out when he could see market opportunities or recognize glaring risks in their positions but could not take decisive action. He eventually realized this was foolish. He was no longer the man. In fact he had not been the man for a long time. They were paying him a good salary with full medical benefits and sticking it out as long as possible seemed the only logical course of action. He no longer had the will to even look for another job in the industry. He was playing out the string and any internal stress would have been foolish and self created. He then focused on dispassionately executing the required trades as seamlessly as possible without any emotion. The FOF business at the new firm was languishing as well. There were no bonuses being paid and most of the staff was miserable and desperately searching for alternative employment opportunities. Despite these grim conditions, Twinkle Toes would saunter into the offices around eleven AM or so every morning and create a loud and annoying spectacle. The man would noisily laugh, shout and holler anything at anyone and it did not matter if they were on the phone or engaged in any other business. Twinkle Toes still loved to insult his staff in a laughing, demeaning fashion while publicly declaring his own market omnipotence. Twinkle Toes regularly claimed to have anticipated each new move in the market or change in performance of a particular hedge fund after the fact, despite the miserable returns of the funds the man was managing. The humbling performance of the new venture had not seemed to affect Twinkle Toes in the slightest. The man was completely delusional. During quiet afternoons, Twinkle Toes would walk around the office with a phone head set on and converse loudly, without caring which of his minions might be distracted from their work. It was the man's way of walking around the room and pissing all over the place to mark territory. The act had grown very old and tiring.

He could see that global financial markets had become much more highly correlated and were becoming less liquid and more unpredictable. In all his years in the market he had never seen a bigger focus on government policy, statements and actions. The same tired stories seemed to get recycled over and over. The only thing that changed was the markets reaction during any given period. The reality that political and economic drama playing out in Greece was rocking global financial markets on a consistent basis, with no resolution over a multi-year period was as unfathomable as it was frightening and pathetic. The Maastricht Treaty established convergence criteria for European Union member states to adopt the euro as their currency. These criteria included controls on interest rates, inflation rates, exchange rates and other measurable economic indicators. The Greeks had never met any of these criteria in the first place. The ECB had turned a blind eye and accepted Greece without really considering the risks involved in this decision. It was only a matter of time from the word go. The Greeks had been borrowing large amounts of money from abroad and then defaulting on the debt every twenty years or so for many centuries. Free money from suckers abroad had always helped fuel the laid back, leisurely Greek lifestyle. It was what they did. There was nothing new here. Except for the euro and the concept of putting monetary union before political confederation. Being accepted into the euro had allowed the Greek government to borrow vast amounts of money over the past decade to maintain their comfortable, welfare state. But they had reached the end game of this current round of external borrowings and it was time to fuck everybody and default and then lay low for a decade or so. By then prosperity should have returned to global financial markets and a new round of suckers, stupid enough to lend to Greece would most likely be back as sure as the sun rises in the east. There was a simple way to solve the problem. There were supposed to be a number of fundamental economic requirements to maintain membership in good standing with the ECB. The Greeks had pretty much thumbed their noses at all of them. They were never going to pay anything back no matter what the ECB said or did. Nobody was getting paid. The ECB needed to throw Greece out of the euro immediately and let the chips fall where they may. Free markets need to be free markets to function properly. Anybody that had lent money to Greece and bought Greek bonds deserved to lose. They had made a bad business decision. How hard was this simple solution? The problem facing the mealy-mouthed, spineless politicians in Europe was that many of their major banks had lent a massive amount of money to Greece relative to the huge levels of free capital they had received from the Central Banks of the world (primarily ECB and the FED) during the past five years, in response to the global credit crisis. Since 2008, the banks had been earning the spread between the free money from Central Banks and the interest paid on Greek bonds to generate easy profits. This had enabled them to show good results to their shareholders and pay themselves large bonuses for a job well done. Former Governor of New Jersey, Jon Corzine busted MF Global, Inc. on a big leveraged bet on Greek debt. Then there was a missing billion dollars of investor's money that nobody could find and Governor Corzine would not comment. The underlying assumption they had all made was that the ECB would never let the Greek Bonds go bust so it was free money to lend to Greece at exorbitant interest rates. But over the past few miserable years the banks had started to figure out that they might have made some bad assumptions about the safety of Greek government debt. In any event, if the ECB pulled the plug on

Greece a number of their private banks would go bust since all the capital related to Greece would have to be acknowledged publicly to be in default. So what? If the banks were so poorly managed and put themselves in this position they deserved to go bust. The European governments could backstop all depositors and pay them first. It was what anybody with any sense would do. Italy, Spain, Portugal and company would step into line real quick after the plug was pulled on Greece. This would be the greatest benefit of all. The whole thing could be over in a couple of months and the world could move. But there was nobody with any true free market spirit, common sense or balls in a position of power anywhere in Europe. Or so it seemed to him anyhow. There was a lot of rhetoric coming out of major Wall Street firms decrying the new levels of financial market regulation that were being implemented in response to the global credit market crisis. In reality, there was nothing new happening here either. Since the dawn of civilization, the moneychangers had always gotten increasingly greedy and reckless in prosperous societies and eventually gotten slapped down. In his mind, the backlash against Wall Street was only beginning and would escalate in the coming years regardless of politics. Everybody had had enough of Wall Street. The classic, bulge bracket Wall Street firm of the past thirty years was a lightly and ineffectively regulated financial institution that had easy access to capital markets. These firms borrowed aggressively to highly leverage themselves, while taking large, complicated unquantifiable risks as well as pinching and poaching aggressively from clients in a remorseless fashion. The only goal was to generate large bonus pools to pay themselves excessively. Wall Street firms operated as pyramid schemes whereby the top guys stuffed the vast majority of the bonus pools into their own pockets. Guys on the production end like himself got paid depending on what they had done and how much the powers that be felt was necessary to keep them around if they were deemed useful. This was the true business model and they were actually, pretty good firms to work for in their heyday if you were motivated mostly by money. On the other hand, time and again owning shares in Wall Street firms had consistently proven disastrous for shareholders. These firms were built to enrich employees not shareholders. It was as simple as that. Markets were going to be more closely regulated and global financial institutions were going to operate less aggressively and with significantly less leverage. Wall Street was going to make less money and most likely continue to contract in the coming decade. Hitters on the Street were still going to make a lot of money but overall levels of employment and average compensation levels would continue to decline. Wall Street was in a long-term bear market. Not necessarily the stock market, but the actual business of Wall Street was going to trend lower for the forseeable future.

Despite his many years in the business, he had developed a somewhat contemptuous attitude towards Wall Street and the people that worked there. When he had gone to graduate business school he had heard a lot of talk about "the best and the brightest" gravitating towards working in the financial markets. As the years went by it had seemed to him that it was more commonly "the neediest and the greediest" that tended to get ahead most often on the Street. If there was one common characteristic he had identified in the people that made the most money on Wall Street it was their relentless self-promotion. Twinkle Toes certainly epitomized the triumph of bravado over substance on the Street. It had become more of a struggle to hide his contempt for the man. As 2011 was coming to a close, the mood on Wall Street was grim. Jobs were being lost and bonuses were being slashed significantly at the banks. Ten years ago, most of the senior sales and trading professionals at Wall Street firms earned salaries around one hundred fifty thousand dollars a year, but with bonuses included they earned five hundred thousand dollars a year on up. Now those that were still around were making around two hundred fifty thousand dollars a year with little bonus opportunity or motivation outside of hanging onto their salaries and medical benefits. The current administration likes to refer to people that make at least two hundred fifty thousand dollars as being rich. In reality, two hundred fifty grand was not all that much money to make working in NYC with its high taxes and outrageous cost of living. In his view, you could probably live just as well on seventy five thousand dollars a year in Pittsburgh vs. two hundred fifty thousand dollars a year in NYC. He knew a lot of Wall Street people that had overspent down through the years and now were grimly holding on, hoping for the return of the good times. He harkened to the words of his old man, "Shit in one hand and hope in the other and see which one fills up first." The good times were not coming back any time soon. Although 2011 had seemed like a very momentous year for financial markets nothing much had really happened in the end. The stock market had violently gyrated up and down and experienced huge volatility before closing the year relatively unchanged. FX markets had followed a similar pattern. Bond markets had continued to grind higher despite the historically, low levels of interest rates. Trading desks at major banks as well as most hedge funds had performed poorly. He had always tried to avoid giving investment advice to friends. But when any of his wealthy friends showed an interest to invest in hedge funds he strongly advised against it. He explained to his friends that giving money to a hedge fund was like going to a casino and paying someone a fixed fee plus a percentage of winnings to gamble on your behalf without taking any risk on their own. There was also a bad selection bias for all the hedge funds aggressively soliciting investors. The few hedge funds that actually had some kind of foolproof scam working to make money were not actively looking for investors. These firms had significantly more capital than they could employ that was begging to get in. The Hedgies in general had not made much money for their investors in a long time. Certainly, not after taking their excessive fees off the top. Hedge funds had performed poorly vs. simple stock market indices for the past decade. Hedgies were by and large looking to grab as much money as they could to book the high fees. If a high net worth individual was solicited for investment in hedge funds the odds were stacked badly against him or her. If he could not dissuade friends from investing in a hedge fund he would buy them a copy of "Fooled by Randomness' by Nassim Taleb. In this brilliant book, Taleb teaches in a colorful but convincing fashion that luck and random events play a much larger role in life in general as well as financial markets in particular, than human beings are naturally able to understand. It was hard to believe that anyone who read this book would still want to invest in a hedge fund. If one of his friends read the book and still wanted to invest in hedge funds than he could only wish them good luck. He had become disgusted with the attitudes among many of his friends and acquaintances still working in the industry. He was hearing almost constant whining and complaining about how bad the markets had become and how they were all getting screwed over on their bonuses. After a number of years on Wall Street, most people tended to believe they deserved to get paid a lot of money regardless of personal contribution and/or overall firm performance. It seemed that 2011 was the year when the good times were coming to an end for a while. Profits were down big time on Wall Street and the stock market valuations of most major firms were in the toilet. The past year had seen significant job cuts on the Street and more retrenchment and downsizing seemed inevitable among the major banks. Bonus numbers were way down and the culture of the industry was changing. The amount of cash compensation was being severely limited at most firms as bonuses were being paid mostly in deferred stock awards with "claw back" provisions. This meant that the firm could take deferred stock bonuses back if individuals and/or the firm did not reach future performance standards. Obviously, it was not appealing to be paid your bonus mostly in stock when the stock market valuation of most Wall Street firms was languishing, let alone the fact that you might not even get your hands on the stock down the road if things did not go well. Despite all the negativity in the air, it was interesting how just about everyone he still knew in the business was holding onto their jobs tightly with both hands. Just like him they realized that alternative employment most likely would never pay as well, even at the new lower levels of compensation on the Street. He had always taken great pride in his work and his abilities as an options trader. But he found little to be proud about on a professional basis during the last couple of years of diligently following Lorenzo's models as they failed to perform in any meaningful fashion. On the other hand, his personal life seemed better than ever even as his career was languishing. He was happily married and they had four dogs that brought much joy and fulfillment into their lives. They had a great group of friends with whom they had grown extremely close. He had cleaned up his act and had lost weight and become much fitter. He had come to the conclusion there was a lot more to life than the stress and pressure of trying to make as much money as possible. He had begun to believe that it would be a huge mistake to spend his whole life chasing after money. He began to accept that his days of making big money were over and it was time to focus his attention on more worthy endeavors. He had stopped recriminating about past missteps and professional opportunities that had somehow slipped away. He became more thankful about the level of financial security that he had been able to achieve despite the many wrong moves he had made in his life.

Early in 2012 they cut him loose. The senior managers at the floundering private investment firm had found another European bank to buy their business. He had to give them a lot of credit for finding another sucker, when all logic indicated that the sucker well should have long since run dry. The pending merger was a good excuse for them to cut staff and bring their cost structure down. He was a big salary and with the fund performing poorly and being run on a purely quantitative basis he was also quite expendable. He had been holding onto his Wall Street career of twenty-seven years like a man holding onto a ledge on a cliff by his fingertips. He had been expecting to get sacked when the merger deal was signed and so it did not come as a surprise. He had long since grown bored with the job and disgusted with working at a firm where Twinkle Toes was a senior partner. He had lost respect for Wall Street in general and was ready to leave the business once and for all. He had just not been able to walk away from the salary and benefits. But it was time to go. In life he had always felt it was very important to understand clearly when it was time to go. Lorenzo was very subdued and apologetic when they had their final discussion and he got his walking papers. He was sure his old friend felt bad about sacking him, but the man had to look out for his own neck first and foremost. There were no hard feelings on his part. It is never pleasant to get fired, but he certainly wasn't all choked up about it this time. In reality, he had felt sweet relief that he was finally closing this chapter in his life. He no longer took any pride in his work. It was time to stop selling out for money and move onto doing something else. He needed to get involved in activity more worthy of his time and effort. He knew what he had become. He didn't much care for it. He was just another Wall Street Journeyman.

The End

CPSIA information can be obtained at www.ICGtesting.com
Printed in the USA
BVOW031858100413

317855BV00001B/37/P

9 781478 719199